Electional Astrology

Electional Astrology

Mary Fortier Shea
M.A. Counseling Psychology

Published by Twin Stars, Unlimited
Mary Fortier Shea
P.O. Box 301
Clinton, CT 06413
www.maryshea.com
maryshea@maryshea.com

Disclaimer
The information in this book is for entertainment and educational purposes only and is not intended as medical, legal, or financial advice. The author and publisher are not responsible for any actions taken based on the contents of this book. The reader is responsible for his or her own decisions, actions, and interpretations of the material. This book does not guarantee specific life outcomes in regard to any electional charts.

ISBN 978-1-930310-33-9

Library of Congress Catalog Card Number:

2026904394

Printed in the United States of America

Electional Astrology

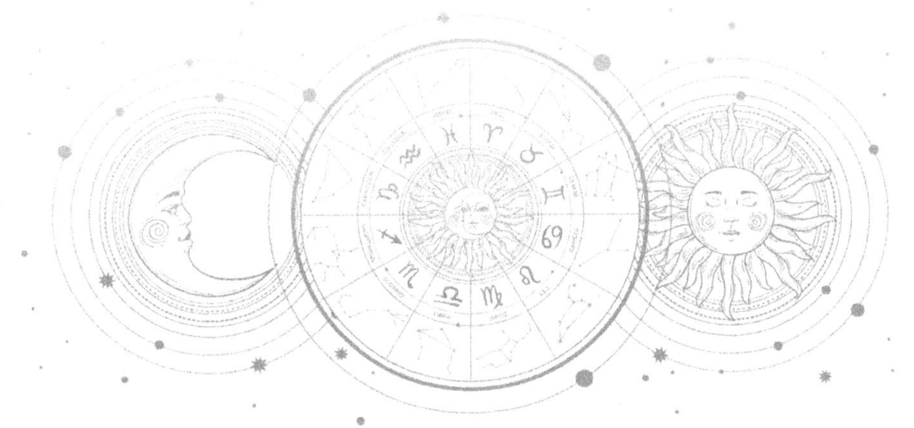

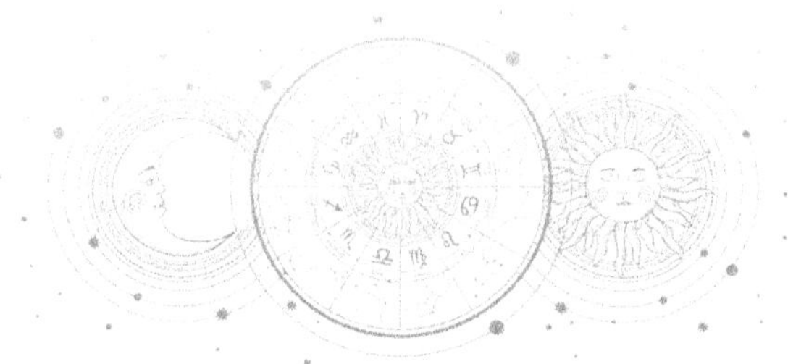

Other astrology books by Mary Shea

Planets in Solar Returns:
Yearly Cycles of Transformation and Growth

Making Choices with the Outer Planet Transits:
Uranus, Neptune, and Pluto

Solar Returns: A Study
Free PDF download at www.maryshea.com
In English, Portuguese, & Spanish

Tomando Decisiones con Tránsitos de Planetas Exteriores:
Urano, Neptuno, Plutón

Spirituality book by Mary Juno (aka Mary Shea)
Heart Journey

Table of Contents

Chapter 6 - Planetary Standing

Chapter 7 - Houses

Chapter 8 - Aspects

Chapter 9 - The Moon's Aspects

Chapter 10 - Moonsign Interpretations

Chapter 11 - Rules

Chapter 12 - Astrological Symbolism as Language

Chapter 13 - Finality

Chapter 14 - Six Steps to Creating an Electional Chart

Chapter 15 - Swim Chart Example

Chapter 16 - Computer Service Complaint

Chapter 17 - Publishing

Chapter 18 - Buying, Selling, or Renting a House

Chapter 19 - Diets and Health

Chapter 29 - Travel

Chapter 30 - Book of Secrets

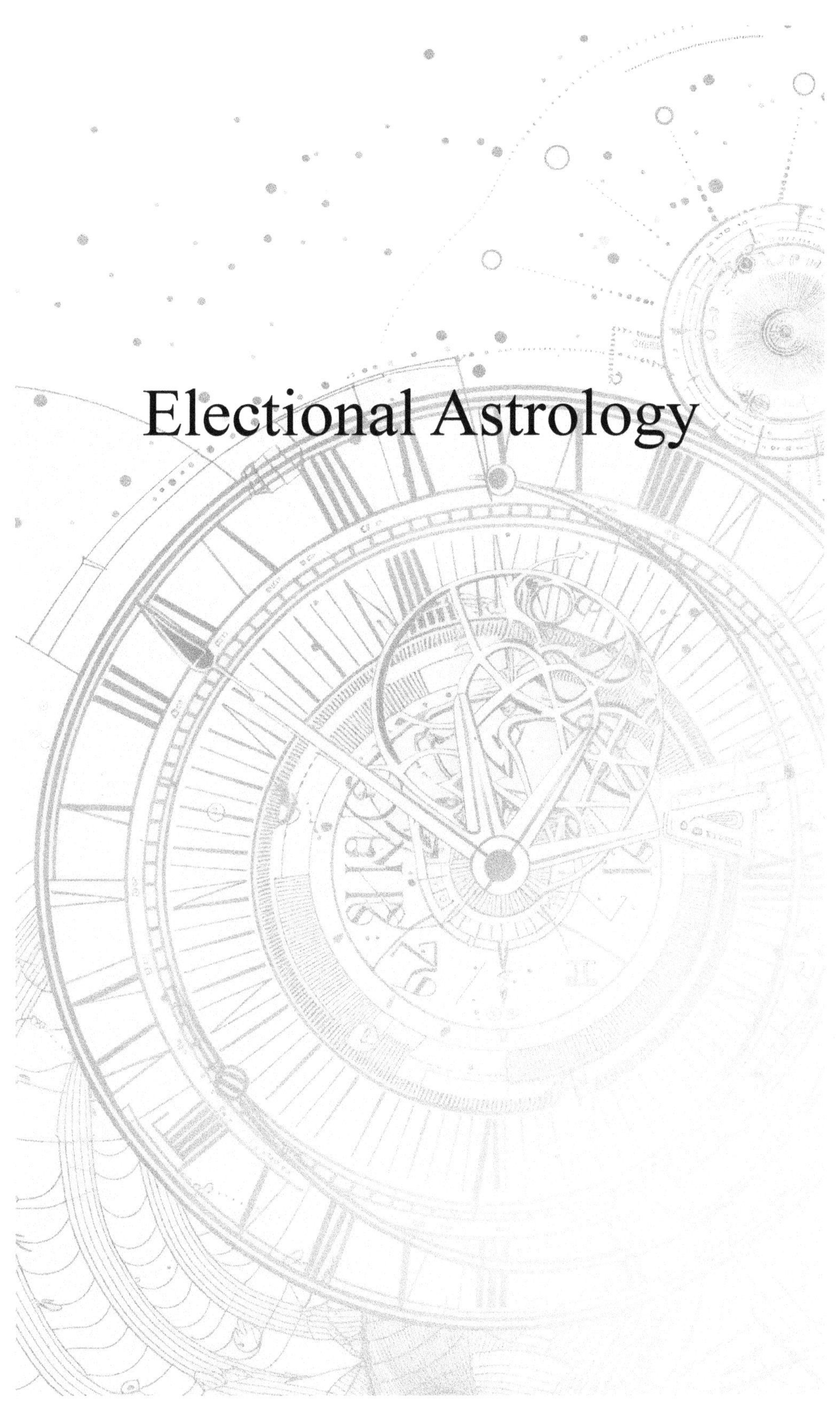

Electional Astrology

Chapter 1

Introduction

Definition of Electional Astrology

Electional astrology is that branch of astrology concerned with selecting the most propitious moment in time for initiating an event, endeavor, project, activity, agreement, contract, business, partnership, marriage, or other important matter. Astrologers have been doing this for ages, for as long as horoscopes have existed, and astrologers were aware of transiting planets. But as you will see, there are several different electional techniques presented in this book. The technique you use might be determined by your goal, or it might be determined by the level of detail you need in order to be successful. Some techniques are more exacting than others and are capable of providing important step-by-step information on how to succeed. Regardless of which technique you choose, all electional astrology techniques depend on your ability to interpret, understand, and utilize favorable astrological weather to inspire you to achieve success despite impossible odds.

Astrological Weather

A gardener knows what vegetables to plant where and when. Different plants require different types of soil, light, and temperatures. Cold weather crops like peas wither in the heat of summer. Other vegetables like tomatoes thrive in hot weather, but succumb to frost and cooler temperatures. A gardener understands the needs of the individual plants, the seasonal changes occurring from one month to the next and acts accordingly. While the plants are maturing, he or she knows what nutrients the plant will need to support growth and how much water to apply. When conditions are right, the plant thrives.

We understand climate as either supportive or detrimental to our garden, but there is also astrological weather which is a mixture of the appropriateness of our intention and the support we can expect from our environment and forces outside our awareness. Just like every vegetable plant, every project, activity, partnership, or event has an innate character with certain requirements necessary for success. A good business partnership requires the blending of individual skills and talents. A personal partnership requires harmony and common goals. Marriage requires love, friendship, and respect. Loans and scholarships involve the transfer of money. To sell your house at a good price, you need to attract a buyer. To buy a home at a lower price, you need the seller to accept your offer. Understanding the goal, the best timing, the nature of the process, and the most appropriate actions you need to take to be successful are crucial aspects of electional astrology.

Unlike climate, astrological weather is very subtle, but at the same time, it is also insightful, and can provide you with information crucial to your success. The goal of every electional astrology technique is to heighten your awareness of this subtlety so you can begin to intuit how to proceed. Using electional charts with good astrological weather increases your possibility for success because you can see your way around challenges.

This book covers the basics of electional astrology in its various forms, and then demonstrates this technique in numerous successful charts. You will learn how the language of astrology can help you make better decisions and guide you through the steps you need to take to be successful in any endeavor. Through astrology, you can pick the most propitious time that resonates energetically with your intention and raises your self-confidence. My hope is that my words and examples in this book will inspire you to use electional astrology to improve your decision-making process and make any goal easier to attain.

What do you want?

Sounds like a simple question, but for some individuals, and/or in certain situations, defining what you want is difficult. To practice electional astrology, knowing what you want is essential. You have to get comfortable with being specific in defining what you want. Energy follows thought, especially when the thought is well-defined and specific. Many times, the search for the best time helps you gain clarity on your intention. Once you have your goal in mind, you are able to focus your attention, and the possibility of attainment improves. Everything in electional astrology starts with desire. What do you want to do, be, have, experience, or give? Once you know the answer to this question, the next step is to translate your desire into astrological symbolism and find a time period that reflects your desire and indicates successful attainment.

My Philosophy Regarding Electional Charts

Before we begin, I need to share with you my philosophy regarding electional astrology. Electional astrology is an art form, not an exact science consisting of hard and fast rules, any one of which can make or break an election. I am not a fatalist. There are no guarantees with electional astrology.

I do not believe that any God, Goddess, or Universal creative force must obey my command if I come up with the perfect electional chart, assuming it exists! Nor do I believe that any God, Goddess, or Universal creative force is waiting with dire consequences should I choose a bad time. When I go through the discussion of electional rules, it might appear that there are right and wrong ways to go about electional astrology, but these are mostly presented for definition and guidance. They are intended to help you gain insight and hone your vision of what you wish to manifest. There are a lot of rules and strictures that I do not follow. I break rules regularly and still succeed. You will note this in the example charts in later chapters of this book. No one rule makes a good election; and no one rule makes a bad election. However, rules can cloak or belie the intuitive nature of electional astrology. You can be so focused on a tree (rule), that you miss the forest (the translation of your vision as seen in the chart and guidance on how to proceed).

I believe that electional astrology helps anyone define his or her specific goal and determine what steps are needed to be successful. But I also believe that the greater your expertise, knowledge, and talent to begin with, the more likely you are to succeed under any circumstances. It has been my observation that those who formulate their plans carefully and bring a lot to the table in the way of skills, intelligence, time, resources, and effort, are not only more likely to succeed, they are also more likely to pick good times astrologically that reflect their process and chances. There is a synchronicity in what we do or don't do. Those who consistently come up short and experience bad luck tend to pick challenging astrological times which reflect their lack of forethought, skills, intelligence, time, resources, and effort. They may be betting on a miracle.

There is not a direct causal relationship between electional astrology and success. Bad timing does not necessarily cause your failure, but a lack of skill, forethought, and preparation will. Good timing merely encourages your success through an interactive, intuitive, and co-creative process. There is not a fatalistic predetermination of success or failure seen in the electional chart, but a non-causal correlation. Success or failure is actually the result of numerous factors reflected coincidentally in the election. If you step back and wait for better astrological weather, you might realize what corrective actions and preparations are needed. Waiting for better astrological weather allows time for helpful intuitive insights to arise, fostering a better chance for success. If you cannot wait, for whatever reason, the election can still provide you with insight. Focus on the challenges you need to face head-on. Work your way through obstacles step-by-step. Electional charts are meant to be informative, not causal. Picking a great electional time never absolves you from participating in a meaningful way.

Electional astrology is not fatalistic since planets do not directly cause or deny your success. Rather, they simply reflect reality at the time of the election. This is similar to Horary Astrology wherein the answer to the question is born at the moment that the horary question is asked, and therefore the answer to your question lies within the horary chart erected for the date, time, and place when the question was asked. Electional astrology functions in a similar capacity. Within any electional chart you choose can be seen the difficulties one might face, the opportunities one might take advantage of, and the pathway to success or failure. In the best of circumstances, the electional chart can address negative tendencies by illuminating the need for the resolution of seen and unseen challenges. Electional astrology can also indicate the best action to take, step-by-step, thereby improving your chances for success. Information like this enables you to apply your skills, intelligence, and efforts in the most appropriate and productive manner. Electional astrology is your guide to success.

Astrology is a symbolic language, and the electional chart must symbolically say what you wish to happen. Hopefully the chart also gives you insight into how this can occur and what your role should be in the process. In this book, you will learn how to search for and erect a good electional chart that reflects your desired outcome. Once you have the chart, you will learn how to interpret the chart and follow the step-by-step instructions included that will lead you to success. A good election chart can indicate how to initiate, proceed, and succeed. In this way, a good election improves your chances for success through a co-creative interaction that fosters insight. Understanding the electional chart will show you how to apply your skills, intelligence, and efforts in the most productive, efficient, and effective manner.

There are some amazing electional charts in this book that defied all odds, but somehow succeeded. In each case, I followed the instructions seen in the electional chart. I have categorized the charts into separate chapters so you can easily find the most appropriate example electional chart to help you with your personal vision or issue. The goal of this book is to make your life easier. May you be prosperous and successful given any challenge or opportunity.

Chapter 2
Horary versus Electional Astrology

Introduction

Some astrologers might think of electional astrology as a child or offshoot of horary astrology. This is because historically electional astrology was expected to follow the same rules as horary. This may no longer be the case. I, myself, was originally trained in horary astrology by Gilbert Navarro who studied extensively with Ivy Goldstein Jacobson for many years. She wrote the book, *Simplified Horary Astrology*, which is still a classic today. I learned all the horary rules, but after I created my first electional chart in 1984 and began to practice electional astrology whenever the need arose, I experienced a shift and saw things differently.

I believe electional astrology has stepped beyond horary's shadow because it is more powerful. Modern astrologers are beginning to see electional astrology as a visionary technique that can inspire an individual to take risks, be productive, and successful when accomplishing difficult tasks despite negative expectations. You can do more with electional astrology than you can with horary. It encourages you to create and manifest the future you can envision.

Horary Charts versus Electional Charts

Horary is a very exacting astrological practice that tends to be fatalistic. You ask a question and record the date, time, and location of the asking. You then erect a chart based on this information. This is the birth chart of the question, and it is believed that the answer to your question is born in the moment of your asking. The question and the answer are one and the same: both are contained in the horoscope of the question. There are numerous exacting rules for interpreting a horary chart. Using those rules, you can read the chart of the question and discover the answer. You might ask, "Where is my wallet?" After you erect a chart for that moment in time at your given location, you will discover clues to help you locate your wallet.

Horary Astrology	**Electional Astrology**
You ask a question to get an answer. You set up a chart for that	You determine your goal or intention and then search for a
Date Time At your location	Date Time At your location
Then you interpret the chart to discover your answer.	when the electional chart will say what you want to happen.

While in horary, you ask a question, then set up a chart for that date, time, and location: the reverse is true with electional astrology. You already know the goal you seek. You know what you want to happen. You want to successfully manifest your desire, whatever that might be. You just need to find a date and time for your location that gives you a chart that reflects your intention and assists you in understanding what steps you need to take to be successful.

I believe electional astrology is more powerful than horary astrology and needs to be seen as a valid technique in its own right, with its own methods for interpretation, and not just a child of horary. When you ask a horary question, you are letting the chart determine the answer which can be tainted by unconscious fears, fatalistic doubts, and anger. Horary charts are not infallible, and they can lead to a dead-end. If the horary chart indicates difficulties or a lack of success, you could give up completely. There would be no incentive to search for a creative option.

On the other hand, when dealing with the same situation, you could decide to do an electional chart instead of a horary. If you choose the best electional time, you gain insight into how to proceed and how to navigate your way around obstacles. You gather information that assists you in the process. You have time to prepare, and you are not trying to plant a garden in the middle of winter. Good astrological weather as seen in the electional chart encourages and inspires you to be creative with the options and resources available to you. Once you begin to believe that you can be successful by factors seen in the electional chart, you willingly work towards achieving your goal.

My best advice is to use a horary astrology chart for those situations you have absolutely no control over. Always choose electional astrology if there is any possibility of empowering yourself and others. You have a lot more freedom with electional techniques which can inspire you if you use them to your advantage.

Electional astrology is a symbolic language, and it is so much richer than the horary rules electional astrology purports to follow historically. You can do more with electional astrology than adhere to make or break rules, and fatalistic predeterminations of success or failure. You can literally write a story with astrological symbolism that clarifies your goal and defines the steps you need to take to be successful. Though I will present some of those horary rules used in electional astrology in a later chapter, think of them as guidelines. Electional astrology is so much more than horary and should not be limited to a set of horary rules.

Chapter 3
Two Approaches to Electional Astrology

Introduction

There are two very different approaches to electional astrology or two different ways to choose the most favorable time to initiate your project or endeavor. One way depends heavily on the individual's natal chart as the basis for a search involving various predictive factors such as transits, progressions, solar arcs, and even solar returns. The elections based solely upon the natal horoscope are called radical elections.

A second electional astrology technique involves a stand-alone electional chart that is based on the transiting planets themselves and their aspects with one another as seen in the ephemeris. These types of elections are called ephemeral elections. They may or may not have any relationship with the natal chart during the electional search or even with the final result. Any natal involvement depends on the significance of the election and its impact on the native. Simple elections for the purchase of an automobile may not be reflected in the transits to the natal chart at all, while the purchase of a home or the establishment of a business is an event of such importance it is likely to be reflected in transiting and progressing aspects to the natal horoscope.

Radical Elections Involve the Natal Chart

Radical elections based on the natal chart may be the most common electional astrology technique used by professional and amateur astrologers. Astrologers have used this technique since horoscopes and transiting planets were first recognized ages ago. An astrologer would scan the transits, progressions, and solar arcs to find a time period with auspicious or favorable aspects to the natal chart. Occasionally the astrologer might also check the solar return if the coming event was highly significant and long lasting. Knowing the nature of the project or the endeavor one wishes to initiate, the astrologer would pick a time period, month, week, or day that looked most beneficial and complementary to the intended goal.

Timing is key with radical elections. For example, you might want Jupiter, known as the greater benefic, to make an applying or exact beneficial transit to the Sun while initiating an important project or endeavor. If the project is imminent, you would want the Jupiter transit to be close to perfecting the beneficial aspect. If you plan to launch your project over a period of several weeks or months, you might allow more time for applying Jupiter to complete the aspect to the Sun. Is your project or endeavor quick and easy, or long term and more involved? Then adjust your timing accordingly. If the project is long and involved, you might search into the future to estimate when the endeavor is expected to be completed. Knowing this in advance can keep things moving forward to completion in a timely manner, avoiding any tendency to procrastination.

When doing a radical election, you can use an ephemeris for your search, but a Transitmaster or a similar listing can be very helpful, making the search process faster and easier. Many computer astrological calculation programs have the ability to produce a detailed chronological listing of your transits, progressions, and arcs over a set period of time. This can be done for whatever time span you choose whether it be long or short duration, and for whatever level of detail you desire. Do you wish to include personal planets or just the outer planets? Most parameters can be customized in the program including aspects and orbs. If you are considering a major transition such as a relocation, career change, or marriage, you should include your secondary progressions and solar arcs in addition to your transits. If you are buying a car, you might only require a listing of your transits. Once you have a Transitmaster, it becomes easy to scan the listing for the most stressful times and also the most beneficial times.

This is a Transitmaster printout generated by Winstar, but something similar

Aspect	Date	Type	P1	P1 Pos	H1	P2	P2 Pos	H2
♄ -- ☍ Asc	07-28-2005	Tra-Nat	♄	01°♌35'	7th	Asc	01°♒35'	1st
♄ -- > 07	07-28-2005	Tra-Nat	♄	01°♌35'	7th	07		
♄ -- ☌ ♄	07-31-2005	Tra-Nat	♄	01°♌58'	7th	♄	01°♌58'	7th
♅ ---- ☌ ♀	08-01-2005	Tra-Nat	♅	09°♓56'℞	1st	♀	09°♓56'	1st
♀ - ☍ ♃	08-12-2005	Pro-Pro	♀	20°♉01'	3rd	♃	20°♏01'℞	9th
♃ -- ☍ ☉	08-27-2005	Tra-Nat	♃	17°♎37'	8th	☉	17°♈37'	2nd
♀ - ✶ ☿	08-30-2005	Pro-Nat	♀	20°♉04'	3rd	☿	20°♓04'	2nd
♃ -- △ ♅	08-31-2005	Tra-Nat	♃	18°♎31'	8th	♅	18°♊31'	5th
♇ ---- SD	09-02-2005	Tra-Nat	♇	21°♐49'	11th			
☽ ☍ ☿	09-06-2005	Pro-Pro	☽	05°♑09'	11th	☿	05°♋09'	5th
♄ -- ✶ ♆	10-04-2005	Tra-Nat	♄	09°♌13'	7th	♆	09°♎13'℞	8th
♃ -- > 09	10-13-2005	Tra-Nat	♃	27°♎23'	9th	09		
♃ -- > ♏	10-25-2005	Tra-Nat	♃	00°♏00'	9th	♏		
♆ ---- SD	10-26-2005	Tra-Nat	♆	14°♒49'	1st			
☽ > 12	10-28-2005	Pro-Pro	☽	06°♑52'	12th	12		
☽ > 12	10-28-2005	Pro-Nat	☽	06°♑52'	12th	12		

is available from Solar Fire, Kepler, Sirius, and many other computerized astrology calculation programs. You can see that this particular listing includes exact transits and progressions. Solar arcs were included in the search but are not listed since they did not occur during this time period. There are both stressful and beneficial periods between late July and late October. Note Saturn's return occurring on July 31st. Saturn returns to natal Saturn conjunct the 7th house cusp. As one might expect, this can be a stressful time involving a relationship. This was a significant time in Joan's life; it was the time of a final separation. Although she and her ex-husband had been divorced for seven years, her youngest child had just graduated college, secured a job, and was renting an apartment. There was no longer a need to maintain the family home, and it had been sold. In late July, Joan is cleaning out the home, donating, selling, giving away, and hauling to the dump the accumulations of twenty years of home ownership. Settlement occurred on August 1st and she and her ex parted ways. This is the last time they saw each other. The sale of the family home truly marked the end of their relationship.

Uranus transits conjunct Joan's natal Venus on August 1st, and Joan received half of the proceeds from the sale of the home. It has always amazed me how specific and revealing the timing of transits, progressions and arcs can be as seen in a Transitmaster. Here the timing occurring at the very end of July and the beginning of August along with the interpretation of the aspects perfectly fit the events occurring. As you look down the column of transits and progressions, note progressed Venus sextiling natal Mercury on August 30th. On August 31st, Jupiter transits trine to Uranus. If you were looking for a good radical electional time, you might choose the end of August. It was at this time that Joan left for an extended European vacation.

When picking a propitious time for a radical election, look for a time period with the best transits, progressions and arcs, while also avoiding a time period with challenging transits, progressions and arcs. Radical elections are most important for life changing events such as marriage, new business, or major relocation. In addition, a radical election search can be used as the initial step in choosing a more detailed election. For example, when electing a marriage time for the following year, a radical electional search can help you focus on the most favorable months. Progressions and solar arcs can be particular important for major events. Run an extended Transitmaster and search through the listing to ascertain the best months or time periods for a marriage.

Ephemeral Elections Involve a Stand-Alone Chart

The second approach to electional astrology is ephemeral elections. The process and result relative to an ephemeral election are totally different from that of a radical election. In fact, these elections may or may not relate back to the natal chart at all depending on the gravity of the situation. Ephemeral elections are based on current and future astrological conditions or astrological weather as seen in the ephemeris and aspectarian. In this technique, you are interested in how the transiting planets interact with one another and with the Moon. Unlike radical elections, you get to choose a specific date, time, and place for the initiation of your project or endeavor. This allows you to erect a stand-alone electional chart that not only relates directly to the transiting planets in the ephemeris, but also reflects your desired outcome and success. It is a valid chart, just like a natal chart, but for the beginning or birth of your project or endeavor. You can interpret this chart just like you would a natal chart.

There is a beauty associated with choosing a specific day, time, and location for an ephemeral electional chart. You begin to use astrological symbolism to tell the story of your goal, process, and success. Astrology comes alive as a language. An ephemeral election is a specific chart which you work from and with. It can tell you what steps to take, what pitfalls to avoid, and how best to proceed. You can gather information and intuitive insights from this chart that will help you be successful. In this way, electional astrology becomes an interactive, creative process that improves your effectiveness in any endeavor. This is a level of detail that a radical election cannot supply. Specificity is limited because there is no chart, just a day or a time period. You might understand the impact that the transits, progressions, and solar arcs are having on your natal chart, but you will not get detailed guidance on how to succeed along with information regarding particular challenges you could face along the way.

Two Approaches to Electional Astrology

Radical Elections	Ephemeral Elections
Radical elections are based on the natal chart. The astrologer searches the native's: • Transits • Progressions • Solar arcs • Solar return then picks a favorable time period or date that looks good for initiating a project or event.	Ephemeral elections are based on the ephemeris & aspectarian. You choose a goal, then the astrologer searches for a: • Day • Time • At your location that yields a chart favorable for your project. The chart includes information on how to proceed.

Picking a Good Moonsign

Within the ephemeris and aspectarian, you are looking for a positive Moonsign with good aspects between the planets and the Moon, paying particular attention to the Moon's last aspect in any given Moonsign. Here is an aspectarian

34　　A COMPLETE ASPECTARIAN FOR　2008

AUGUST

Date	Time	Aspect	B/G
	03 34	☽ ∠ ♀	b
	05 18	☽ ⚺ ☉	g
	05 29	☽ ⚹ ♄	
	06 08	☽ ⚺ ☿	g
	06 43	☽ □ ♆	b
	08 29	☉ ⚺ ♄	
	17 28	☽ ☍ ♃	B
	20 22	♀ ▽ ♅	
	22 13	☽ ⚹ ♂	G
31 Th	05 31	☽ △ ♅	G
	06 15	☽ ∠ ♄	b
	06 22	☽ ⚺ ♀	g
	12 12	☽ ⚹ ♃	G
	16 29	♀ ☍ ♅	
	18 22	☽ ♎	
1 Fr	00 03	☽ ∠ ♂	b
	06 17	☽ □ ♅	b
	07 16	☽ ⚺ ♄	g
	09 40	☽ ‖ ♀	G
	10 13	☽ ☌ ☉	D
	14 06	☽ ‖ ☉	G
	14 47	☿ ⊥ ♂	
	15 52	☽ ☌ ☿	G
	17 07	☽ ‖ ♇	D
	17 28	☽ □ ♇	b
2 Sa	02 21	☽ ⚺ ♂	g
	03 00	☿ □ ♇	
	04 25	☽ ‖ ☿	B
	06 16	☽ ‖ ♆	D
	09 18	☽ ☍ ♆	B
	11 27	☿ ▽ ♃	
	13 19	☽ ☌ ♀	G
	18 59	☽ △ ♇	G
	20 10	☽ □ ♃	b
	20 59	☽ ♍	
	22 25	☽ ‖ ♄	B
3 Su	05 30	♀ ‖ ♆	
	05 58	☿ ± ♅	
	10 58	☽ ☌ ♄	B
	17 30	☽ ⚺ ☉	g
	19 55	☽ ‖ ♂	B
	22 16	☽ △ ♃	G
	22 48	☽ ‖ ♅	B
4 Mo	02 22	☉ ‖ ♇	
	02 23	☿ ‖ ♇	
	02 23	☉ ‖ ♇	
	04 42	☽ ⚺ ☿	g
	09 13	☽ ☌ ♂	B
	12 02	☽ ‖ ♅	B
	22 36	☽ ∠ ☉	b
	23 47	☽ ⚺ ♀	g
5 Tu	00 16	☽ □ ♇	B
	02 28	☽ ♎	
	04 53	♀ △ ♇	
	05 08	☽ ‖ ♅	B
	06 35	☽ ‖ ♅	B
	08 05	☿ ± ♃	
	12 59	☽ ∠ ♆	b
	13 49	♀ □ ♃	
	17 32	☽ □ ♆	b
	17 52	☽ ⚺ ♄	g
	20 55	☉ □ ♇	
	23 23	☿ ‖ ☌	
6 We	04 20	♀ ♍	
	04 49	☽ ⚹ ☉	G
	05 00	☽ □ ♃	B
	05 46	☿ ▽ ♅	

Date	Time	Aspect	B/G
	06 33	☽ ‖ ♄	B
	06 46	☽ ∠ ♀	b
	06 56	☉ ▽ ♃	
	14 54	♂ ‖ ♅	
	18 19	☽ ‖ ♀	G
	18 38	♂ ☍ ♅	
	18 40	☿ ☍ ♆	
	20 03	☽ ⚺ ♂	g
	22 00	☽ △ ♅	G
	22 37	☽ ⚹ ☿	D
	22 41	☽ ∠ ♄	b
7 Th	01 35	☽ ‖ ♆	D
	06 11	☽ ‖ ☿	G
	09 02	☽ ⚹ ♇	G
	11 26	☽ ♍	
	11 51	☽ ‖ ☉	G
	14 54	☽ ⚹ ♀	G
	16 45	☽ ‖ ♇	D
8 Fr	01 10	☽ □ ♅	b
	02 54	☽ ∠ ♂	b
	03 59	☉ ± ♅	
	04 19	☽ ⚹ ♄	G
	09 27	☿ ▽ ♆	
	14 34	☽ ∠ ♇	b
	14 46	☿ ‖ ♆	
	15 01	☽ ⚹ ♃	G
	20 20	☽ □ ☉	B
9 Sa	04 09	☽ ‖ ♃	G
	06 59	☽ △ ♅	G
	09 06	☽ □ ♀	B
	10 28	☽ ⚹ ♂	G
	18 18	☿ △ ♇	
	20 04	☿ □ ♃	
	20 36	☽ ⚺ ♇	g
	20 53	☽ ∠ ♃	b
	21 02	☽ □ ☉	B
	23 10	☽ ♐	
10 Su	09 39	☽ □ ♀	B
	10 51	☿ ♍	
	17 08	☽ □ ♄	B
	22 00	☉ ⊥ ♂	
11 Mo	02 58	☽ ⚺ ♃	g
	14 06	☽ △ ☉	G
	19 21	☽ □ ♅	B
	21 31	☽ ⚹ ♆	G
12 Tu	00 25	☉ ± ♃	
	02 24	☽ □ ♂	B
	09 04	☽ ☌ ♇	D
	11 42	☽ ♑	
	20 22	☽ △ ♃	G
	22 52	☽ □ ☉	G
13 We	03 31	☽ ∠ ♆	b
	04 57	☽ △ ♀	G
	05 29	♀ ‖ ♄	
	06 04	☽ △ ♄	G
	14 43	☽ ☌ ♃	G
	17 03	♀ ‖ ♄	
14 Th	05 20	☉ ▽ ♅	
	06 57	☽ ⚹ ♅	G
	07 05	☉ ‖ ♆	
	07 05	☽ □ ☿	b
	09 04	☽ ⚺ ♆	g
	11 57	☽ □ ♄	b
	13 50	☽ □ ♀	b
	14 35	☽ ‖ ♃	G
	17 09	☽ △ ♇	G
	20 20	☽ ⚺ ♇	g
	22 56	☽ ♒	
	23 33	☿ ‖ ♄	

Date	Time	Aspect	B/G
15 Fr	07 43	☉ ☌ ♆	
	11 57	☽ ∠ ♅	b
	19 59	☿ ☌ ♄	
	23 32	☽ □ ♂	b
16 Sa	00 36	☽ ⚺ ♃	g
	00 50	☽ ‖ ♇	D
	01 06	☽ ∠ ♇	b
	15 12	☽ ‖ ♆	D
	16 20	☽ ⚺ ♅	g
	18 23	☽ ☌ ♄	D
	18 52	☽ ‖ ☉	G
	21 16	☽ ☌ ☉	B
17 Su	00 16	♀ △ ♃	b
	04 36	☽ ∠ ♃	b
	05 14	☽ ⚹ ♇	G
	06 15	♂ □ ♇	G
	07 46	☽ ♓	
	12 06	☽ ‖ ♄	B
	12 25	♂ ± ♆	
	20 21	☽ ‖ ☿	G
	20 26	☽ ‖ ♀	G
	22 15	☿ ‖ ♀	
18 Mo	01 23	☽ △ ♃	G
	01 46	☽ ☍ ♄	B
	08 01	☽ ⚹ ♃	G
	09 00	☽ ☍ ☿	B
	10 02	☽ ‖ ♅	B
	11 26	☽ ☍ ♀	B
	23 07	☽ ‖ ♂	B
	23 13	☽ ☌ ♅	B
19 Tu	01 13	☽ ⚺ ♆	g
	04 16	☽ ‖ ♂	B
	10 03	♂ ♎	
	11 41	☽ □ ♇	B
	14 10	☽ ♈	
	14 22	☽ ☍ ♂	B
	17 29	☽ ‖ ♅	B
20 We	00 28	☽ ‖ ☿	G
	02 19	☽ ‖ ♀	G
	03 50	☽ ∠ ♆	b
	12 52	☽ □ ☉	b
	13 15	☽ □ ♃	B
	14 02	☽ ‖ ♄	B
	18 00	☉ □ ♃	B
21 Th	01 04	☽ ‖ ☉	G
	04 01	☽ ⚺ ♅	g
	05 59	☽ ⚹ ♆	G
	06 51	☉ △ ♇	
	10 21	☽ □ ♄	b
	10 28	☽ ‖ ♆	D
	15 44	☿ ☌ ♂	
	16 11	☽ △ ♇	G
	16 53	☽ △ ☉	G
	18 38	☽ ☌	B
	23 39	☽ ‖ ♇	D
22 Fr	02 28	☽ □ ♀	b
	02 45	☽ □ ♀	b
	05 50	☽ □ ♅	b
	10 25	☿ ‖ ♅	
	12 23	☽ △ ♄	G
	16 52	☽ △ ♃	G
	17 54	☽ □ ♇	b
	18 02	☉ ♍	
23 Sa	00 14	☽ □ ☌	b
	06 13	☽ ‖ ♅	G
	06 32	☽ △ ♃	G
	06 37	☽ ‖ ♃	G
	07 22	☽ ⚹ ♅	G
	07 31	☽ △ ☿	G

Date	Time	Aspect	B/G
	09 19	☽ □ ♆	B
	15 49	♀ ☍ ♅	
	18 16	☽ □ ♃	b
	21 48	☽ ♊	
	23 50	☽ □ ☉	B
24 Su	00 11	☿ ▽ ♆	
	02 52	☽ △ ♂	G
	12 15	♀ ‖ ♅	
	13 58	♀ ▽ ♆	
	15 42	☽ □ ♄	B
25 Mo	09 52	☽ □ ♅	B
	11 50	☽ △ ♆	G
	13 56	☽ □ ♀	B
	16 03	☽ □ ☿	B
	21 52	☽ ☍ ♇	B
26 Tu	00 19	☽ ♋	
	05 58	☽ ⚹ ☉	G
	07 43	☽ □ ♂	B
	09 41	☿ ‖ ♂	
	12 59	☽ □ ♆	b
	18 35	☽ ⚹ ♄	G
	21 47	☽ ☍ ♃	B
27 We	09 02	☽ ∠ ☉	b
	12 11	☽ △ ♅	G
	18 57	☽ ‖ ♃	G
	20 05	☽ ∠ ♄	b
	21 11	☽ ⚹ ♀	G
28 Th	00 13	☽ ⚹ ☿	G
	01 11	☿ ± ♆	
	01 37	☿ □ ♇	
	02 51	☽ ♎	
	12 17	☽ ⚺ ☉	g
	12 44	☽ ⚹ ♂	G
	13 31	☽ □ ♅	b
	20 53	♀ ‖ ♂	
	21 48	☽ ⚺ ♄	g
29 Fr	01 06	☽ ∠ ♀	b
	01 32	☽ ‖ ♇	D
	01 52	☽ □ ♇	b
	02 50	☿ ♎	
	04 34	☽ ∠ ☿	b
	07 24	☉ ⚺ ♂	
	08 50	♀ ± ♆	
	09 51	♀ □ ♇	
	14 24	☽ ‖ ♆	D
	15 39	☽ ∠ ♂	b
	17 14	☽ ☍ ♆	B
30 Sa	02 15	☽ □ ♃	b
	02 26	☿ ‖ ♀	
	03 44	☽ △ ♇	G
	04 54	☉ ‖ ♄	
	05 29	☽ ⚺ ♀	g
	06 18	☽ ♍	
	09 20	☽ ⚺ ☿	g
	12 49	☽ ‖ ♄	B
	13 15	☽ ‖ ☉	G
	14 41	♀ ♎	
	19 04	☽ ⚺ ♂	g
	19 58	☽ ☌ ☉	D
31 Su	00 25	☿ ‖ ♃	
	02 21	☽ ☌ ♄	B
	04 31	☽ △ ♃	G
	06 49	☽ ‖ ♅	B
	13 03	☽ ‖ ☌	B
	14 22	☽ ‖ ☌	B
	19 44	☽ ☍ ♅	B
	21 51	☽ ‖ ♀	G

SEPTEMBER

Date	Time	Aspect	B/G
1 Mo	00 23	☽ ‖ ♀	G
	09 02	☽ □ ♇	B
	10 18	☽ ‖ ☿	G
	10 25	☽ ‖ ♂	B
	11 44	☽ ♎	
	12 14	☿ ‖ ♂	
	16 00	☽ ‖ ♅	B
	16 23	☽ ☌ ♀	G
	20 55	☽ ☌ ☿	G
2 Tu	01 18	☽ □ ♆	b
	03 58	☽ ☌ ♂	B
	06 17	☽ ‖ ☉	G
	06 28	☽ ⚺ ☉	g
	09 20	☽ ⚺ ♄	g
	10 17	☽ ‖ ♄	B
	10 59	☽ □ ♃	B
3 We	05 23	☽ △ ♆	G
	11 38	☽ ‖ ♆	D
	13 07	☽ ∠ ☉	b
	13 59	☽ ∠ ♄	b
	17 09	☽ ⚹ ♇	G
	17 25	☿ □ ♆	
	17 37	☿ ‖ ♅	
	20 02	☽ ♏	
4 Th	02 00	☉ ☌ ♄	
	02 09	☽ ‖ ♇	D
	07 10	☽ ⚺ ♀	g
	07 42	☽ □ ♅	b
	12 07	☽ ⚺ ☿	g
	16 21	☽ ⚺ ♂	g
	17 41	☉ △ ♃	
	19 25	☽ ⚹ ♄	G
	20 29	☽ ⚹ ♃	G
	20 43	☽ ⚹ ☉	G
	22 21	☽ ∠ ♇	b
5 Fr	13 08	☽ △ ♅	G
	13 23	♀ □ ♆	
	13 59	☽ ‖ ♃	G
	15 45	☽ □ ♆	B
	16 02	☽ ∠ ♀	b
	20 59	☽ ∠ ☿	b
	23 46	☽ ∠ ♂	b
6 Sa	02 15	☽ ∠ ♃	b
	04 10	☽ ⚺ ♇	g
	07 11	☽ ♐	
	17 54	☉ ‖ ☿	
7 Su	01 26	♂ ‖ ♅	
	01 35	☽ ⚹ ♀	G
	06 20	☽ ⚹ ☿	G
	07 42	☽ ⚹ ♂	G
	08 02	☽ □ ♄	B
	08 27	☽ ⚺ ♃	g
	14 04	☽ □ ☉	B
	14 52	♂ ⚺ ♄	
	21 05	♂ □ ♃	
8 Mo	01 19	☽ □ ♄	B
	02 47	☽ ⚺ ♄	
	04 03	☽ ⚹ ♆	G
	04 13	♃ Stat	D
	05 09	☿ □ ♃	
	16 43	☽ ☌ ♇	
	17 44	☽ ☌ ♇	
	19 45	☽ ♑	
	23 18	♃ △ ♄	
9 Tu	03 13	♇ Stat	D
	10 13	☽ ∠ ♆	b
	14 58	☉ ‖ ♂	

from *Raphael's Astronomical Ephemeris of the Planets' Places* for 2008. The first step in creating a good ephemeral election is finding a good Moonsign. For example, the Moon in Aries, starting on Tuesday, August 19th, at 14:10 has a final Moon aspect trine Sun on Thursday, August 21 at 16:53, two days later. Before the Moon trines the Sun, you can see a lot of other aspects in between including oppositions, squares, sextiles, and trines. Those are just the zodiacal aspects. There are also contra-parallels to Uranus and Neptune, along with four parallels to Mercury, Venus, Saturn, and the Sun. Parallels and contra-parallels do count in electional astrology, and the Moon is allowed all of her applying aspects before leaving the sign, even if it is several days later. From the Moon's entry into Aries to the final aspect trine to the Sun, all the aspects in-between might be significant.

What you want to avoid when searching for a good Moonsign is something like the Moon in Gemini seen on Saturday, August 23rd. The Moon enters Gemini at 21:48. The Moon's final aspect is an opposition to Pluto. While the Moon is in Gemini, it also squares the Sun, trines Mars, squares Saturn, squares Uranus, trines Neptune, squares Venus, and squares Mercury. Squares and oppositions in any Moonsign can indicate challenges. The Moon's last aspect, an opposition to Pluto, indicates complications before all is said and done. Although there are some good aspects in this Moonsign, the ending opposition to Pluto would not be considered a positive conclusion to any matter. It is the ending of any Moonsign, as well as the process along the way, which is important in ephemeral elections. You want to succeed easily, so choose a good Moonsign with a good final Moon aspect.

You are also looking for a time when "good" planets are in "good" aspects to one another. Good planets are normally considered to be the Sun, Moon, Mercury, Venus, and Jupiter, but this may or may not be the case given specific signs, aspects, and your desired outcome. In electional astrology, Jupiter and Venus are almost always positive. Jupiter is commonly referred to as the greater benefic while Venus is referred to as the lesser benefic. In addition to picking strong, beneficial planets, you want them aligned with good aspects. Good aspects are normally considered to be trines, sextiles, parallels, contra-parallels, and sometimes conjunctions, (depending on the planets involved). Besides focusing on beneficial aspects, you want to avoid competing negative aspects like squares and oppositions especially from malefic planets. These are normally considered to be Mars, Saturn, Uranus, Neptune, and Pluto, but again, everything is relative. Future chapters will address the interpretations for planets and aspects in greater detail, but in electional astrology there must be positive and negative indications of benefit, stress, and success. Please note, definitions in this book related to good, bad, positive, negative, beneficial or malefic do not and should not be used in natal interpretation. Electional astrology has black and white lines of distinction and natal astrology does not.

Choosing a Specific Time within a Moonsign

The Moon denotes the activity in an electional chart, and the Moon is allowed all of her applying aspects until she leaves the Moonsign, even if this is across several days. Just as it is important to pick a Moonsign with good aspects and a good final aspect for the Moon, it is also important to choose a good starting point within the Moonsign.

	17:14	☽♌
	18:23	☿☌♀
	21:43	☽∥♂
29	00:54	☽⊼♅
	08:22	☉#☽
	09:24	☽⊼♂
	17.27	☽#♀
	21:01	☽☍♆
	22:39	☽∥♄
30	00:25	☽#☿
	01:48	☽#♂
	02:13	☽△☿
	03:01	☽△♀
	03:44	☽✶♃
	10:19	♀✶♃
	14:54	☽△♇
	19:38	☽⊻♄
	21:07	☿✶♃
	23:10	☽△☉
		☽♍

In this example, the Moon enters Leo at 17:14 on the 28th, but the Moon does not leave the Moonsign for two days. The Moon's final aspect is a trine Sun at 23:10 on the 30th. Even if the Moon's final aspect is two days away, it still counts as the end result of your election.

Since the Moon indicates the activity in an electional chart, and the Moon is allowed all of her applying aspects until leaving the sign, process is important as well as the final result. When choosing a Moonsign, look for good aspects along the way in addition to a positive final Moon aspect.

Once you have chosen a good Moonsign, choose a good starting point within the Moonsign. Looking at the Moon in Leo aspects, you will note that the Moon makes an opposition to Neptune at 21:01 on the 29th. If you do not want this aspect applying in your electional chart, you could choose a later time. If your elected time is 00:25 on the 30th, the opposition to Neptune is in the past and does not apply to future activity. You have choices within every Moonsign on when to initiate your endeavor, what the process will look like moving forward, and how the electional chart will reflect your goal.

Three Moonsign Choices

1. Choose a Moonsign with a good final Moon aspect (Result)
2. Choose a Moonsign with good interim aspects (Process)
3. Choose a good Moonsign starting point (Avoid challenging aspects)

The Moon's previous aspects can indicate past or present conditions at the time of the election chart. This is in addition to the Moon's ability to indicate future developments as the Moon moves forward toward the Moon's final aspect. The Moon and its aspects are major indicators of movement and change within the electional chart.

What Tools You Will Need

When doing an ephemeral election chart, you will need an ephemeris with an aspectarian that includes the Moon's sign, the Moon's ingress and egress, and all the aspects that the Moon makes within a Moonsign including declinations (i.e. parallels and contra-parallels). As shown in the aspectarian example in this chapter, I have used *Raphael's Astronomical Ephemeris of the Planet's Places*, because everything is sequential in one column, but any aspectarian that meets the above-mentioned criteria will do. It is also possible to calculate and print out an aspectarian from many of the computer astrological calculation programs.

I also highly recommend a rulership book. You can use either Lee Lehman's, *The Book of Rulerships: Keywords from Classical Astrology*, or *The Rulership Book*, by Rex Bills and Kristen Brandt Riske. These are reference books you can use to discover what planets or houses are related to your intention in any electional chart you wish to erect. A rulership book along with a good ephemeris with aspectarian are the tools you will need to construct your own ephemeral elections.

Ephemeral Elections Versus Radical Elections

Many astrologers believe that the ephemeral electional chart takes precedence over the transits and progressions to the natal. In some cases, this is true as the ephemeral election is a stand-alone chart independent of the natal chart. On the other hand, I believe the best elections work with the natal chart and the transits, progressions, and solar arcs when the event is of great importance. The association with the natal chart depends somewhat on the gravity of your intentions.

Sometimes you are given months to come up with a marriage or business chart. If you are electing a chart for a major event, doing a radical study first of the transits, progressions, and solar arcs to the natal chart can help you zero in on the best time period. Once you have defined your likely time period, whether it involves one month or several months, your focus should shift to the ephemeris and aspectarian which details the interactions of all of the planets. It may occur to you that certain planets in certain signs fit your goal more so than others. For example, Venus in Taurus or Libra could be an appropriate choice in a wedding chart. These are not the only Venus placements you might use for a marriage, but if either sign fits with your bride and groom, your search period is thereby defined. If you are doing an electional chart for a business, you might choose certain planets that reflect the nature of the business. Regardless of the signs you focus on, you want to utilize the best planets with the best aspects within the best Moonsign you can find. And when the ephemeral election falls within a good time period as seen through a radical election search, you are able to combine the best of both worlds, radical and ephemeral, resulting in the best chance for success.

Chapter 4

Two Kinds of Ephemeral Elections

Introduction

There are two different kinds of ephemeral elections, "character elections" and "activity elections." Although they both involve initiating an endeavor at a specific date, time, and place, and erecting a stand-alone chart, they have very different purposes. As you will see, character elections form an entity such as a marriage, business, or partnership that has character. On the other hand, activity elections rarely form an entity and can be more appropriately described as "to-do" elections. They are erected with a specific purpose in mind, such as lowering the price of a house you wish to buy or applying for a scholarship. The successful accomplishment of a goal is what's most important.

There are no perfect electional charts, whether character or activity. There is only the best chart given the selected time period whether it be a day, week, or month. Within any electional chart, you can see your hopes, intentions, resources, and support, but also your fears. Most importantly, you can envision your path to success in the chart and the steps you need to take. Present in the chart are also any challenges you need to face and surmount, otherwise you may fail. Electional charts are mirrors of one's innermost thoughts and feelings. Everything in the electional chart is information that can prepare you for the journey, guide your steps along the way, and improve your chances for success.

Character Elections

Character elections are the type of elections most astrologers and many people are familiar with. They establish an entity that has an enduring character or quality. These types of electional charts are used for marriages, partnerships, businesses, incorporations, organizations, and groups, just to mention a few examples. The essential element and purpose of this type of election is to establish a real presence that manifests and expresses a character that can last over a period of time. The important thing to remember is that once established and set in motion, the entity you create has a chart just like a natal chart. You can look at the transits and progressions to see how the character or quality of the entity created evolves and endures. You live with a character election chart, sometimes for years.

Because the nature and quality of character elections are lasting, you want to think in terms of process and dynamics. What will the chart look like moving forward into the future? Is there a balance of power? What are the strengths in the chart and what are the challenges? (There are always challenges since there are no perfect charts.) Do the planets in the electional chart enhance the natal charts of the participants? For example, in a marriage election, you want the chart to complement both the bride and the groom so that the marriage brings out the best in each. You want the election to reflect their combined and individual wishes in forming this union. Do they want children? Will they practice a common religion? What do they see as their roles in marriage? Where is there agreement, and what are the areas of disagreement? Most importantly, how will they make their love last.

Character Election Examples

Establish an entity that has a character or enduring quality.	Emphasizes process, harmony, & chart dynamics of the planets.
• Marriage charts	• We want our love to endure.
• Partnerships / contracts	• We want our talents to blend & complement each other.
• Business & corporations	• Our business should grow & succeed financially.
• Organizations	• Our charitable organization should help others.
• Groups	• We need harmony within our support group.

Creating a character election is generally more involved than creating an activity electional chart. It can be an in-depth process. Not only do you have to understand the goal of the entity being formed and be able to reflect that in the electional chart, but you also need to investigate how the election will affect each of the individuals involved. This means looking at the individual natal charts for the participants. For this reason, it is always good to do a radical electional search first. Choose a time period that is beneficial and complimentary to the natal horoscopes of the participants. When you scan all the transits and progressions, you should see things come together in a common time period that is good for everyone involved. Within this mutually beneficial time period, look for a chart that complements both individuals. This technique of doing a radical search first and then shifting to an ephemeral election is particularly important when doing a marriage or partnership election. You want the strengths and energies of the individuals to balance each other out, and the best way to do this is to select a time period that is good for all those involved.

Activity or "to do" Elections

Activity elections are also known as "to do" elections because they are meant to accomplish a specific goal or result such as buying a home for less or selling a house for more. These elections are task oriented and only last as long as it takes to successfully complete an endeavor. The timing may be short-term, as little as minutes, or long-term and lasting over several years when goals are complex. Activity elections usually do not form an entity. You can create an activity election around any purpose you desire. Besides buying or selling a house, activity elections can be used to secure a loan, apply for a scholarship, get a book published, file a consumer complaint, initiate a lawsuit, apply for a job, or seek acceptance into a school or club. These are just a few examples, but there is no limit to the reasons for using an activity electional chart. If you can envision your goal and find the appropriate astrological weather in the ephemeris and aspectarian, you can erect a chart to initiate your endeavor. Your goal can be lofty or mundane, complex or simple. The possibilities are endless.

Activity or "To-do" Election Examples

Accomplish a specific result. They are usually short term, and they do not form an entity.	Emphasize outcome, actions to take & the activity Moon
• Sell or buy a house	• I must sell my house immediately
• Get a loan or scholarship	• I need startup cash for a business.
• Apply for a job	• I want to get the bid for this construction job.
• Publish a book	• I want an agent to get my book published.
• File a consumer complaint	• My purchase was defective & I want a new replacement.

The beauty of a good activity election is that the chart can help you understand the process moving forward, and even tell you how to succeed by providing specific instructions. An exchange of information occurs between the electional chart and the creator of the chart. The exchange might be intuitive, it might be intellectual, it might be a gut reaction. The mind expands to see movement within the chart. Many or all of the interim Moon aspects can suggest step-by-step guidance regarding actions you need to take and tasks you need to complete in a timely manner. In addition, the overall chart will have a lot to say about the path to a successful conclusion.

Another benefit of creating an activity electional chart is that it has measurable outcomes. If you practice creating ephemeral elections regularly, your astrological skills will sharpen over time. You can use these charts in ordinary situations to make life easier for yourself. Character elections are not generally measurable. With an activity election either you are successful, or you fail. Results tend to be clear-cut, black or white. Unless you are a professional astrologer, you might not erect many marriage or business charts. These are not everyday needs, especially for the amateur. But an activity election can be used for common endeavors and be most helpful even in mundane situations. There are many times when you can use an activity election chart.

Below is a breakdown of the various electional astrology techniques. Radical elections are totally different from character and activity elections. The tools, techniques, and processes you use for radical versus ephemeral elections entail different skill sets. I believe ephemeral elections give you a lot more information because you have a chart you can interpret. They also allow you to use astrological symbolism as a language to write the story of your success.

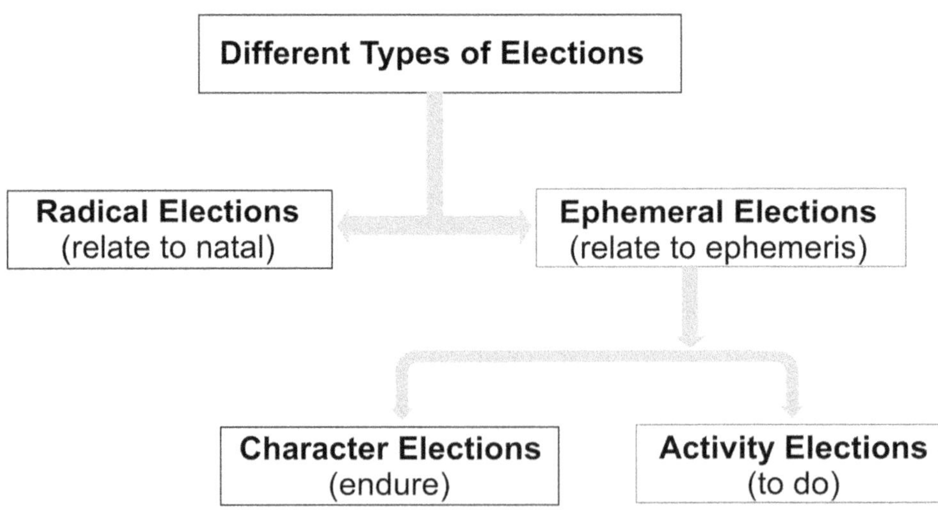

The Innate Value of Ephemeral Electional Charts

An ephemeral electional chart is like a vision board. It is a statement in concise symbols (planets, houses, and aspects) of what you wish to happen or manifest. It embodies your goal in astrological notation. Both the process of finding a good electional time for your endeavor, and the subsequent implementation of the steps needed to succeed, stimulate a creative problem-solving mindset.

During the search for the best electional time, you must weigh various options as you work to translate your goal into astrological symbolism. There are many things to consider. What future Moonsign or Moonsigns are of the highest quality? What are the best planets to represent your intention? What houses should you focus on? What aspects would work to your advantage? What Moon aspects would you prefer to avoid? Can you imagine planets as people and the aspects as interactions?

Just as importantly, what electional times and charts do you reject? Why do you reject them? Do you reject them out of anxiety and fear, or concrete problems you wish to avoid? If the same issues keep coming up in your search, you probably must address them regardless, or you need to seriously expand your search calendar. As much information and guidance can be gleaned from the charts you reject as the final chart you choose.

The very act of searching for and choosing an ephemeral election chart stimulates one to think ahead, plan, and prepare. This is why electional astrology goes far beyond horary rules and takes on a life of its own. Electional astrology is an art form and creative process that helps you navigate life issues and gain insight into solutions. It helps you to see beyond the problem and seek a solution.

The more you put into your project, with or without an electional chart, the more positive and productive the outcome. It is also true that the more confident you feel, the more likely you are to succeed. Optimistic thoughts tend to lead to success, and this is where a good electional chart can be most helpful, raising your self-confidence. If you can see the goal in an electional chart, you will believe that it can happen. The greatest gift an astrologer can give to any individual is a "sense of vision" of how good the future could be along with guidance on how to get there.

Draw on all of your abilities to be successful. Let the positive interpretations associated with the electional chart stimulate your creative impulses, allowing you to develop new avenues for success previously not considered. Let the challenging interpretations caution you to consider possible proactive solutions to future problems which could affect your project negatively. By perceiving difficulties before beginning a project, they can be circumvented, counteracted, or corrected. Use any negative interpretations seen in the chart to troubleshoot situations. You can overcome difficulties with practical solutions and common sense. With electional astrology you can be inspired to reach higher, try harder, persevere despite impediments, and succeed against all odds.

In this book, I will be presenting numerous examples of electional charts, both character elections and activity elections. Some of these charts worked despite impossible odds. I will show you how to construct a good election using astrological symbolism so that the chart says what you want to happen. I will teach you to see planets as people, and aspects between planets as interactions between people. The chart houses can indicate either things or locations. Now that you know the different types of electional charts and understand their point of origination, let's begin to see the planets as people within the electional chart.

Chapter 5
The Sun, Moon, and Planets

The interpretations presented here and elsewhere in this book may not be what you are used to, or what you would normally find in other books on electional astrology. That is because some of these definitions were taught to me directly by Gilbert Navarro. We joined forces in 1986 and wrote the *Good Days Action Planning Guide*, for twenty years. It was a yearly electional astrology planner with interpretations for each day. The definitions, interpretations, and insights contained in this chapter and in other chapters in this book stem from my interactions with Gilbert, and my own work as an electional astrologer over the past forty years.

The interpretations in this chapter and many of the chapters which follow, are not meant to be applied to natal horoscope interpretation. In electional astrology, you need to clearly determine positive, negative, plus, and minus options in order to make sense of the chart and render a decision. These black and white distinctions should only be used in electional astrology charts as these interpretations are inappropriate for natal chart readings.

Introduction

Viewing the planets as people in the electional chart can give you clues to their actions and responses to your project or request. Are they supportive or are they a deterrent? There can be both positive and negative interpretations based on either the nature of the planet, its standing, or its aspects. If the planet has good standing either in rulership or exaltation, and good aspects, you are more likely to view that planet's interpretation in a positive light. Here is someone who might be able to help you realize your goal. If the planet has poor standing in detriment or fall, or is peregrine with difficult aspects, you are likely to avoid using that planet in a significant way in your election. A person represented by this planet might be too weak to assist you. Even worse, this could be someone who will thwart your efforts and block your path to success. This is probably never truer than with Pluto, which is commonly seen as a malefic or negative significator in many situations. It is important to remember that any planet in your election can have bearing on the chart interpretation even if that planet is secondary to the story and outcome you are trying to represent.

The Sun in an Electional Chart

Rulership	Leo
Exaltation	Aries
Detriment	Aquarius
Fall	Libra

The Sun usually indicates a male, but not always. The Sun is an important planet in any electional chart because it is frequently seen as an indication of success when strong and well-aspected. A person represented by the Sun might be an important person or one of high station, like a boss or authority figure. It is someone who has earned respect and might be famous or well-known. You can benefit through the efforts of this person if your significator or the Moon makes a good aspect to the Sun. Since the Sun never turns retrograde, it represents a person who is less likely to disappoint you. Only retrograde planets can indicate disappointment. Consider carefully when the Moon applies to a negative aspect to the Sun, especially if it is an important significator. Even if the Moon goes on to make positive aspects, and even if the Moon's final aspect is a good one, success might be tainted or less than it could have been. You can recover from a difficult aspect to the Sun, but it takes effort and creativity to make up for lost influence. Should the Moon make an applying parallel or contra-parallel to the Sun after a square or opposition, things can certainly turn around. You can win back the positive support you lost by adjusting your strategy. A good Moon aspect to the Sun in any chart is nice, but not essential. There are other planets to represent supportive people.

Combust the Sun, Under the Sunbeams, & Cazimi

A planet within 8 1/2 degrees of the Sun, applying or separating, and in the same sign and house as the Sun is considered to be combust the Sun unless it is saved by being in mutual reception. The conjuncting planet represents someone who might be overwhelmed by closeness to a powerful person. He or she can get burned by someone who is much stronger while his or her own vitality can be somewhat reduced as a result. Mercury is never weakened while combust the Sun since it is considered to be the Sun's messenger; however, the individual might be anxious. Mars conjunct the Sun is not considered combust. It is strengthened by the heat and proximity when conjunct the Sun. This individual might become more forceful.

A planet plus or minus 17 degrees of the Sun is under the sunbeams. The planet and the Sun need not be in the same sign. Closeness to the Sun still has an overwhelming effect, similar to being combust the Sun, but to a lesser degree. It is only mildly unfortunate. The person represented by the planet under the sunbeams might be timid, passive, or lacking in power in comparison to a more forceful individual.

Any planet within 0 degrees and 17 minutes of the Sun is known as Cazimi and is greatly strengthened in this position. The closeness does not burn, but instead enhances chances for success. The individual represented by a planet this close to the Sun is in a favored position, supported by an important person. The Moon is Cazimi 30 minutes of time before the exact conjunction to the Sun and 30 minutes of time after.

Positive Interpretations for the Sun

an important person	rules success in general
an adult male	authority figure, boss. or superior
a commanding presence	famous person
has power over the matter at hand	someone who can help you
keeps commitments & promises	delegates work to others
is respected	can be kind
accepts services and favors gratis	has money he or she did not earn
in a position to gain more or less	clumsily playful
able to benefit others	is superior in some way
in control	sports-loving
shines a light	someone with masculine traits

Negative Interpretations for the Sun

can be cruel	an indication of failure
can deny or thwart you	authority who stands in your way
might burn you figuratively	someone who overshadows you
tends to be insecure	commands a place beyond ability
self-indulgent	gambler, reckless speculation
improvident	financially irresponsible
lacking foresight	in debt
extravagant	dominates or controls

The Moon in an Electional Chart

Rulership	Cancer
Exaltation	Taurus
Detriment	Capricorn
Fall	Scorpio

☽ As the Moon moves through its Moonsign, it indicates activity and change according to its house placement and major aspects. The Moon usually represents a grown woman or someone who is emotional, sensitive, maternal, or caring. The Moon rules mothers or those who nurture, and domestic situations in the electional chart. Whether in the home or outside of the home in the community, this is a person who volunteers and works for free even though she is very capable. She easily develops and accomplishes a diversity of tasks and functions for others.

Positive Interpretations for the Moon

is the activity of the election chart	change related to house placement
feminine energy, receptive traits	strongly influenced by mother
someone willing to work for free	a woman, mother, maternal
family member	takes a subordinate position
develops projects for others	a nurturing person
completes a diversity of functions	rules trivial or minor matters
someone sensitive and sympathetic	someone maternal
emotional, placid, genteel	yearns to be carefree
the home, residence	a domestic situation
eventually relieved of obligations	involved in domestic affairs
cares for children	a commoner
owns real estate	is looking to buy a property

Negative Interpretations for the Moon

easily imposed on, meek	mommy's boy
subject to fads and current fashion	defers to the decisions of others
fluctuates too much, inconstant	someone facing domestic upsets
too attached to mother	missed educational opportunities
someone moody, overly emotional	subject to emotional swings
not always dependable	common, not cultured
one who may fear his or her father	burdened by many responsibilities

Mercury in an Electional Chart

Rulership	Gemini, Virgo
Exaltation	Virgo, Aquarius
Detriment	Pisces
Fall	Leo, Pisces

☿ Mercury can represent a person of either gender. Generally, the individual is young, but still knowledgeable. It depends somewhat on Mercury's standing and aspects. On one hand, Mercury can represent someone who is very intelligent and has the information or facts that you need, an expert. On the other hand, Mercury can represent someone who is ill-informed, uneducated, lacking in common sense, or prone to making poor decisions. Someone who is impractical, impatient, and restless. This person may not be dependable. When Mercury is poorly aspected and has no standing, all communications and revelations should be verified. You would be wise to investigate any information thoroughly.

Positive Interpretations for Mercury

young person, male or female	gives advice and acts as an agent
minds someone else's business	has the information
mind can change if changing signs	does research
knowledgeable person, expert	carries a message, letter, or reply
has the facts or details	forms an agreement
great in an emergency	can be persuaded, can be persuasive
a communicator	is clever, skillful
subject to correction	susceptible to change
sibling, brother or sister	able to adapt
rules trivial matters	quick to make decisions
highly intelligent	disseminates information
good in an emergency	detail oriented

Negative interpretations for Mercury

someone misinformed	has inaccurate information
too easily swayed or persuaded	changes mind when changing signs
impatient	changes mind if changing direction
tends to be restless	a busybody who gossips
nervous, anxiety ridden	shrugs off mistakes

indecisive, hesitates	does not research thoroughly
trivializes matters	makes poor decisions
a liar who misrepresents	someone secretive
withholds information	might be mentally ill
impractical	experiences or causes delays

Mercury Retrograde

Mercury turns retrograde three to four times a year. Retrogradation normally lasts for three weeks. The effects associated with the retrogradation may begin a few days before Mercury turns retrograde and continue until the day Mercury turns direct again. New situations which appear on the day that Mercury becomes stationary or turns retrograde may be best left to develop during the retrograde period. A sense of urgency can push you to make snap decisions or take immediate action. Don't be rash! This is not a good time to buy on the spur of the moment without thorough investigation. Major purchases may be reduced in price after the retrograde period, and you can save money by waiting. Impulsive choices and slapped-together impromptu projects are more susceptible to problems, reversals, new considerations, modifications, mix-ups, mistakes, or delays in correspondence and decisions. Long-term or well-planned projects and decisions are less subject to error. It's urgency which causes mistakes.

The three-week retrogradation period should be a time of introspection and research. If you delay action and keep track of your thoughts during this time, you might see an evolution in your thinking process. Insights gained during Mercury retrograde can be invaluable and set you on a correct course for the future.

While Mercury is retrograde, it rules everything that begins with an "R" like reply, repeat, rewrite, replace, renege, rescind, recall, rethink, recondition, recover, record, reconcile, reclaim, redo, return, renegotiate, renovate, repair, and reverse a decision. You are more likely to change your mind while Mercury is retrograde, and when it changes sign or direction. The change may be major or minor. Mercury retrograde is beneficial in situations where you want to successfully complete a task you failed at before.

Mercury retrograde is best when it is at its fastest in the middle of the retrogradation. Speed equals intellect and the ability to make good decisions. A slow Mercury can indicate a tendency to make poor decisions. If Mercury is slow, information might be slow in coming and with difficult aspects, it could come too late or not at all. It is more important to do things in a good Moonsign when the Moon is making good aspects and the Moon's final aspect is positive than to try to avoid a Mercury retrograde period entirely. Life can continue normally.

On a good day, (when the Moon's aspects are positive), you can successfully repeat a task, get a reply, or have something repaired, replaced, or repealed. You can make good decisions or start a project so long as you leave room for adjustments. Good days allow for corrections. There may be something you don't know, but things can turn out well anyway. A lack of information doesn't have to seriously affect the outcome. If the Moon's aspects are good and you fail, the matter still turns out well. Failing might have been beneficial in the long run. It is better to fail with good moon aspects than succeed with bad moon aspects.

On a challenging day, (when the Moon's aspects are negative), while Mercury is retrograde, a lack of information becomes a factor in your difficulties. These days, you tend to think too slowly or make decisions too quickly.

Special Rules that Apply to Mercury

According to some astrologers, Mercury is never burnt out by being combust the Sun since it is the messenger to the Sun and needs to communicate. Within 17 degrees of the Sun, Mercury is under the sunbeams and tends to show someone who is anxious, but not debilitated.

Mercury rules information. When the Ascendant in an electional chart is Mercury ruled, and especially when the Ascendant falls in Gemini, an important piece of information maybe inaccurate. There is something to be corrected, and the person initiating the election should be warned to research further.

Venus in an Electional Chart

Rulership	Taurus, Libra
Exaltation	Pisces
Detriment	Aries, Scorpio
Fall	Virgo

♀ Venus represents a young woman, maiden, or girl. In electional charts that require funding, Venus can indicate the person with money and/or resources needed to pay expenses. This might involve your personal money, or the money supplied by others. Financing could involve a loan, mortgage, scholarship, reward, or gift. High priced possessions might be sold off. Venus is the lesser benefic, while Jupiter is considered to be the greater benefic. Venus' standing in the electional chart might indicate how expensive any process will be, what type of funding could be available, how it could be acquired, and when.

In any relationship election such as a marriage or partnership, Venus can represent the relationship itself, the wife, spouse, mistress, or either partner. In general, Venus rules cooperation between all parties. At its best, this entails mutual benefit.

Positive Interpretations for Venus

feminine energy	partner or spouse
woman, young woman, girl	cooperative or diplomatic individual
someone kind, a loving disposition	attractive
agreeable, sweet disposition	a person you can benefit from
someone socially acceptable	well-versed in diplomacy
a good negotiator	promotes harmony, is peace-loving
works to improve situations	innocent of ulterior motives
enjoys creature comforts	financially well-off or wealthy
soft-spoken, gentle demeanor	romantic and loving
well-mannered, cultured	less trouble, more gain for all
volunteers, a charity worker	someone donating time & resources
emphasizes inner qualities & values	security oriented

Negative Interpretations for Venus

socially unacceptable person	unpleasant
isolationist, recluse	course, crude, or vulgar
someone unkind	disagreeable
may concede to keep peace	ill-mannered
refuses to compromise	a hoarder, too materialistic
careless with money, extravagant	non-materialistic
elitist, snob, uncaring	unattractive
financially poor, penniless	someone not likely to benefit you
possessive	unloving
focused on outer physical beauty	emphasizes outer qualities

Venus Retrograde

Venus is retrograde for 5 weeks. Some years, it is direct for the whole year. While Venus is retrograde, you may not be able to depend on an external manifestation of beauty, love, and/or money. This is a time when you are meant to reflect on the inner value of your experiences and not get hung up on the outer display. Events associated with beauty may not take place as planned since they may be tainted or marred in some way. Immaterial and intangible gifts are especially important during this period as material and monetary rewards may be delayed. Money or possessions you expect to acquire might not appear until Venus turns direct. If you buy something as a financial investment, it may not accrue the way you thought it would. If you purchase a luxury item, you may not be pleased with it.

This is a great time to volunteer for nonprofit projects or charity work. Relationships started during this time might be associated with inhibitions. These should be brought to light and discussed. One can experience unusual attractions. Perhaps a relationship can only survive as a behind-the-scenes or clandestine affair. A tendency to withdraw or isolate is possible. Outward assurances and displays of love and affection are not readily evident. Something may be withheld, and if this is so, disappointments are likely. Sometimes existing relationships may be up for review. This is a good time to renew existing relationships and contact old friends and lost lovers. On a different, inner level, a very strong spiritual connection can be made if the focus is on mutual fulfilment.

Values may be more closely attuned to the individual's aesthetic appreciation, and therefore may be less consistent with societal preferences and standards. One can see unique beauty in what might appear ordinary to others. One's taste in material objects might depend on the emotional qualities and memories associated with those objects. Price or status becomes unimportant.

On a good day, (when the Moon's aspects are positive), you will be able to make the transition from outer to inner qualities. New insights help you to assess relationships accurately. Financial returns are more likely.

On a challenging day, (when the Moon's aspects are negative), the defects in the external display will be especially annoying. Relationships will be frustrating and financial returns are delayed, absent, or only partial.

Mars in an Electional Chart

Rulership	Aries, Scorpio
Exaltation	Capricorn
Detriment	Taurus, Libra
Fall	Cancer

♂ Mars generally represents a masculine person such as a man or boy, but instead can represent a woman who is commanding and assertive. Mars indicates a fighter, whether one who fights for him or herself literally or figuratively, or advocates for someone else. When Mars is strong by sign, house placements, or aspects, it signifies someone capable of self-motivation and independent action. He or she tends to work quickly, and projects are usually done on time. Mars is not associated with procrastination. Rather, a Marsian person will resist attempts at delay and refuse to be thwarted or limited while striving towards a goal.

Mars might relate to someone who is hotheaded and quick to respond aggressively or argumentatively. One does not mince words. When under duress, speech is fiery and cutting. On the other hand, the individual represented by Mars knows when to abandon a lost cause. What is quick to ignite can be quickly extinguished. Mars can be an energizing force in any electional chart, especially when it is well-aspected, well-placed by house, or exalted in Capricorn.

Positive Interpretations for Mars

masculine energy	a male, man, young man, or boy
someone brash	a go-getter
an initiator, self-starter	effective debater
assertive, defends his or her rights	competitive person
a fighter protecting self-interest	able to advocate for others
acts quickly, sooner than expected	self-motivated individual
a force of nature, someone dynamic	energizes situations
able to work independently	outspoken
knows what to cut out	knows to abandon a lost cause
goal oriented, strives	courageous
brave fighter, soldier	strategizes
independent	fast worker

Negative Interpretations for Mars

may be the transgressor	argumentative, intimidates
conflicted, resentful	is angry or hostile
injured or may have a scar	carries a grudge, never forgets
unruly personality	a brat or upstart, reacts too soon
aggressive person	can be cruel
picks fights, may fight dirty	sharp tongued, cutting
aims to win at all costs	thinks the ends justify the means
crude personality, not polished	manipulates
pushy, a bully	self-destructive, self-defeating
comes armed with weapons	prone to self-sabotage
misbehavior when far from the Sun	an overpowering force

Mars Retrograde

Mars is retrograde for sixty to eighty days once every two years. It can be direct for a whole calendar year. Whenever any planet is retrograde, there is a tendency to be more reserved in certain situations. Your hesitation causes you to review your past behavior and look for new ways to respond in the future.

Through this process, you can begin to refine your responses. As you go back over situations, (either in your mind or in reality), you can do things differently, making corrections in the way you handle events.

While Mars is retrograde, you review the way you handle anger, self-defense, self-motivation, and sexual relationships. During this period, outward anger or conflicts may not be appropriate; there are other ways to win wars or make your point. You are open to handling anger-producing situations differently, and may try passive-aggressive behavior, manipulation, arbitration, or subtle power plays, whatever seems more appropriate.

If you do not normally assert yourself, you may be forced to defend yourself during a Mars retrogradation. Whatever your tactics, you must give some thought to what you are doing. If your tactics do not work or are inappropriate to the situation, your anger will continue to build while Mars is retrograde, and you can expect anger to manifest full-blown by the time Mars turns direct. If you have seriously wronged or angered another person with your inappropriate responses or acts of aggression, you can also expect the backlash to occur as Mars turns direct. Issues involving a lack of self-motivation or sexuality are also important during this time and should be addressed.

On a good day, (when the Moon's aspects are positive) while Mars is retrograde, assertive techniques will work to your advantage, and you are more likely to be successful when you take the initiative. You can respond appropriately to any situation.

On a challenging day, (when the Moon's aspects are negative), while Mars is retrograde, responses tend to be inappropriate. Your inability to handle a conflict will hurt you. You react when you should not, or do not respond when you should. Self-motivation can be a problem. You may be motivated in the wrong direction, doing the wrong thing, at the wrong time, or with the wrong people. When taking action, you are either too early or too late, and never on the mark. Sexual relationships started on a difficult day while Mars is retrograde may be disappointing.

Special Rules that apply to Mars: Mars is never combust the Sun, as he is the one who defends the Sun. Mars is favored, and actually becomes stronger when near the Sun.

Jupiter in the Electional Chart

Rulership	Sagittarius, Pisces
Exaltation	Cancer
Detriment	Gemini, Virgo
Fall	Capricorn

♃ Jupiter is the greater benefic and represents someone with a generous and forgiving nature, especially when Jupiter is in the 7th house. This person is optimistic about life in general and will meet you more than halfway in any exchange. Jupiter represents someone who has great respect for the rule of law and can be a judge, arbitrator, or a fair and honest person who seeks to settle matters honorably and out of court. An individual associated with religion or spirituality such as a priest or rabbi, a philosopher, or professor of higher education are all examples of Jupiterian individuals. Because Jupiter is a huge planet, it is associated with big ideas and plans that can expand or grow. Place Jupiter in the most appropriate house for maximum benefit.

In a sign of detriment or fall, a person indicated by Jupiter will not practice what he or she preaches. This person might be disadvantaged in some way. If he or she meets you more than halfway in any situation, it will be to his or her detriment and your advantage.

Positive Interpretations for Jupiter

the greater benefic, protective	benefactor who assists you
optimistic person, jovial, playful	meets you more than halfway
honorable, honest, keeps promises	willing to help those less fortunate
forgiving, especially if in 7th house	is younger than a Saturnian person
tends to be blunt	someone who inspires others
able to reconcile, an arbitrator	tends to like expensive things
may raise the price, or pay extra	promotes growth and expansion
charitable, generous, hopeful	a teacher, publisher, intellectual
cooperates, peace-loving	defers to settle matters honorably
respects laws, a judge	someone who settles out of court

Negative Interpretations for Jupiter

suffers from foot in mouth disease	may not practice what s/he preaches
may renege on a promise	lazy, too placid
makes inappropriate jokes	gluttonous
lacks concern about any threats	a moral snob, questionable ethics
not ambitious	materialistic
can be a hypocrite	exaggerates, boasts, lies
wasteful, overindulgent	expensive, over charges
prone to all forms of excess	decisions are unjust or arbitrary
unchecked growth, out of control	can be too much of a good thing
misguided generosity	success costs more than it is worth

Jupiter Retrograde

Jupiter is retrograde for six months out of every year; this is not considered a major concern in any election chart. Jupiter has a twelve-year cycle and is exalted in Cancer once every twelve years. The Moon's final aspect to a retrograde Jupiter might have some bearing. The interpretation depends on the Moon's aspect to Jupiter, Jupiter's sign, and standing. More information can be found in Chapter 9: The Moon's Aspects.

Saturn in an Electional Chart

Rulership	Capricorn, Aquarius
Exaltation	Libra
Detriment	Cancer, Leo
Fall	Aries

♄ Saturn can represent a mature male or elderly person. He or she is a trainer, a teacher, or someone who expects you to get it right. The goal is excellence, and a person represented by Saturn can push you to be the best that you can be. Saturn is a tough disciplinarian and is sometimes known as the greater malefic, but a Saturnian person or situation can actually reward you better than a Jupiterian person or situation when you put in the extra effort.

Saturn rules practicality, persistence, and cause and effect reality, especially as it relates to work. When you improve your technique or effort, something better can always happen. A Saturnian individual learns through failure or criticism. A Saturnian teacher allows student failure while supplying structure and support. You might be asked to try again and again with more effort to make any dream a reality. Nothing is given and everything has to be earned. Saturn has been called the cosmic tripper. It represents a person or circumstance that demands perfection. You will be tripped and thwarted until you do your best. When working with Saturnian energy, you cannot cut corners, but in the end, your success will be impressive.

Positive Interpretations for Saturn

an older person, perhaps wiser, male	authority figure, boss
teacher, expert in a field of study	practices what Jupiter preaches
an organizer, good planner	slow. purposeful movement
is realistic, serious, cautious	provides structure
honors traditions, a conservative	executive, head of an organization
knows how to shrink or decrease	follows the rules and regulations
aware of limitations, a disciplinarian	government representative

strives for excellence	can reward you better than Jupiter
is practical, stable, patient	understands cause and effect
will put forth great effort	someone persistent, never gives up
benefits through learning	benefits from experience
awareness of causality	knowledge acquired through failure
never accepts less than your best	trips you until you get it right

Negative Interpretations for Saturn

greater malefic	slows you down, thwarts & delays
can be cruel, cold, stern	acts later than expected
unforgiving	makes you face the harsh reality
puts a damper on things	demands impossible perfection
miserly, overly thrifty	teaches by allowing failure
appears without warning	hypercritical, tough love
tough taskmaster	suspicious, aloof
withholds out of meanness	manages without authority
"the devil to pay"	has the ability to permanently injure

Saturn Retrograde

Saturn is retrograde for six months out of every year; this is not considered a major concern in any election chart. Saturn has a twenty-nine-year cycle and is exalted in Libra. The Moon's final aspect to a retrograde Saturn might have some bearing. The interpretation depends on the Moon's aspect to Saturn, Saturn's sign, and standing. More information can be found in <u>Chapter 9: The Moon's Aspects.</u>

Uranus in an Electional Chart

Rulership	Aquarius
Exaltation	Scorpio
Detriment	Leo
Fall	Taurus

♅ Unlike the other planets in our solar system, Uranus spins on its side rather than on a more upright axis. Similarly, a Uranian individual marches to the beat of a different drum and carves out his or her own path. Uranus represents someone who thinks differently, dresses differently, and behaves differently. He or she stands out in a crowd. This is someone who does not follow tradition, any organized religion, societal norms, or predetermine male-female roles. Instead, this person questions everything, and endeavors to be the test case for most rules or restrictions. "That regulation is fine for everyone else, but it does not fit my situation!"

The dual nature of the Uranian person is that he or she is both brilliant and erratic, innovative and unpredictable. He or she is an impersonal, free thinker who is ahead of his or her time, and will inspire you as long as you do not become dependent. On the upside, the person represented by Uranus will seek to modernize what is old, update what is no longer applicable, and improve what could be working better. He or she has the ability to cut through the red tape propagated by Saturnian individuals and institutions.

Negatively, Uranus can represent a disruptive influence in your electional chart. It is never what you expect it to be no matter how prepared you are. You can cover all your bases and still be surprised.

Positive Interpretations for Uranus

an inventor or innovator, genius	an original, a non-conformist
someone who cuts through red tape	gets around restrictions
spontaneous personality, carefree	ahead of his or her time
a newcomer, someone just arrived	freedom fighter
always advocating change	changeable chameleon
seeks improvement & modernization	rule changer, rule challenger
seeks to evolve, enlighten	believes in the exception to the rule
one who updates or reforms	does things differently
brilliant, insightful	looks different, eclectic dresser
takes on heroic ventures	mentally quick
beats the structure of Saturn	unconventional

Negative Interpretations for Uranus

highly unusual, possible weirdo	disorganized, disruptive
never what you expect	divorced, separated, never commits
undependable, unpredictable	rebel without a cause
contrarian, objects to proceedings	functions outside of society norms
separates, breaks relationships	eccentric, informal
out of control, loose cannon	ignores rules, exception to the rule
promotes revolution	hermit, loner, estranged, disappeared
accident prone	never what you expect

bearer of undesirable surprises	unstable, adds to the instability
modernizations that don't work	renovations run amok
too impersonal	crazy genius

Uranus Retrograde

Uranus is retrograde for six months out of every year; this is not considered a major concern in any election chart. Uranus has an eighty-four-year cycle and is exalted in Scorpio. The Moon's final aspect to a retrograde Uranus might have some bearing. The interpretation depends on the Moon's aspect to Uranus, Uranus's sign, and standing. More information can be found in Chapter 9: The Moon's Aspects.

Neptune in the Electional Chart

Rulership	Pisces
Exaltation	Gemini
Detriment	Virgo
Fall	Sagittarius

Ψ   Neptune represents the dreamer who is inspired to go beyond or higher with any endeavor even though this might not be realistic. Every dream starts with imagination and inspiration, but at some point, the individual must work to manifest the dream with a plan. The beauty of the visions lies with Pisces, but the execution of the vision belongs to the material world and the organizational ability of Virgo. This is not an easy transition to make. For this reason, Neptune rules uncertainty. The translation of the vision into manifestation is many times "iffy."

Neptune rules the highest of the high, (a spiritual person, an artist, or someone who serves others), or the lowest of the low, (a drug addict or alcoholic). There is a fine line between the two groups. A Neptunian person in very intuitive, but easily fooled or misguided because distinctions are subtle. For this reason, the influence of a Neptunian person can cloud any issue though his or her intent is not to be untruthful or misleading. When Neptune is prominent in your election chart, you must deal with a level of uncertainty and confusion.

Positive Interpretations for Neptune

insightful, idealistic, visionary	follows hunches, someone intuitive
spiritual person, prays, meditates	very sensitive, compassionate
good Samaritan, one who sacrifices	wants to serve others or a cause

dedicated to higher principles	follows a calling or purpose
can be persuaded or influenced	open to suggestions
enhances, decorates	able to create an image
imaginative, inspired, inspirational	creative, artistic, musical, poetic
provides surreptitious assistance	secretiveness is advantageous
able to go with the flow	humanitarian, kind, gentle
stays true to highest ideals	charitable, one who donates
imaginative, dreamer	intuitive, psychic

Negative Interpretations for Neptune

airhead or flake, vague or weird	iffy influence, easily fooled
unknown or vague information	deceptive, misleading, a fraud
has incorrect information	confused, confusing, indecisive
too easily persuaded, overwhelmed	always uncertain, lack of clarity
oblivious and totally unaware	wanders without direction, aimless
forgetful, not good at explanations	creates an illusion
scandalized, caught in a scandal	drug addict, alcoholic, complainer
undefined, unclear or missing facts	perhaps impermanent

Neptune Retrograde

Neptune is retrograde for six months out of every year; this is not considered a major concern in any election chart. Neptune has a one-hundred-and-sixty-five-year cycle around the Sun and relative to earth. The Moon's final aspect to a retrograde Neptune might have some bearing. The interpretation depends on the Moon's aspect to Neptune, Neptune's sign, and standing. More information can be found in Chapter 9: The Moon's Aspects.

Pluto in the Electional Chart

Rulership	Scorpio
Exaltation	Aquarius
Detriment	Taurus
Fall	Leo

People who organize focus groups or endeavor to sway public opinion carry characteristics associated with Pluto. Power and control can be the name of the game from large corporations to those who manipulate and monopolize. Numerous expectations and demands can be brought forth by a Plutonian person who complicates whatever you are attempting to accomplish.

This might delay or derail progress. Things are never simple and straight forward regarding Pluto. There are layers and layers of mystery and intrigue that someone brings to the table making any process more involved than it need be.

An individual represented by Pluto might be a researcher or investigator trying to uncover the truth or solve a crime. Unfortunately, he or she may not dig deep enough. There is a tendency not to be thorough.

Pluto represents someone who is missing in action, either on purpose or through no fault of his or her own. He or she might not show up at a previously scheduled event or appointment. Even in a crowd, Pluto indicates a person who remains a detached loner. A lack of reliability is a factor. Consider a backup plan for important events.

An individual represented by Pluto works best in isolation and needs to focus without interruption. This is someone who can streamline operations, discard duplicates, and reorganize the office. These abilities represent the positive qualities associated with Pluto, but the dark side remains. Here is someone who can control or manipulate people and circumstances for person gain.

Positive Interpretations for Pluto

major organization or corporation	power broker
able to lead and control	a manager, boss
can be a good researcher	acquires in-depth information
one who investigates	discovers what is hidden
a detective or police person	works undercover
allows voting by proxy	have a backup plan if absent
discards outdated material	streamlines & organizes office
organizes focus groups	able to motivate the public at large
works best alone or in seclusion	isolation increases focus
enjoys mystery & intrigue	handles insurance matters
is detached	avoids distractions

Negative Interpretations for Pluto

manipulates, monopolizes	drama queen, or drama junkie
serious complications	overly controlling, micromanages
poor researcher	incomplete information & research
abandons tasks, people, situations	complicates matters & situations
missing in action at a crucial time	unreliable under pressure
does not fit in or mingle well	complicated loner

wannabe groupie	can be vulgar or crude
conspiracy theorist	spreads gossip and rumors
can discard important information	hides documents & possessions
delays progress with demands	compounds trouble & problems
group for nefarious purposes	rebellious
undercover personality	generally guilty of something
hidden or subversive agenda	insurance fraud, bungled claims
sways public for personal gain	possible criminal activity
requires a backup plan or proxy	isolates

Pluto Retrograde

Pluto is retrograde for six months out of every year; this is not considered a major concern in any election chart, especially when it is not your significator. Pluto has a two-hundred-and-forty-eight-year cycle around the Sun relative to earth. The Moon's final aspect to a retrograde Pluto might have some bearing. The interpretation depends on the Moon's aspect to Pluto, Pluto's sign, and standing. More information can be found in <u>Chapter 9: The Moon's Aspects.</u>

Conclusion

These are just some of the interpretations for the planet representing people or personal characteristics. Positive and negative keywords have been presented to assist you in seeing people and dynamics in your election chart. Some of these interpretations you already know, while some might be new to you. The planets are actors or items in an election chart. They help to write the story regarding the manifestation of your vision. They are clues to the activities, interactions, and dynamics relevant to your vision's successful conclusion.

Chapter 6
Planetary Standing

Introduction

When choosing planets to represent you or your goal in an electional chart, you want to pick the strongest planets with the best aspects, and most appropriate and beneficial house placement. Planets reflect strength according to their sign, house placement, element, and angularity. In most electional charts, it is advisable to choose planets in rulership or exaltation, either by sign or house as the most important significators. Planets can also have some limited standing by being in an element that they rule, a house that they rule, or by being angular.

Standing and Natal Interpretation

It is worth mentioning again, I don't use standing for natal planets. I do not look on natal Mercury in Pisces as being in detriment or fall, or to have any disability. There have to be positives and negatives in electional astrology, but I do not use the same interpretation and considerations in natal astrology.

Planets in Rulership

☉	♌		♃	♐ ♓
☽	♋		♄	♑ ♒
☿	♊ ♍		♅	♒
♀	♉ ♎		♆	♓
♂	♈ ♏		♇	♏

Planets with Standing in Rulership by Sign

A planet in a sign that it rules has dignity and rights in the matter at hand. A planet's special powers when in rulership will be reflected on the person it represents. In most cases, this individual and his or her actions can create an advantage through actions perceived intuitively within the electional chart and planetary interactions. It is important to note what planets are in rulership, their house placements, and aspects to determine the most beneficial way to proceed, what opportunities might be available, and what actions to take. Rulership has its privileges. Learn to recognize them and use them to your advantage.

Planets in Rulership Represent an Individual who:

has rights in the matter at hand
he or she belongs
has dignity
has an advantage in the proceedings or is in control of the proceedings
is generally trusted and respected
is in the right place at the right time
behaves appropriately given the circumstances
is only doing what he or she should be doing
encounters only expected problems
gains assistance in his or her endeavors
is capable and qualified
is healthy and/or fit
is likely to be aware of opportunities as they arise
tends to have some control or power over the proceedings
works to avoid problems

Planets with Standing in Rulership by House Placement

You can improve the standing of any planet through house placement. Planets can be in rulership, exaltation, detriment, or fall by residing in the corresponding house of rulership, exaltation, detriment, or fall. Standing in rulership by house placement occurs when a planet is in a house that it naturally rules. For example, Sun in Virgo gains dignity by house placement when it is in the fifth house. Even though the Sun is not in a sign it rules, it is dignified by house. The person represented by a planet that has standing by house placement is in a favorable position, but probably has less influence or power when expressing his or herself. Rulership by sign may relate more to the individual's strength of character and intellectual abilities, while rulership by house placement may relate more to the individual's circumstances. Standing according to house placement is seen as less advantageous than standing according to sign.

A planet in a house wherein the sign on the cusp of the house is a sign of rulership for that planet lends dignity to the planet even if the planet is in a different sign. For example, if the Sun in Virgo is in the fourth house and Leo is on the cusp of the fourth, the Sun has some standing by house placement. This does indicate standing, but again it is somewhat limited. Under this rule, a planet can be peregrine by sign, but dignified by house. This indicates that though the person ruled by the planet may have problems or character defects that limit his or her chances for success, he or she is in a good place and possibly has some control over the situation that will support success.

Planets in Detriment

☉	♒		♃	♊ ♍
☽	♑		♄	♋ ♌
☿	♐ ♓		♅	♌
♀	♈ ♏		♆	♍
♂	♉ ♎		♇	♉

Planets with Standing in Detriment by Sign

Planets in detriment are not necessarily weak, though they can be, but they do indicate challenges. The individual represented by a planet in detriment is disadvantaged in some manner, probably because he or she is outside of one's normal territory. Someone may be trying to succeed in the enemy's camp. Planets in detriment show that there is no support system. Others will not lend assistance and may resent the intrusion. The individual can succeed against all odds and against opposition, but may have to resort to less than conventional or kosher means. This will require great effort and perhaps, in the end, the individual will be too weak and debilitated to take an important part in any proceedings.

Planets in Detriment Represent an Individual who:

is wrong
has little or no rights in the matter at hand
is unable to act
is at a disadvantage
meets with opposition
does not belong
is not welcomed
is in the enemy camp
is not appreciated regardless of what he or she is doing
is not where he or she should be

is doing what he or she should not be doing
might function outside the law, rule, or norm
is incapable and/or unqualified
may be weak
could be unhealthy

Planets with Standing in Detriment by House Placement

Planets can be in detriment by house placement and not just in detriment by sign. Detriment by sign may relate more to the individual's character, while detriment by house placement may relate more to the individual's circumstances. A planet in a house that is opposite a sign that it naturally rules, even though it is not in a sign of detriment, is somewhat disadvantaged. For example, Mercury in Cancer in the ninth house is in detriment by house placement. The person represented by a planet in a detrimental house might be in a difficult situation, but is generally impacted less by negative and inhibitory influences than if in detriment by sign.

A planet in a house wherein the sign on the cusp of the house is a sign of detriment for that planet means that the individual's circumstances are not likely to be supportive or beneficial. For example, if Jupiter in Libra is in the fifth house and Virgo is on the cusp of the fifth, Jupiter is in detriment by house placement. The environment is not as welcoming as it could be. Challenges exist.

Planets in Exaltation

☉	♈		♃	♋
☽	♉		♄	♎
☿	♍ ♒		♅	♏
♀	♓		♆	♊
♂	♑		♇	♒

Planets with Standing in Exaltation by Sign

A planet is the strongest and most effective in its sign of exaltation. It indicates someone with clout and power in the matter at hand. This individual is more likely to receive assistance, and could benefit greatly from special treatment. He or she will be welcomed, respected, and honored. In most situations, he, she, or it can rise to a higher position and display a remarkable improvement.

Planets in Exaltation can Represent an Individual who:

is the honored guest
is welcomed, and his or her actions are also welcomed
is appreciated, and his or her actions are appreciated
has clout, and his or her influence has clout
is sitting pretty, is comfortable
can rise to a higher position in the present situation
is very comfortable
can have his or her cake and eat it too
is likely to receive and benefit from assistance or special treatment
works to avoid problems

Planets with Standing in Exaltation by House Placement

You can improve the standing of any planet by placing it in a house of exaltation. This occurs when a planet resides in a house naturally ruled by its sign of exaltation. For example, Venus in Cancer is exalted by house placement when it is in the twelfth house. Even though Venus is not in a sign of exaltation, standing improves and the planet is in a more favorable situation. Exaltation by sign may relate more to the individual's character, while exaltation by house placement may relate more to the individual's circumstances. The person represented by a planet in exaltation by house placement can have opportunities and circumstances that are more beneficial, but has less power to express his or herself than when in a sign of exaltation.

A planet in a house wherein the sign on the cusp of the house is a sign of exaltation for that planet lends standing to the planet even if the planet is in a different sign. For example, if Jupiter in Leo is in the fifth house and Cancer is on the cusp of the fifth, Jupiter has exaltation by house placement though it is somewhat limited. Under this rule, a planet can be peregrine by sign, but exalted by house. This indicates that though the person ruled by the planet may have problems or character defects, he or she is in a welcoming place and possibly has some influence over the situation.

Planets in Fall

☉	♎		♃	♑
☽	♏		♄	♈
☿	♌ ♓		♅	♉
♀	♍		♆	♐
♂	♋		♇	♌

Planets with Standing in Fall by Sign

A planet in fall is opposite its sign of exaltation. The individual who is represented by a planet in fall is not necessarily weak and still can succeed using other than traditional or kosher methods. When planets are in fall, the ends can justify the means. Individuals are unlikely to get any assistance and will feel that they are not welcomed. Their tendency will be to do something, knowingly or unknowingly, wrong and end up having to apologize. In the worst-case scenario, there can be a fall from grace.

There are situations where you might use a planet in detriment or in fall to represent you. Suppose you have bad credit, but you still want to successfully apply for a loan. With great aspects you can still get a loan even though you are not qualified. If you file a complaint or start a lawsuit, the ruler of the 7th should be in fall, be at fault, and to blame. You, on the other hand, want to be in rulership and have rights in the matter.

Planets in Fall Represent an Individual who:

is wrong
is at fault or to blame
able to do something requiring an apology
likely to do something he or she should not be doing
is incapable
can be unqualified
might not be healthy
isn't welcomed, and neither are his or her actions
can experience a fall from grace
might cheat to succeed
ends tend to justify the means

Planets with Standing in Fall by House Placement

Planets can be in fall by house placement. Fall by sign may relate more to the individual's character, while fall by house placement may relate more to the individual's circumstances. A planet in a house that is naturally ruled by its sign of fall, is somewhat disadvantaged even though the planet is not in a sign of fall. For example, Venus in Leo is in fall by house placement whenever it is in the eighth house. The person represented by this planet can be in difficult circumstances though the challenges might not be as inhibitory if the planet was in fall be sign.

A planet in a house wherein the sign on the cusp of the house is a sign of fall indicates fall by house placement even if the planet is in a different sign. For example, if Jupiter in Aquarius is in the seventh house and Capricorn is on the cusp of the seventh, Jupiter is in fall by house placement though challenges will not be as strong as when Jupiter is in fall by sign.

Planets with Standing in Regard to Element

A planet is strengthened when it is in an element that it rules. For example, the Moon rules Cancer, a water sign. When the Moon is in Pisces, the Moon represents someone who is in his or her element and therefore has some standing.

Planets with Standing in Regard to Angularity

Planets have accidental dignity by being angular when in the 1st, 4th, 7th, or 10th houses, especially when they are close to the cusp. This indicates some standing in regard to the matter as hand, though power and influence are limited.

Peregrine Planets Lack Standing

Peregrine planets are not lucky enough to be in a sign, house, or element that they rule. A planet that is in an element that it rules, is not peregrine. Peregrine planets indicate someone who is roving and aimless. They are weak and wandering without a sense of direction. Their vibration is pointless in regard to the matter at hand. They may be ineffective and easily led, misled, manipulated, or taken advantage of. They are not dependable unless saved by being in mutual reception. Peregrine planets need a tighter orb in order to function in the electional chart. In most or all electional charts, you would not want to be represented by a peregrine planet.

A planet is not peregrine if it has standing by sign (even detriment or fall), house placement, or element. A planet can seem peregrine by sign, but then be dignified or exalted by house. This situation indicates that although the person may have problems or character defects, he or she is in a good place, and may have special consideration because of circumstances.

Peregrine Planets Represent an Individual who:

has no standing
is weak
can be taken advantage of
wanders aimlessly without direction
has a vibration that is pointless in the matter at hand
is far off base

is not dependable unless saved by mutual reception
is ineffective and lacks strength
is led, misled, or easily manipulated
is susceptible to difficult aspects
needs a tight orb to function in an electional chart

Chapter 7
Houses

Introduction

The houses are the places where the electional activity takes place. They set the stage for events to unfold. They can also represent the people or matters related to your election. I use a Placidus, Tropical Chart. These are the more common definitions for the houses in an electional chart. Should you require more detailed information, there are three books I would recommend. You can use *The Rulership Book*, by Rex E. Bills & Kris Brandt Riske, *The Book of Rulerships: Keywords from Classical Astrology*, by Lee Lehman, or *The Astrological Thesaurus - House Keywords (Book 1)*, by Michael Munkasey.

The 1st House

In an electional chart, the 1st house rules several important areas, some of which are not normally associated with the 1st house in a natal reading.

the initiator	The 1st house always rules the person or entity initiating the project or event. This is the person who sets the wheels in motion. The person is represented by the ruler of the sign on the 1st house, any planets in the 1st house, and the activity Moon unless the Moon is the ruler for a significant other person or factor in the chart. (* See 1st house interception exceptions below.)
remaining	The 1st house rules "here," where you are now. It is the house of remaining as opposed to the 7th house which is the house of removing. The 1st house is where you wish to remain while the 7th house is where you wish to go.
the present	The 1st house rules the present and current conditions, including anything one might want to change.

health & body	Because the 1st house represents the initiator, it is also an indication of the initiator's health and physical condition.
the plaintiff	In any lawsuit, the 1st house rules the plaintiff who initiates the lawsuit, while the 7th rules the defendant.
* 1st house interception	A sign intercepted in the first house and any intercepted planets in the first house do not rule the initiator. They are more likely to rule a possible impediment to progress or success. This is especially true if there is an intercepted planet contained in the 1st house interception. The interference noted by the interception may or may not be serious or difficult to overcome.

The 2nd House

money & possessions	The 2nd house in the electional chart has interpretations that are similar to natal interpretations in that it rules money, resources, securities, movable possessions, earning ability, wealth, gain, and personal property.
income and expenses	The 2nd house rules both income or funds earned and personal expenses whether discretionary or not.
future	Where the 1st house rules the present, the 2nd house rules the near future and when the sign on the 1st house is the same as the sign on the 2nd house, matters tend to stay the way they are from the present extended into the near future. This can work to your advantage in an electional chart when you want matters and conditions to remain the same.

The 3rd House

communication, negotiations, contracts & books	The 3rd house rules all forms of communication, and anything written including books, letters, messages, written contracts, or agreements. This house might include the process of negotiation though the other person would be represented by the appropriate house.

cars	Cars and local means of transportation such as bicycles and buses are ruled by the 3rd house.
information & technology	All forms of information and methods for gathering or disseminating information including advertising and technology such as computers, electronic equipment, phones, and the internet are ruled by the 3rd house.
education	A grade school education and coursework are ruled by the 3rd house.
distant future	Where the 1st house is the present and the 2nd house is the near future, the 3rd house can represent the distant future when the election involves timing.
trips	If you are planning a short distance trip or visit, look to the 3rd house regardless of how you travel.
siblings	Siblings are family members and can be ruled by the 4th house unless the focus is specifically on brothers and sisters.
neighbors & neighborhood	When buying a house, the 3rd might indicate the surrounding neighborhood.
bylaws	Established rules, bylaws, or standards set by a local community or organization are reflected in the 3rd house.

The 4th House

real estate & unmovable property	First and foremost, the 4th house rules immovable property such as any home you hope to sell including undeveloped land and business real estate. The 4th also rules any house, building, or lot you hope to buy. Planets in the 4th house can increase the value of the property while malefics here are cautionary and might indicate a problem, seen or unseen.
home & domestic situations	The 4th house also rules the domestic situation, people living in the home whether coming and going, any improvements taking place, and the need for repairs.

motherhood & family	Motherhood and pregnancy can sometimes relate to the 4th house as well as the 5th. The 4th house is also associated with all family members in general.
end of the matter	The 4th house is called "the end of the matter house." Planets in the 4th house of any electional chart may have bearing on the outcome.

The 5th House

price	Real estate purchases or sales are relevant to the 4th house, but the 5th house is the price of the property. Benefics here can indicate an increased price while malefics can indicate a price reduction whether buying or selling.
children & pregnancy	The 5th house rules children as one might suspect. Pregnancy can be seen in this house or in the 4th house of motherhood.
creativity & hobbies	Creative projects and artistic endeavors belong in the 5th while writing is ruled by the 3rd and publishing is ruled by the 9th house.
love affairs & romance	The 5th house rules love affairs and unbonded or undefined one-on-one relationships which may or may not be sexual or stable, but are usually romantic, exciting, and may involve courtship. Marriages, betrothals, and partnerships are seen in the 7th house.
recreation	This house rules fun, entertainment, both indoor and outdoor recreation, events of this nature, and gambling

The 6th House

paid work or volunteered	The 6th house rules all work whether paid or unpaid, coworkers, employees, the office environment and decor. Included as work is volunteer service. Any changes in the office routine, employee benefits, or job descriptions would be ruled by the 6th house.

caregivers	Caregivers for sick or elderly individuals are ruled by the 6th house. Doctors are ruled by the 7th house.
management	The 6th house might refer to low level management or an immediate supervisor as opposed to a 10th house boss or authority figure. If you are a manager yourself, the 6th house can relate to your employees and people you plan to hire.
office & its organization	The 6th house rules a home office or an office at a place of business, and its organization or lack thereof.
diet & nutrition	If you wish to diet or improve your health through nutrition, you would focus on the 6th house.
animals	The 6th rules pets, small animals, farm animals, and those who care for them. Veterinarians are professionals and therefore ruled by the 7th
sickness, health, & healing	While health of the initiator is seen in the 1st house, disease, healing, and the means to heal are associated with the 6th house.
tenants	If you are a landlord, your tenants are represented in the 6th house.

The 7th House

marriage & partnerships	The 7th rules marriage, spouses, partners, & partnerships along with all bonded or contractual relationships.
separation & divorce	The end of a relationship in separation and divorce is also related to the 7th house.
unknown person	The 7th is the house of the unknown or undesignated person. If you are selling your house, the prospective buyer is described by the 7th, but if you are buying a house, the seller is seen in the 7th.
lawsuits & defendant	Lawsuits and the defendant in any lawsuit are represented by the 7th house. The plaintiff, as the initiator in any lawsuit is shown in the 1st house.

agreements, disagreements, & contracts	If there are benefics in the 7th house, the person you are dealing with is more likely to be honorable. Agreements can be reached and contracts signed.
cooperation & competition	While conjunctions in the 7th house can indicate cooperation, depending on the planets involved, they can instead indicate competition, especially when the 1st house and the 7th house are at odds with oppositions.
conflict & opponents	If there are malefics in the 7th house, disruption or a conflict of interest is possible. Opponents and adversaries, whether malefic or not would be indicated by oppositions from the 7th house to the 1st.
removing	As noted under the 1st house, the 7th house is the house of removing. It can indicate where you wish to go or to be, while the 1st house is where you are presently and perhaps likely to remain. If the ruler for the 1st house has crossed over to the 7th house, this can show the initiator's desire to relocate.
influence & advice	If the ruler of the 1st house crosses over to the 7th, this can indicate that he or she is subject to decisions and influence of a 7th house person. This may or may not be to the 1st house person's benefit. Consultants are also ruled by the 7th house.

The 8th House

other's money	The 8th house is associated with other people's money, most notably the spouse's or the partner's, but it can also rule money from inheritance, gifts, settlements, royalties, retirement accounts, investments, alimony, palimony, and shared resources.
debts, loans, taxes & bankruptcy	When it comes to having shared money, the opposite is also true. The 8th house rules taxes, debts, financial losses, bad investments, and bankruptcy whether yours or your partner's.
credit	Your credit rating is reflected in the 8th house.

wills, trusts & legacy	Those who wish to put their affairs in order will find that the 8th house rules wills, legacies, and trusts whether revokable or not.
surgery	Surgery is also ruled by the 8th.
insurance	All forms of insurance are related to the 8th house, and especially problems with claims or settlements.
sex & sexuality	In a marriage or partnership election that includes a sexual aspect to the relationship, sexual compatibility might be seen in the 8th house.

The 9th House

higher education & knowledge	The 9th house rules higher education and lectures usually found in colleges, universities, conferences, and seminars. Grade school education is seen in the 3rd house.
publishing	Books are in the 3rd house while editors and publishing houses are ruled by the 9th house. This includes self-publishing.
foreign travel & long journeys	Long journeys, especially voyages and trips overseas or to foreign countries relate to the 9th house. Ethnic heritage and interaction with different cultures even without travel is referred to in the 9th.
religion & faith	Any religion or religious ritual is ruled by the 9th. Spirituality and spiritual experiences occurring outside of religion such as visions or dreams are related to the 12th house.
philosophy & beliefs	A philosophy or belief system whether religious or not has its impact in the 9th house.
legalization	Legal matters that do not involve a lawsuit or a contentious situation are ruled by this house.

The 10th House

career, business & employment	The 10th house is a career and business house, especially regarding professionals and self-employed individuals.
accomplishment & ambition	Ambition or the desire to be successful in any career endeavor is ruled by the 10th house. The ends might not justify the means if there are malefics here.
superiors & the boss	Higher level management, employers, bosses, company owners, the governing board of a company, and the company itself are indicated by the 10th house.
fame & reputation	These are people who might be well-known, famous, important, or have a reputation and prestige, whether positive or negative.
the law, judge & the courts	In a any legal case before a court of law, the 10th rules the judge and the decision.
father & parents	While mother and motherhood are ruled by the 4th house, father, fatherhood and parents in generally are ruled by the 10th because they are seen as authority figures.
government	Because a government and government agencies have authority, they are ruled by the 10th.
success 10th	What is significant to note is that the 10th house is known as "the success 10th." This might apply to any electional chart you choose. It never hurts to have a strong 10th house when electing a time, but this should not be the primary goal when your intention does not specifically involve 10th house issues.

The 11th House

salary	Job or business salary is ruled by the 11th, (2nd to the 10th)
groups	The 11th house rules all groups, regardless of their purpose, whether a self-help group, book club, or volunteer neighborhood clean-up service. Any group or club should have a common focus and purpose.

group membership	If you wish to join a group or organization, the 11th house rules group membership and your ability to relate to the other members.
friendships & unbonded relationships	Friendships, acquaintances, and unbonded relationships are ruled by the 11th house.
humanity & humanitarian concerns	Any organization or group that is focused on providing humanitarian services to those disadvantaged is indicated in the 11th house.
liberty & freedom	As the 11th house is normally ruled by Aquarius, freedom from unnecessary restrictions, red tape, or regulations might apply in regard to the interpretation and goal of some electional charts.
hopes & wishes	Your dreams for the future are seen in the 11th house.

The 12th House

silence, seclusion, & spirituality	The 12th house might bode well for someone pursuing silence, seclusion, meditation, or a spiritual retreat. Electional charts are suitable for pursuing spiritual advancement and insight.
hospitals & rehabilitation	No one looks forward to being hospitalize, either for medical or emotional reasons, but if you must be admitted, make it a beneficial and healing experience where healing can occur.
drugs	Whether prescription, over the counter, or street drugs, they are ruled by the twelfth house.
prisons & punishment	The 12th house rules prisons, possible detention for whatever reason, and the prisoner or detainee.
enemies	While open adversaries are in the 7th house, hidden enemies are ruled by the 12th house.
atonement	The 12th house is more than a simple apology. It also involves restoration.

exile	Voluntary and involuntary exile is ruled by the 12th.
disappointment	Disappointment and perhaps the reasons for disappointment is ruled by the 12th house.
secret & hidden matters	Anything hidden or kept secret is ruled by the 12th house.
large animals	Large animals such as horses or farm animals are ruled by the 12th house.
the past	This house rules the past. When the sign on the 12th is the same as the sign on the 1st house, your past follows you into the present. You have brought matters and problems down on yourself. This is good to know since you can take corrective action.

Interceptions

Interceptions generally indicate some form of interference or limitation no matter which houses they fall into and especially when planets are contained in the interception. There is a break in the power of those houses when the signs do not have a cusp. This may or may not be a problem, and may or may not affect the outcome of your election. Many astrologers try to avoid interceptions, but it's not always possible in some far north and south latitudes and when signs of long or short ascension are involved.

Planets on the House Cusp

Planets on the cusp of the next following house are entering a new area or environment and may have influence in both the old and new house placement. If a planet is just inside a house cusp, it has recently left an old situation and entered a new arena. The transition from one house to another might be relevant to the electional chart interpretation.

Chapter 8
Aspects

Introduction

The relationship between two planets is called an aspect. Aspects in the electional chart can show agreement and combined efforts or problems and impediments you must address to be successful with your election. There are seven major aspects: the conjunction, sextile, square, trine, opposition, parallel, and contra-parallel. The first five are zodiacal aspects while the parallel and contra-parallel depend on declination. The major aspects appear to have the strongest interaction. The minor aspects are the semi-sextile and the quincunx. Minor aspects are supporting aspects only and are interpreted to confirm what is already seen or suspected by the major aspects. In any electional chart, the ideal is to have at least three aspects confirming your interpretation and expectation.

Orbs

Orbs are the distance from an exact aspect. Orbs are flexible and can be adjusted to accommodate configurations in the chart or your own personal preferences. Any orb can be increased depending on the strength of the planets by sign, angularity, rulership, exaltation, and when mutually applying. Mutually applying aspects involve one direct planet applying to a retrograde planet. These planets can have a greater orb as they are reaching for one another.

You might consider tightening an orb when planets are in detriment, fall, peregrine, or the aspect is separating. The orbs for separating aspects are generally smaller than those for applying aspects. Orbs should be smaller and tighter when planets are mutually separating because the direct planet has passed the retrograde planet and now both have turned their backs on each other. They are moving away from the aspect and out of range. They do not wish to interact any longer.

An eight-degree orb is commonly used, but does not immediately cease to exist at eight degrees and one minute. The closer the aspect is to being exact, the stronger the aspect is. The strength of any aspect gradually diminishes with increasing distance from exactness.

Applying and Separating Aspects

You must distinguish between applying and separating aspects in an electional chart to understand the unfolding of future events. The dividing point between separation and applying is the time of the election chart. All exact aspects that occurred before the time of the election are separating aspects and may or may not relate to past events and actions that have already occurred. All exact aspects that will occur after the time of the electional chart and have yet to be perfected are applying. They can relate to future events and actions still to take place in your progress toward a successful conclusion.

In an electional chart, the faster planet is the one either applying or separating. The Moon is the fastest planet followed by Mercury, Venus, Mars, then Jupiter, and so on in almost all cases. The only exception might be if a personal planet is stationary, (either Mercury, Venus, or Mars), turning retrograde or direct. This can alter the interpretation of the electional chart. Planets that are in the same degree indicate that the aspect is partile. This emphasizes their importance in the matter at hand.

Conjunction - Major Aspect - 0 degrees - 8-degree orb

A conjunction is generally thought to be a cooperative aspect bringing together whatever is represented, whether individuals with other people, a person with his or her possessions, or visionaries with their goal. A conjunction between two or more planets indicates coming together, mutual respect, consolidation, joining forces, and agreeing on important matters. This is especially true when the planets are benefics. On the other hand, the planets might represent two or more people or elements that disagree. Difficulties can result in competition or a conflict of interest depending on what planets are involved.

Conjunctions are thought of as a mixed aspect since the interpretation is not necessarily good or bad; it depends on the planets involved. If the planets are benefics, the interpretation could be very positive. If the planets are malefics, the interpretation is more likely to be negative. If there is one benefic and one malefic, the interpretation might be mixed. It depends on the combination, the planets involved, their signs and standing.

Conjunctions indicate a stronger focus on one particular issue, task, or area of life, especially when the planets are in the same sign and house. Several planets conjunct can create a single-minded sense of purpose or obsession. If the planets are in different signs and/or different houses though conjunct, the interpretation becomes more complex and perhaps less focused. Benefics split between houses and signs can be less promising than when they are in the same sign and house. Some conjunctions are a combination of traits that are not easily blended or managed. This creates an inner turmoil that can be a distraction, especially when malefics are involved and there are stressful aspects to other planets.

Positive Conjunction Keywords

success	support	cooperation	agreement
assistance	unity	focus	alignment
mutual respect	combination	consolidation	joint effort
brings together	helps	utilizes	energizes
consolidates	adds to	gives new options	comes together

Negative Conjunction Keywords

disagreement	impediment	depletion	is stuck with
conflict	makes demands	subtracts from	hinders
inhibits	thwarts	delays	limits

Sextile - Major Aspect - 60 degrees - 8-degree orb

The sextile is next in power to the conjunction. It is a communication aspect. Good communication makes any project easier and more successful. Listen to expert advice whenever it is given. This is a very mental aspect, so you want to discuss, share, and brainstorm your plans with those you trust. Because sextiles are associated with the 3rd and 11th house, friends and siblings might give you good feedback and encouragement. Sextiles indicate good support and assistance toward being successful.

Cooperation is also implied by this aspect. Although sextile planets are not in the same element like two trine planets, their elements are compatible, fire with air and earth with water. Planets in fire and air represent individuals who are more likely to share ideas, information, and knowledge while planets in earth and water are more likely to share resources and feelings. As always, when the aspect is out of compatible elements, the interpretation might be less promising.

Planets that are sextile in an electional chart represent opportunities that may or may not be seized, but require some effort. Individuals are more likely to seize an opportunity when the faster planet is moving to conjunct the slower planet in the future. Individuals are less likely to seize the opportunity when the faster planet moves to a square aspect next in the future.

Advice is important. Discussions tend to stay on the mental level. You want someone to talk to and brainstorm with whether you are dealing with a friend, acquaintance, or a sibling. Relationships among participants tend to be friendly rather than sexual. You are most likely good buddies. This is a harmonious aspect, and cooperation is implied. Short trips may be important to success, but long trips are limited to simple comings and goings.

Positive Sextile Keywords

ease	encouragement	gives feedback	informs
support & assistance	ideas & information	knowledge & expertise	seized opportunity
communication	resources	cooperation	befriends
shares ideas with others	provides opportunities	makes things easier	gives someone a chance

Negative Sextile Keywords

laziness	missed opportunity

Square - Major Aspect - 90 degrees - 8-degree orb

Squares indicate difficulties through internal or external tensions and obstacles you need to address and overcome. These obstacles can come as a complete surprise even after you have committed to a course of action. They are generally unexpected. This might be due to a lack of research and planning. The type of problems you encounter can be described by the planets involved in the square aspect.

When internal obstacles arise, you can work against yourself, especially if you are not clear about your intentions. Dilemmas will mandate decisions about basic preferences and methods. Short-term expenses can compete with long-term goals. Financial instability and limited resources might foster fear, doubt, and lack of confidence. You must figure out a way to integrate conflicting internal needs, or you will sabotage your own efforts.

Squares can instead indicate an external conflict of interest. Objections can come from an individual, administrative body like a government agency, natural limitations related to weather or climate, and commercial competition.

The point is, whether internal or external, there is most likely a problem to address. Squares can cost you and any success you achieve might not be worth the cost in lost resources and wasted effort. You only succeed when you find a way to deal with impediments. The greater the number of squares in an electional chart, the greater the number of obstacles you must address. If you intend to be successful regardless of difficulties to the contrary, you need to put in extra effort.

Positive Square Keywords

does not deny success	success comes with a cost	the cost may be prohibitive	strong planets can overcome
can be overcome but at a cost		builds the strength to overcome	

Negative Square Keywords

difficulties	competition	dilemmas	success at a cost
self-sabotage	obstacles	losses	denial
lack of approval or permission	unanticipated problems	high costs & much effort	hindrances & delays
trouble-making aspect	something is withheld	fosters suspicion & anger	ends in estrangement
setbacks	undue pressure	stressful	calculated risks
blockages	loss of control	stops	pressures
forces	isolates	weakens	ignores
injures or hurts	does not respect	thwarting	abandonment
change of plans	might regret	broken promises	a conflict of interest

Trine - Major Aspect - 120 degrees - 8-degree orb

△ The trine aspect, along with the sextile, is next in power to the conjunction. It indicates expected good fortune which is rarely a surprise. Events, circumstances, and positive results are anticipated well in advance. An innate ease is associated with trine planets and influences seen in an electional chart. Sometimes, progress can be made without a complete awareness of the process. If you do not easily succeed, there are enough resources and options for you to make adjustments. You have the ability to shift your focus and succeed in another manner or area. You are not locked in.

For example, if you are plagued by frequent travel away from your home office, you might change to a mail order business with drop shipments. You can schedule this on your phone from anywhere. It is important to remember you have options, you can adjust, and then you succeed. Changes might be subtle, but they allow you to be successful in the end. Trines show the ability to adapt, and this can be the key to success.

A planet in trine aspect is likely to represent a person who will assist you or cooperate in the matter at hand. This is a harmonious aspect that implies cooperation on many levels. Relationships tend to be helpful and can either be sexual (related to the 5th house) or spiritual (related to the 9th house). Because trine planets tend to be in the same element, (fire, earth, air, or water), there is a compatibility and common purpose. Personality traits are expressed easily and without inhibitions. People, elements, and circumstances are in tune with one another. If the trining planets are not in a common element, the interpretation might be less promising.

Contrary to popular opinion, trines are not always beneficial. They imply very little resistance to any difficulty. Should there be a major conflict or impediment, one might not have the drive to overcome any difficulty. In addition, when good fortune is anticipated, one can be oblivious to any negative influences or collateral damage.

Positive Trine Keywords

easy success	momentum	gives ease	can be effortless
support	resources	anticipation	good luck
compatibility	assistance	adaptation	helpful
benefits	gives freely	promises success	satisfies
understands	sympathizes	forgiving	is compatible
expected good fortune	cooperation with others	full-blown opportunity	others readily offer help
never a surprise	in-tune	harmony	timely

Negative Trine Keywords

fail to overcome impediments	unrealized potential	little resistance to difficulty	blind to negative influences
laziness	wasteful	oblivious	procrastination

Opposition - Major Aspect - 180 degrees - 8-degree orb

The opposition is an aspect of awareness. It indicates a problem you are probably already aware of, but need to comprehend more fully; consequently, the opposition is a learning aspect. Those who oppose you or your project are indicated by the planet opposing your significator or the ruler for your project. The nature of the opposing planet, its sign, and placement will describe the person or circumstances in your way and the reasons for any objection. In most situations, you must give something up to be successful. If you are asked to give up more than you will gain, you will probably drop matters entirely. Under the best of circumstances, you can negotiate a compromise, especially if a third planet is sextile and trine the opposing ends. A third person with a good relationship to both parties helps to balance perspectives and prevent polarization.

The opposition aspect is associated with the 1st and 7th houses. The individual's needs and desires are pitted against the needs of a relationship or the needs of another person. In some situations, there is no middle ground, no room for compromise leading to never resolved seesawing points of view. Individuals are pulled between two mutually exclusive perspectives or situations. Disagreements can lead the parties involved to pull apart and eventually separate. Planets mutually applying to an opposition indicate that both parties choose to go their separate way.

Positive Opposition Keywords

complements	exchanges	new awareness	stands up to
negotiation	arbitration	makes up for	trades
fights with awareness	success at any cost	revisited point of view	forced reconsideration

Negative Opposition Keywords

conflict of interest	separation	compromise	lack of approval
disagreement	opposition	contradiction	uneven exchange
having to give in order to get	success with a cost or loss	alternative points of view/opinions	necessary change in plans
rejection	stoppage/ends	dissolves	gives in to
stands in the way	loss	drops matters	poor trade
tendency to drop matters	abandons when too costly	give up something to succeed	blind-sided awareness

Parallel - Major Aspect - 1-degree orb by declination

// The parallel and contra-parallel are both considered the good side of a conjunction, and they are powerful aspects. They are based on declination. When two or more planets are in the same north or south declination from the equator within one degree, a parallel aspect is formed.

Parallels bring people and things together despite any planetary incompatibility or differences related to sign, standing, or negative interpretation. Interpretations for parallels are always positive and represent the best sides of the planets involved. The people brought together can be very compatible or totally incompatible, it does not matter, but the alliance will still be good. Assistance commonly comes from two totally different fields of interest or skill sets. In an electional chart, when using a parallel, you can form an alliance with someone regardless of how you feel about the other person. Parallels make strange bedfellows, and diversity furthers your chances for success.

Parallels indicate permanent help from others, especially from family members, friends, or those you know. New relationships tend to become permanent, become strong bonds that you hope will last forever. It is a strong final Moon aspect and can indicate "yes!"

Parallel Keywords

mutual benefit	alignment	"as good as done"	permanent help
leads to success	lasting alliance	conjoined forces	positive result
good side of a conjunction	attainment with others	overcome differences	benefit through diversity
aligns different forces	concludes favorably	supportive family & friends	makes strange bedfellows
bring together	sustained support	agreements	good final aspect

Contra-parallel - Major Aspect - 1-degree orb by declination

Contra-parallels are considered the good side of a conjunction and just as powerful. Like parallels, they are based on declination. When two or more planets are with one degree of declination, but one is in north declination while the other is in south declination, a contra-parallel is formed.

Contra-parallels bring people and things together despite any incompatibility or differences related to sign, standing, or negative interpretation. Regardless of how you feel about the other person, the alliance will be good.

The difference between the parallel and the contra-parallel is that assistance and alignments are not permanent. With the contra-parallel, any help you receive is temporary. It only lasts for as long as it needed and solely for the matter at hand. Most commonly, you join forces with professionals you hire. You may hire them to handle your project completely or to fill in with partial assistance as needed. The professionals you hire probably have expertise you do not have. They have a different mindset or skill set. Any friends or family members who assist you, also only do so temporarily.

Contra-parallel Keywords

professional help	limited alignment	"as good as done"	temporary help
leads to success	brief alliance	conjoined forces	favorable result
good side of a conjunction	attainment with hired others	overcome differences	benefit through diversity
agreements	brings together	paid help	good final aspect

temporary or partial assistance	temporary alliance	concludes favorably	makes strange bedfellows

Quincunx - Minor Aspect - 150 degrees - 2-degree orb

The quincunx is a minor zodiacal aspect halfway between an opposition and a trine. It is generally interpreted of as a lack of ease or instability, similar to an off-balance or three-legged table. It's a call for change and one needs to make an adjustment. The quincunx can be considered a difficult aspect, especially when confirming an already negative interpretation. The phrase commonly associated with the aspect is, "change your mind and settle for less." The option to make a change is a by-product of the trine influence while the need to make a change is a by-product of the opposition. Adjustments can be temporary or permanent as this aspect relates to either the 6th or 8th house. Since the 6th house is a mutable house, change can be temporary, but since the 8th house is fixed, any change can be long-lasting.

Quincunx Keywords

lack of ease	instability	change your mind	reorganization
forced to make necessary changes	permanent or temporary adjustment	less than perfect options	having to settle for less

Semi-sextile - Minor Aspect - 30 degrees - 2-degree orb

The semi-sextile aspect is a minor aspect. It is considered to be neutral, neither outright beneficial nor negative. Because it relates to the 2nd and 12th houses, it generally refers to timing, either in regard to the future or the past. It can be interpreted in elections when timing is important.

Semi-sextile Keywords

related to the past when timing	related to the future timing	considered a neutral aspect	neither beneficial nor negative

Chapter 9
The Moon's Aspects

Introduction

The Moon is the fastest moving body in an electional chart. The speed of the Moon may indicate how quickly matters develop and settle. The Moon is slow when traveling approximately eleven degrees a day, and considered fast when it is traveling fifteen degrees a day.

The Moon is of upmost importance in an electional chart unlike the Sun which is more important in natal interpretations. The Moon denotes action and is called the "activity of the election chart." She represents the developing power in an electional chart and rules all change that occurs. Her aspects as she moves through the Moonsign help to identify events, changes, and progressive steps toward the end result. Wherever the Moon is found by house in the electional chart, change is most likely to happen.

The Moon is allowed all of her applying aspects until she leaves the Moonsign. The better the Moon's aspects, standing, and placement, the more likely the chance of success. It is important to distinguish between applying and separating aspects. The time of the election is the point for determining separating versus applying aspects. Previous Moon aspects are separating and may have little to no significance in electional chart interpretation. The more applying aspects there are, the more action and change one can expect.

You might have a lot of good aspects in an electional chart, but of all of the Moon's aspects, the Moon's final aspect is the most important because it denotes how things will end; the better the final aspect, the better the ending and chance for success. In addition to choosing a Moonsign with a good final Moon aspect, also choose good interim aspects for developmental ease. If you want to begin, progress, and end well, choose good interim and a good final Moon aspect.

Generalizations about the Moon's Final Aspects

Below is a list of aspects, some considered positive and some considered negative. In general, it is better to fail with a positive final Moon aspect than to succeed with a negative final Moon aspect. A positive final Moon aspect might work out best for all involved in an unexpected manner with an alternate result. With squares, oppositions, and difficult conjunctions, the success you achieve might not be the success you hoped for or wanted.

Moon's Final Aspect a Conjunction

When the Moon's final aspect is a conjunction, the effect can be either positive or negative. When the Moon's final aspect is a conjunction to the Sun, Mercury, Venus, or Jupiter, easy success is more likely, and more support is given. You also tend to have more options and resources available.

Final conjunctions to the malefics (Mars, Saturn, Uranus, Neptune, and Pluto) can indicate success at a cost depending on the standing of these planets by sign and house. More is taken or withheld and there is some loss or fee charged, but you can be successful. It takes more to be successful, and complete success may be withheld. Negative results are even more likely when the Moon's final aspect is a conjunction is to a retrograde malefic.

Moon's Final Aspect a Sextile

When the Moon's last aspect is a sextile, success is usually implied, but it is important to note if the sextile is a sinister sextile wherein the moon will next square the sextiled planet. In this case, the opportunity presented by the sextile is less likely to manifest completely. If the Moon will next apply to a conjunction to the planet previously sextiled, the opportunity is more likely to be realized.

Moon's Final Aspect a Square

When the Moon's final aspect is a square, success will be difficult and will require extra effort. Overcoming the obstacle may cost you more than any success will be worth. This depends somewhat on the malefic's standing by sign and house. For this reason, you may abandon your project. The planet squared will describe the nature of the problems you will encounter and where extra effort will be needed.

When the Moon's final aspect is a square to a retrograde planet, success, if achieved, might never be as you hoped. A final square to a retrograde planet can indicate lasting damage, especially if the planet is in a fixed sign. Final squares to retrograde malefics indicate that you may regret the course of action you have chosen.

Moon's Final Aspect a Trine

When the Moon's final aspect is a trine, not much effort is required on your part in order to succeed. Others readily offer to help. For this reason, the trine is sometimes considered the lazy man's aspect.

Moon's Final Aspect an Opposition

When the Moon's final aspect is an opposition, you must give something up to be successful. If you are asked to give up more than you will gain, you will probably drop matters entirely. Those who oppose you or your project are indicated by the planet opposing the Moon. The nature of this planet will describe the person or circumstances in your way.

Moon's Final Aspect a Parallel

When the Moon's last aspect is a parallel, you succeed because of permanent alliances you form and the assistance you receive. A thing is as good as done. Generally, this is a good final aspect; however, sometimes it is not enough to overcome other difficulties indicated by the Moon's aspects.

Moon's Final Aspect a Contra-parallel

When the Moon's final aspect is a contra-parallel, you succeed because of the temporary alliances you form and the assistance you receive. Usually this is a good final aspect, but sometimes it's not enough to overcome other difficulties indicated by the Moon's aspects.

Moonsign Characterization

The characterizations below attempt to define the types of Moonsigns one might encounter. These interpretations relate to aspects the Moon makes including the final aspect the Moon makes as it moves through a sign. Aspects might correspond to the opportunities or assistance you receive, problems you encounter along the way, or in the final result. The interpretation most closely associated with your experience is the one most likely to occur. These interpretations are intended to be a simple guide for the reader and are not to be considered complete.

It should be remembered that great days, good days, and even challenging days are not interpreted in regard to common, daily, ongoing activities. If it is something you do habitually or regularly, the Moonsign aspects do not necessarily apply. Only take notice of the Moon's aspects when you are actually initiating a project or event. These classifications are for electional astrology only, not for everyday occurrences. In fact, when the Moon's final aspect is a square, it can be a good time to work on continuing projects or daily tasks. You can feel energized enough to get a lot done.

Great Day

Great days are few and far between. Some years, only a couple great ones will occur during the calendar year; some years will not have any. Use these days to your advantage when they occur. You can succeed easily with little or no opposition, obstacles, delays, or conflicts. Planetary conditions are especially favorable since not only is the Moon's final aspect very good, but also many of the Moon's other aspects are good and the day has something extra special such as many planets in rulership or exaltation. Take advantage of the opportunities, assistance, and resources offered to you.

Good Day

You are likely to succeed on a good day if you take advantage of the opportunities and assistance to overcome any problems. The Moon's final aspect is good, and the majority of the Moon's other aspects are also good, but you may encounter some problems on the road to success since the Moon will make one or two difficult aspects. Obstacles can be overcome.

Neutral Day

There are two kinds of neutral days. In the first category, the final aspect is good indicating that you can succeed; however, the Moon's previous aspects indicate that you encounter a lot of difficulty along the way. The problems you encounter, not the outcome of events, warrant the downgrade from good to neutral. In the second category are "blah" days, too neutral to be either positive or negative with a weak final aspect like a parallel or contra-parallel after several stressful aspects. In either case, problems are not too difficult, but also not easy, and success is limited.

Challenging Day

Challenging days tend to end poorly. The problems you encounter could cause you to fail despite any help you receive. The Moon's final aspect is negative, and your chances of succeeding are decreased. You may also encounter serious problems along the way from beginning to end from which you can't recover. When attempting to initiate something on a challenging day, carefully consider all the possible problems you could encounter.

Specific interpretations for the Moon's Aspects

Moon-Sun

Conjunction to the Sun on a good day - An important person joins forces with you to make your project a success. Authority figures approve and provide you with the support you need. It is important to remember that the Moon can be either combust the Sun or Cazimi even on a good day. The Moon Cazimi the Sun occurs thirty minutes of time before the New Moon conjunction to the Sun, and thirty minutes of time after the conjunction to the Sun. This is also the dark of the Moon. Caution is warranted as there may be things you do not know. I do not avoid or favor any Moon phase whether waxing or waning.

Conjunction to the Sun on a challenging day - You can get burned by someone who is much stronger or more powerful. You are starting out from a poor or disadvantaged position. Perhaps there is a strike against you. Situations are not healthy, or you, yourself, can be ill. Actions are hampered. Your timing is off. This is a better time to close down than to start something new. It is important to remember that the Moon can be either combust the Sun or Cazimi. This is also the dark of the Moon. Caution is warranted as there may be things you do not know.

Dark of the Moon or Dying Moon situation - This phase may last approximately twenty-four hours, more or less depending on the speed of the Moon. It is when the Moon's crescent is no longer visible in the sky and before the time of the New Moon. When this occurs, caution may be warranted. There are many factors unknown to you. You are probably not well-informed at this time, and you might be better off waiting for further developments, especially if your timing is off. Generally, this is a better time to close down operations than to start something new.

New Moon situation - This phase may last approximately twenty-four hours, more or less depending on the speed of the Moon. It is the time between the new Moon and when the crescent first becomes visible. This is a time associated with new beginnings. When the Moon is last over the Sun, changes tend to be well-timed. You may start out from a poor or disadvantaged position, especially if resources are low. This temporarily limits your ability to succeed since you are probably starting from scratch. Information may be slow in coming. Caution is warranted as there may be things you do not know. You could be ill-informed. Perhaps there is a strike against you. Problems can be readily apparent or completely unknown. Actions can be hampered because plans and circumstances are not fully developed.

Sextile to the Sun - You succeed through the help of an important person or authority figure. He or she may provide you with an opportunity or the assistance you need to be successful. When the Moon's final aspect is a sextile to the Sun, but the Moon will square the Sun next in a future Moonsign, it is possible that the opportunity and assistance are not as strongly defined or as successful as one might hope. This is called a sinister sextile. If the Moon will conjunct the Sun next in a future Moonsign, success is much more likely to occur.

Trine, parallel, or contra-parallel to the Sun - You succeed through the help of an important person or authority figure. He or she may provide you with an opportunity or the assistance you need to be successful. Progress tends to occur in a timely manner.

Square or opposition to the Sun - You may have a problem with a superior or formidable opponent. Someone in authority objects to your project, and unfortunately, this person has some control over you and can inhibit your progress. You can still succeed, but matters will cost you more in resources than they are worth. You must give up something to get something accomplished. Most likely, your timing is off. Are you rushing ahead at an inopportune moment? Cruelty or the threat of cruelty can exist. Does someone have an axe to grind? Your success can be thwarted for any of these reasons so be prepared with alternate plans. These aspects should be avoided in a surgery election as success is crucial in those situations.

Moon - Mercury

Conjunction, trine, parallel, or contra-parallel to Mercury - You receive needed information, and bright people and agents assist you. Successful negotiations lead to agreements. You make good decisions. This is a good time for all mental activities including writing, studying, reading, and communicating.

Sextile to Mercury - When the Moon's final aspect is a sextile to Mercury, you succeed because you carry a good idea to completion. Others share their expertise and knowledge. Negotiations and resulting agreements lead to success. When the Moon's final aspect is a sextile to Mercury, but the Moon will square Mercury next in a future Moonsign, it is possible that the information is not complete. This is called a sinister sextile. If the Moon will conjunct Mercury next in a future Moonsign, accurate and complete information is more likely available.

Square or opposition to Mercury - Disagreements occur and you cannot reach an agreement with others. You may be basing your actions on incorrect information or making poor decisions. Anxiety and stress-related illnesses are possible. You worry, perhaps needlessly. Emotions conflict with rational assessments and may even defy logic. You might deal with discrimination for various reasons. Someone can have an attitude problem. Be careful what you say or put into writing, or you may regret it. Private information becomes public, and skeletons come out of the closet. When the Moon's final aspect is a square or opposition to Mercury, you may fail because others have information they should not have, and they use this information against you. On the other hand, perhaps you do not get the information you need to be successful. Consequently, you fail because your actions are based on misconceptions and incorrect facts.

Moon - Venus

Conjunction, trine, parallel, or contra-parallel to Venus - A kind person, possibly a woman helps you. You receive the financial backing, money, or resources you need. Conditions are comfortable. Little effort is required, but actions still lead to success. Situations feel stable and secure. Agreements are reached, compromises are fair, cooperation is important and easily attained. Matters are very pleasing to the eye or the senses. Beauty and artistry are evident. You succeed for all or any of the above reasons.

Sextile to Venus - A kind person, possibly a woman, helps you. You receive the financial backing, money, or resources you need. Conditions are comfortable. Little effort is required, but actions still lead to success. Situations feel stable and secure. Agreements are reached, compromises are fair, cooperation is important and easily attained. Matters are very pleasing to the eye or the senses. Beauty and artistry are evident. You succeed for all or any of the above reasons. When the Moon's final aspect is a sextile to Venus, but the Moon will square Venus next in a future Moonsign, it is possible that success is tainted in some way. This is called a sinister sextile. If the Moon will conjunct Venus next in a future Moonsign, easy success is likely.

Square or opposition to Venus - A social faux pas or error is possible since there is a tendency to respond in less than socially acceptable ways. Someone is cheap, tacky, crude, gushy, or gaudy. Comments are tasteless and clothing is not in fashion. Purchases or events are expensive and not as nice as expected. Relationships can be strained. Endeavors are not worth the expense, and you could have gotten a better deal at another time.

Moon - Mars

Conjunction to Mars on a good day - If push comes to shove, you must fight for your rights. Know your rights and state them clearly. Any battle might become contentious when you stand your ground. A break in relationships may occur over important issues. You may be forced to cut someone off. This is a good time to be courageous. Do your best in any challenge and eliminate the competition.

Conjunction to Mars on a challenging day - Push comes to shove, and you must fight for your rights. Know your rights and demand that they be respected. Any battle might become fierce when you become defiant and stand your ground. A break in relationships might occur if you feel forced to cut someone off or out of your life completely. Any game or sport will have strong competitors.

Sextile to Mars - You receive help from someone who is assertive or aggressive. He or she helps you fight for your rights or even does the fighting for you; consequently, you sustain less damage. You can win the battle easily. Taking the initiative gives you the edge. This is a time when you are able to motivate yourself and you motivate others in the process. When the Moon's final aspect is a sextile to Mars, but the Moon will square Mars next in a future Moonsign, it is possible that you do not seize the opportunity to defend your rights completely or timely. This is called a sinister sextile. If the Moon will conjunct Mars next in a future Moonsign, you are on solid ground defending your rights. You know what needs to be done and you do it.

Trine, parallel, or contra-parallel to Mars - You receive help from someone who is assertive or aggressive. He or she helps you fight for your rights or even does the fighting for you; consequently, you sustain less damage. You can win the battle easily. Taking the initiative gives you the edge. This is a time when you are able to motivate yourself and you motivate others in the process. When the Moon's final aspect is a trine, parallel, or contra-parallel to Mars, you succeed by fighting for your rights, motivating others, or taking the initiative.

Square or opposition to Mars - You overreact or move too quickly. You may hurt yourself or someone else if you are careless and angry. Disagreements, confrontations, conflicts of interest, arguments, or even fights are possible. You do not know when to give up or back down. Someone may reject your efforts. Stop and think, are you championing a lost cause? Are you putting your worst foot forward? Someone is excessively angry, and success is not worth this kind of battle. Though others may infringe on your rights needlessly, you meet strong opposition. In the end, you probably abandon your endeavor.

Moon - Jupiter

Conjunction, trine, parallel, or contra-parallel to Jupiter - You can be successful even when you should not have been successful. You receive help from a very optimistic and generous person who gives you hope. If there were problems in the past, all could be forgiven now. Your beliefs are confirmed. The possibility of teaching and publication exists. You make wise purchases and have the money to cover your expenses. Expectations are met or exceeded. Ethical behavior is noticed, and it pays off. Most situations improve.

Sextile to Jupiter - You can be successful even when you should not have been successful. You receive help from a very optimistic and generous person who gives you hope. If there were problems in the past, all could be forgiven now. Your beliefs are confirmed. The possibility of teaching and publication exists. You make wise purchases and have the money to cover your expenses. Expectations are met or exceeded. Ethical behavior is noticed, and it pays off. You are successful even when you should not have been. When the Moon's final aspect is a sextile to Jupiter, but the Moon will square Jupiter next in a future Moonsign, it is possible that benefits are not as good. This is called a sinister sextile. If the Moon will conjunct Jupiter next in a future Moonsign, benefits, assistance, and resources should be available to you.

Square or opposition to Jupiter - You or someone you are involved with has questionable ethics and/or morals. What you are trying to do might not be sanctioned by society, and someone objects. Hypocrisy is commonly an issue. Your beliefs are challenged and perhaps you must totally change your beliefs or religion. Relationships can be stressful, and amicable separations are possible. Decisions are unjust and favoritism might be the cause. Expectations are not met, especially when they are exaggerated. You tend to expect a lot more than you get. If you do by chance get what you asked for, it won't really be what you wanted in the long run. Someone is overindulgent. Purchases and events are expensive, gaudy, too extravagant, or excessive. Wastefulness is evident. More growth than you need occurs and excess can become harmful. Too much of a good thing is cumbersome. Someone's generosity might be misguided. When you are in a tough situation, others give you little hope or encouragement. You can be successful, but success costs you more than it was worth. If you drop the whole thing for any reason given above, all is forgiven.

Moon - Saturn

Conjunction, parallel, or contra-parallel to Saturn on a good day - You can receive assistance from someone who is older, wiser, or more experienced. It is to your advantage to heed good advice. Matters slow down, but when delays occur, wait patiently. You succeed with careful, step-by-step planning. Focus on organizing talents, skills, and resources into a well-choreographed process to create a smooth transition. Be frugal with resources. You can succeed on a shoestring budget without having to give anything up.

Conjunction to Saturn on a challenging day - Matters take a lot longer than expected. Delays are frustrating and sometimes purposeless. You can get caught up in red tape with difficulty navigating bureaucratic regulations. Someone might have an axe to grind and withholds out of meanness. Not all players play nicely. Older people, in particular, might block your progress or weigh you down. In the end, you may fail because of a technicality, or because someone is stingy and won't give you what you need to succeed.

Sextile to Saturn - You receive help from an older or more experienced person. He or she is well-seasoned and an expert in the field. Time works to your advantage. Go slow when matters move slowly; speed up when matters move quickly. You succeed through careful planning, persistence, and determination. One hand washes the other, and someone owes you one. You have earned a favor. Ask for assistance and you may receive help over a long period of time. When the Moon's final aspect is a sextile to Saturn, but the Moon will square Saturn next in a future Moonsign, it is possible that good advice is not followed. This is called a sinister sextile. If the Moon will conjunct Saturn next in a future Moonsign, expertise, assistance, and resources should be available to you.

Trine to Saturn - You receive help or good advice from an older, wiser, or more experienced person. He or she is well-seasoned and an expert in the field of endeavor. It is to your advantage to accept assistance. It can sustain you over a long period of time. You succeed through careful planning and being organized. There may be temporary delays, but time works to your advantage. Be patient and persistent. One hand washes the other. If someone owes you a favor, it is time for reciprocation.

Square or opposition to Saturn - Matters take too long and to no beneficial end. Delays are caused by rules, regulations and immovable structures which impede and inhibit rather than support. You get caught in red tape. Any concessions come with a string attached making compromise almost impossible. Though relationships are difficult, separations are rarely complete because issues continue. A problem person may have an axe to grind and withholds out of meanness. Others are stingy or greedy and want something for nothing. Older, more experienced individuals may be particularly problematic, but worn-out notions will not work for you. Machines and tools can be outdated, ineffective, or malfunctioning. You can fail simply because matters take too long.

Moon - Uranus

Conjunction, parallel, or contra-parallel to Uranus on a good day - These aspects suggest that success occurs from short-term alliances that work to initiate changes. You cut through red tape by being creative and innovative. You do not have to do things a particular way simply because "it has always been done this way." Think outside the box. Circumstances demand modernization and you are wise to update procedures and systems. At this time, matters move quickly and change leads to success.

Conjunction to Uranus on a challenging day suggests that circumstances are unstable and individuals are erratic. Disruption occurs in many areas of life. Relationships are stressful and severed ties or separations may occur. Matters move forward quickly and end without warning, leaving you unprepared. When you rush ahead, you make snap decisions with limited insight. This leads to unfortunate and preventable mistakes. To make circumstances worse, unexpected and undesirable surprises await you. Attempts at modernizations can fall short. Renovations run amok. You might fail for the above reasons.

Sextile to Uranus - You receive surprise assistance in your quest to make changes. Someone helps you cut through red tape or shows you a new way of doing things. The changes you make are likely to be successful and advantageous. Communicate with others and you might get a lucky break. Shared insight improves on results. When the Moon's final aspect is a sextile to Uranus, but the Moon will square Uranus next in a future Moonsign, it is possible that changes are not made as easily as you hoped. This is called a sinister sextile. If the Moon will conjunct Uranus next in a future Moonsign, success comes suddenly, probably through the changes you make.

Trine to Uranus - You receive surprise assistance in your quest to make changes. Someone helps you to cut through red tape or shows you a new way of doing things. The changes you make are likely to be successful and advantageous. Communicate with others and you might get a lucky break. Shared insight improves on results. Success comes suddenly, probably through changes you make.

Square or opposition to Uranus - Unexpected or undesirable surprises occur causing disruption and instability. Separations or breaks in relationships leave you stranded. You cannot make headway when you are constantly putting out fires. Matters proceed too quickly, and you are caught unprepared; consequently, mistakes happen. Decisions are not the best. Modern conveniences don't work as well as they should. Renovations run amok. There is a lack of unity among friends, groups, or participants. You are not all on the same page. Democratic processes break down. Freedom becomes an issue. Problem solving becomes difficult when interruptions break your concentration. You might fail because of circumstances beyond your control. Surprise obstacles or objections are also your downfall.

Moon - Neptune

Conjunction, parallel, or contra-parallel to Neptune on a good day- These aspects can suggest that you are very idealistic and creative. Spiritual concepts attract you and you are trying to uplift situations and those around you. You act with compassion and sensitivity toward others. In every way, you are just trying to help others. You are charitable and give of your time, effort, and resources. You receive surreptitious assistance from others without knowing why or who is assisting you.

Conjunction to Neptune on a challenging day suggests that you are misinformed and your actions are based on a misconception. Secret information is revealed about you or your endeavors to your disadvantage. You become confused about procedures or uncertain in regard to goals. Forgetfulness, disorganization, and/or addictions to drugs or alcohol contribute to your inability to succeed. Others deceive and defraud you, or you deceive yourself. You do not have the ability to assess people and circumstances; consequently, you associate with untrustworthy people. Scandals and schemes develop around you or about you whether true or not. Despite good intentions, there are some people you cannot save.

Sextile to Neptune - You get unexpected help, possibly from an unknown or unexpected source. Assistance can be surreptitious and maybe you do not realize what's being given. People appreciate your high ideals. You are compassionate and respond to the needs of others. Secrets and intuitive insight give you the edge. Confusion and uncertainty can prove to be an asset. You succeed because you are able to go with the flow and stay true to your ideals. When the Moon's final aspect is a sextile to Neptune, but the Moon will square Neptune next in a future Moonsign, it is possible that your intentions are misunderstood. This is called a sinister sextile. If the Moon will conjunct Neptune next in a future Moonsign, others support your helpful intentions and efforts.

Trine to Neptune - You get unexpected help, possibly from an unknown or unexpected source. Assistance can be surreptitious and maybe you do not realize what's being given. People appreciate your high ideals. You are compassionate and respond to the needs of others. Secrets and intuitive insight give you the edge. Confusion and uncertainty can prove to be an asset. You succeed because you are able to go with the flow and stay true to your ideals.

Square or opposition to Neptune - Secret information is revealed to your detriment. Truth may be elusive, and perhaps you cannot acquire the information you need. Information can be inaccurate, in which case actions are based on misconceptions. It is difficult to determine what is real and true. Misunderstandings develop between participants. You go through a period of confusion and uncertainty when nothing is guaranteed. Forgetfulness contributes to your confusion. You can be deceived or defrauded by your associates, especially if you are so idealistic that you lose touch with reality. You are scandalized by another's actions or caught in a scandal of your own making. Addictions impair your performance or the performance of those you depend on. You blindly trust untrustworthy people. Your goals are derailed by someone ill or in need of immediate help. In the end, you cannot save everyone.

Moon - Pluto

Conjunction, parallel, or contra-parallel to Pluto on a good day - These aspects suggest you can get rid of worn-out, useless things. Streamline your project and eliminate unnecessary steps and expenses. Though your research is not complete, you have enough information to chart your course and succeed as long as you address any complications that arise. Someone might be missing at an important event, but this can work to your benefit. Your greatest success might come from joining forces with a group.

Conjunction to Pluto on a challenging day suggests that matters fail because of a missing person or complications you cannot overcome. Others reject your efforts and abandon you. Vulgarity mars the proceedings making any event distasteful. Research is incomplete to the extent that you don't know what you're talking about, and others sense your lack of understanding and knowledge. What you don't know hurts you because no one will tell you what the gossipers are saying about you. You are out of step with society and might be considered an outcast.

Sextile to Pluto - You align yourself with a powerful group of people and they offer you assistance. You gain an advantage when someone is missing from important proceedings. You have enough information to succeed though your research is not complete. Save time and resources by streamlining your project. Undercover associates lend a hand from behind the scenes. Though you succeed, success comes with complications. In the end, you must make corrections to retain any success, so patch holes, fix errors, and straighten things out. Handle complications with attention to details. When the Moon's final aspect is a sextile to Pluto, but the Moon will square Pluto next in a future Moonsign, it is possible that complications are very difficult to handle. This is called a sinister sextile. If the Moon will conjunct Pluto next in a future Moonsign, complications are likely to be manageable.

Trine to Pluto - You align yourself with a powerful group of people and they offer you assistance. You gain an advantage when someone is missing from important proceedings. You have enough information to succeed even though your research is not complete. Save time and resources by streamlining your project. Undercover associates lend a hand from behind the scenes. Though you succeed, success comes with complications. In the end, you must make corrections to retain any success, so patch holes, fix errors, and straighten things out. Handle complications with attention to details.

Square or opposition to Pluto - An important person is missing at a crucial point in time, and this is a major problem. Matters must be handled by proxy, but this is not a good fix. Psychological complexes color the event or the interpretation of the events. Vulgarity mars the proceedings and others are offended. Circumstances become very complicated, people become very difficult. More than likely, you must deal with unscrupulous characters. Your research is incomplete and inadequate. What you do not know does hurt you. You are out of step with society and isolated in some way. Others reject or abandon you.

Moon Void of Course

The Void of Course Moon indicates "nothing to worry about" or "nothing will happen." If you begin a project during a Void of Course Moon, it may not succeed or ever develop. Decisions made during a Void of Course Moon may never be acted upon. The good news is that disturbing information heard at this time may not be worth worrying about. You might choose this time slot to initiate an activity if you want it to fail or to at least limit the consequences resulting from your actions or the actions of another. For example, if you do not want new ideas to be accepted by others, choose a Void of Course Moon time for their presentation. Nothing of consequence will evolve. If you do not want the IRS to audit your income tax, mail it on a Void of Course Moon.

You can be successful when the Moon is Void of Course by picking a time when the Moon makes a good applying aspect to the Part of Fortune indicating nothing but success. I avoid a Void of Course Moon in an electional chart because I prefer to see the activity Moon making good aspects to planets.

Eclipses

A solar eclipse occurs when the Sun and the Moon are conjunct within 5 degrees of the node. A lunar eclipse occurs when the Sun and Moon oppose each other within five degrees of the nodes, and the earth is aligned between them.

The interpretation is that the affairs in the house or houses in which the eclipse (Sun and/or Moon) occurs will be changed or upset. The disruption is likely to be more upsetting when the eclipse is conjunct, square, or opposing a malefic.

Solar Eclipses

When the Sun is eclipsed by the Moon, the Moon blocks out the Sun's light. The Moon rules activity and change. Activity might get out of control and eclipse an event and its purpose. Occurrences can be either good or bad depending on whether it is a good day or a challenging day. Trines and sextiles to the eclipse point improve conditions while squares and oppositions from malefics indicate unfavorable conditions. Instability can go either way. A solar eclipse signals a critical or tenuous situation which must be handled carefully. Perhaps so many people are involved in your event that everyone ends up tripping over each other. Complications arise from too many people stirring the pot. Surprises can knock you down for the count making it difficult to proceed or recover. Important people can lose standing. Perhaps there is a change in leadership. Your position is reassessed when resources dwindle, and you may have to start from scratch.

Lunar Eclipses

When the earth eclipses the Moon, the earth blocks out the Moon's light. The event gets out of hand because an important person, represented by the Sun, might take over the festivities. He or she may be grandstanding, but his or her presence alone may be enough to force you to change your plans. Activities can become chaotic or completely stalled. Eclipses can be either beneficial or difficult depending upon whether this is a good day or a challenging day. Trines and sextiles to the eclipse points improve conditions while squares and oppositions from malefics indicate unfavorable conditions. A lunar eclipse can signal a critical or tenuous situation which must be treated carefully. Instability could go either way. If two forces are pitted against each other, this will hurt the event.

Occultations

An occultation occurs when the Moon eclipses a planet. The occultation aspect is essentially a conjunction, but the interpretation is modified slightly. If the Moon occults Mercury, Venus or Jupiter, you do not benefit to the extent that you thought you would. For example, you may be missing important information when the Moon occults Mercury or you may not get as much money as you expected when the Moon occults Venus. Occultations to Mars, Saturn, Uranus, Neptune and Pluto indicate that results are not as bad as indicated. For example, surprises won't be as bad with the Moon-Uranus occultation. To better understand the meaning of any occultation, read the Moon's conjunction aspect to the planet. Adjust the meaning to be slightly less benefic or less malefic.

Moon's Final Aspect a Refranation

5	03 24	☽ □ ♆
Mo	07 31	☽ ♑
	08 09	♀ # ♆
	13 46	♀ ♌
	14 44	☽ △ ♃
	16 05	♀ ☍ ♆
	17 03	☉ // ♀
	19 12	☽ ✶ ♄
6	15 14	☉ # ♆
Tu	17 10	☽ △ ♅
	21 34	☽ △ ☿
7	04 40	☽ ✶ ♆
We	08 42	☽ ♒
	08 48	☽ ☌ ♆
	11 39	☽ ☍ ♀

There are two types of refranations. In a zodiacal refranation, a planet leaves the sign before the Moon can aspect it. For example, you are represented by the planet Venus, and I am represented by the Moon. We are invited to a party, and I want to connect with you at the party. When I arrive, you are across the room in a doorway and ready to leave. By the time I cross the crowded room, you're gone, and we never connect.

In this example aspectarian, the Moon is in Capricorn. Venus is in Cancer, but quickly moves into Leo. The Moon would have opposed Venus in late degree of Cancer, but Venus has left the sign. This is a true zodiacal opposition Venus refranation. Checking the aspects Venus makes once the Moon is in Aquarius, it is evident that the refranation aspect was an opposition.

The second kind of refranation involves a planet turning retrograde or direct. When the Moon is applying by aspect to a planet which will change directions before the Moon leaves the sign, it indicates someone changes his/her mind and this change affects your plans. In this situation, I do connect with you, but you have changed your mind about an important matter we previously agreed on. This change affects my plans. If the refranating planet turns retrograde, you don't keep a promise. If the refranating planet turns direct, you refuse to stay out of the picture. Your presence causes me to alter my plans.

13	02 44	☿ ✶ ♀
Sa	03 15	☽ ✶ ♃
	04 39	☽ ♓
	06 57	♀ △ ♄
	14 43	☽ ✶ ☿
	15 12	☽ ☌ ♄
	15 39	♂ # ♆
	15 50	☽ △ ♀
	23 52	☽ # ☿
14	02 16	☽ // ♄
Su	03 28	☽ # ♃
	13 22	☽ ✶ ♅
	21 17	☽ ✶ ☉
15	02 30	☽ △ ♂
Mo	02 56	☽ ☌ ♆
	03 17	☿ D
	07 56	☽ ♈

In the aspectarian on the right, the Moon is in Pisces, and the Moon makes a sextile and contra-parallel to Mercury while it is retrograde. At 3:17 on the 15th, Mercury turns direct and may renege on any previous agreement.

All refranations carry the meaning that something is dropped. This can be a good or bad thing. The supporting planet is the Moon's final aspect disregarding the refranating planet. A supporting aspect shows if an advantage may be gained by dropping all/ part of a project, or if events grow more difficult. Not all refranations have supporting aspects. There is no supporting aspect in the aspectarian with the Pisces Moon. In the previous aspectarian, the Moon sextile Neptune would be considered the previous, supporting aspect.

Refranation conjunction, sextile, square, trine, or opposition

Something is dropped and the entire project probably falls through. People may pull out of the deal, leave the scene, or refrain from further action, leaving you stranded. Money runs out. Ideas prove to be incorrect. With a refranation conjunction, sextile, or trine, the outcome may not be successful, or matters may be dropped. With a refranation square or opposition, matters will be dropped before things could end badly.

Refranation semi-sextile

Things are iffy, especially those matters pertaining to jail, hospitalization, possessions, money, or plans for the future. You can safely use this time for a one-time event with no plans for the future. A refranation semi-sextile is not important enough to make the matter drop.

Refranation quincunx

Things are iffy, especially for matters related to work, health, shared resources, bank loans, insurance, and diet. Projects may be dropped, but most likely you will change your plans and settle for less. Adjustments are made when you can't get what you want.

Moon's Final Aspect to a Retrograde Planet

When the Moon makes a final aspect to a retrograde planet, conditions are less than stellar, but you still can succeed.

On a good day, you can successfully repeat a project or task. Even though you may have failed before, this is a good time to try again. You are more likely to succeed this time, but with all first-time projects, success will tend to be qualified in some way, depending on the type of day. Success may be delayed, come at an inopportune time, or you may no longer desire what you have been striving for.

On a challenging day, you may tend to repeat the same mistakes you made before. Difficulties on these days seem harder to take and the effects might be longer lasting. Final squares to retrograde malefics indicate that you will regret the course of action you have chosen. The final aspect to a retrograde planet, even a difficult one, means that you can try again, but you are less likely to do so if the retrograde malefic is in a fixed sign.

Moon's Final Aspect to a Returning Retrograde Planet

Unlike zodiacal refranations when a planet leaves the sign before the Moon can aspect it, retrograde planets can return to a sign changing the Moon's final aspect. When the Moon's final aspect is to a returning retrograde planet, it indicates someone or something, shows up unexpectedly and their presence effects that outcome of your project. For example, you are at a party and someone you never expected to see and didn't know was invited, suddenly appears. This changes your experience at the party which might be a good thing or a difficulty.

In this aspectarian, the Moon is in Pisces. Pluto is retrograde at zero degrees of Aquarius. Pluto enters the late degree of Capricorn at 9:47 on the 11th and becomes the Moon's final aspect, a sextile Pluto retrograde at 13:20 on the 11th. This indicates that complications are likely to arise unexpectedly. There is also a zodiacal Mercury sextile refranation as Mercury leaves Taurus and enters Gemini at about the same time, at 10:27 on the 11th. Perhaps information is unavailable and this complicates the situation.

Day	Time	Aspect
09	02 12	☽ ∦ ♅
Fr	04 24	☽ □ ☿
	05 02	☽ ∦ ☿
	10 14	☽ ♓
	19 02	☽ ⚹ ♃
	21 14	☿ ⚹ ♆
	22 16	☽ ☌ ♄
	00 36	☽ ∦ ♃
10	08 09	☽ ∥ ♄
Sa	13 23	☿ ∥ ♅
	19 31	☽ □ ☉
	21 21	☽ ⚹ ♅
11	09 09	☽ ☌ ♆
Su	09 47	♇ ♑
	10 26	☿ △ ♇
	10 27	☿ ♊
	13 20	☽ ⚹ ♇
	13 20	☽ ♈

Moon's final conjunction, sextile, or trine to a returning retrograde planet

Someone or something appears on the scene unexpectedly to help you succeed. This person or thing wasn't initially involved, but appears and joins your endeavor along the way.

Moon's final square or opposition to a returning retrograde planet

Someone or something appears on the scene unexpectedly to thwart your efforts or oppose your project. Obstacles seem to appear out of nowhere, making it difficult, if not impossible, to continue and succeed.

Chapter 10
Moonsign Interpretations

Introduction

Understanding the basic nature of the Moon's sign can give you an idea of how to proceed toward success and what tactics to use when seeking to realize your vision. It is not necessary to begin your electional search by choosing a Moonsign that has particular characteristics, or a particular interpretation related to your vision. In fact, it would be ill-advised to think of step one as choosing the Moonsign with the closest interpretation to what you want to happen and then look for a chart. There are ten planets, twelve houses, and numerous astrological factors to choose from. There are many ways to arrive at the electional chart interpretation that you want, and some are more important than others.

For example, when choosing a time for marriage, you do not have to limit your search to a Moon in Libra. Any Moonsign can be appropriate for a marriage depending on the couple. It is more important to choose planets in good standing with good Moon aspects, and especially a favorable final Moon aspect than to choose a Moon in Libra. You could choose Venus in Libra or an Ascendant in Libra instead. You could focus on planets in the seventh house.

Where the Moonsign interpretations are most helpful is in the final analysis and interpretation of the electional chart when you are deciding how to manifest your vision. The sign on the Moon can describe the nature of change, and how you might attempt to complete tasks. The interpretations are provided to give you insight into the steps you need to take, and your attitude and perspective while taking them.

Aries Moon

The Moon in Aries represents someone who is positive by nature. The individual tends to be self-reliant, sometimes acting without thinking and often relying on instincts, gut feelings, and second nature reactions. There is a tendency to be fearless, defiant, sometimes offensive, and physical. The individual might not consider how actions could affect others. Because of this, the Moon in Aries has an edge in accomplishing goals. The tendency is to reject any direction from others and to take the lead, sometimes as a pacesetter or pioneer, often in charge. A brash attitude can make this the "brat Moon."

The Moon in Aries is associated with new, innovative, or original projects that can be accomplished quickly, before anyone loses interest. Matters should be geared to produce immediate results. Delays should be avoided since patience will be limited. Projects that require a self-centered attitude are in the Arian style. Use this time to take the initiative and work independently. You can be assertive or even aggressive with this Moon sign.

On a good day, you can succeed with the Moon in Aries despite the objections of others. If you know you are right and need to proceed without letting others stop you, choose this Moon sign. You will feel as if you were given a mandate to succeed. Be assertive. You will want to do things your way. Take the initiative and try something new. Aries can be spirited, the original feminist, spontaneous, courageous, honest, intense, and fiery.

On a challenging day, you can be too aggressive when aggressiveness is inappropriate or unnecessary. Your selfishness or total disregard for others seriously hurts your project and your chances for success. Aries can be quick tempered, insecure, and impatient. There is a tendency toward fragile confidence and impulsive foolhardiness.

Taurus Moon

When the Moon is in Taurus, the individual tends to be very deliberate and careful. Development is slow, but steady. One does things on purpose. This is not a time for spontaneity. Everything is considered and reconsidered in the interest of self-protection and personal security. Methods tend to be tried and true. This often takes the form of following a book or formula, a tradition or precedent. You tend to take the high road and not want to dirty your hands by being unscrupulous. Any injury to another is generally unintentional. Your actions rarely offend, and your activities are usually welcomed. You gain respect because of what you are attempting to do. Choose this Moon sign if you want your project or idea to have clout.

On a good day, you operate as comfortably as you can, from a cushy chair surrounded by pillows. Success comes easily because others admire your "noble cause" or they treat you as an honored guest. Extra consideration is given to your needs. Expect better and you can rise to a higher position. The Taurus personality is charming, good-natured, loyal and gentle. The tendency is to be slow to anger. Taurus might have constant support while nurturing the building process.

On a challenging day, you get sucked in because matters seem to go well, but then the most admirable projects can go awry. Your urge for self-protectiveness may lead you to coverup your mistakes, thereby compounding your problems and making the situation more serious. Taurus can be stubborn, possessive, greedy, jealous, materialistic and self-protective. The tendency is toward slow assimilation.

Gemini Moon

The Moon in Gemini tends to be impersonal. Choosing this Moon might indicate you are operating under a misconception. Are you are misinformed or uninformed, although you think you are well-informed? Suspicions tend to be groundless, but you should investigate. You rethink your project a number of times because adjustments are necessary. Matters seldom run according to plan, do not turn out the way you expected, but still, you are successful. This is a good time to ad-lib life or make things up as you go. If need be, you can do two things at once. All forms of communication including rumors and gossip are consistent with this Moonsign. Documents and papers might be particularly important. Use go-betweens, agents, secretaries, and young people to assist you. Visits and short trips are likely.

On a good day, things can turn out well despite the instability and inaccurate information. Gemini is adaptable, versatile, and humorous.

On a challenging day, inaccuracies are never corrected, consequently, you make poor decisions. You can be too smart for your own good and no one will be able to convince you that your thinking is flawed. Your reactions to inconsistencies, distractions, and contingencies are ill-considered. The flake factor is operating. You forget what you should be doing now because you are thinking too far ahead. Gemini tends to lack depth, flitting from one thing to another, and generally inconsistent in all things. Sometimes they are all logical with little to no emotion. There is a tendency toward anxiety and nervousness.

Cancer Moon

The Moon in Cancer involves many changes, usually developed for others and quite often without receiving or expecting payment in return. Individuals tend to take a subordinate position. This Moonsign is associated with home, family, and certain inalienable rights. Family matters and responsibilities may complicate the task at hand. Obligations need to be fulfilled and resolved. Your project can foster dependency in others or give them a sense of security. Activities tend to involve ordinary or common tasks. Individuals can be emotionally attached to material items, eventually leading to accumulation. You probably have the right to be doing whatever you are doing. If someone tries to break into your home, you have the right to defend yourself and property. The activity might involve returning something which is out of place.

On a good day, matters run smoothly and any problems you have are problems you expected to occur. You have rights in the matter at hand, exercise them.

On a challenging day, even if you think things are going smoothly, you fail. Your project is complicated by emotional or domestic considerations. You tend to react impulsively rather than think clearly and logically.

Leo Moon

While the Moon is in Leo, one might tend to be insecure and uneasy. The tendency is to act under delegated authority only. You do not have authority of your own, but you can act on behalf of another who is an authority in his/her own right. Presentation is important to the events at hand and an experienced spokesperson may be used. Activities tend to be based on passion. Your enthusiasm augments your chances for success, and you are more likely to take risks. Risk is the order of the day. You will probably take chances or be reckless, often with the funds or the possessions of others. Extravagant purchases and self-indulgence are possible. This is a good Moon sign for entertainment, fun, and enjoyment.

On a good day, everything tends to run smoothly, and you feel elated. Exaggerating the facts can work to your advantage. Sins tend to be forgiven, and you are not always held responsible for your actions. You feel justified under the circumstances and can make a case in your defense. This is a good time to please those in authority, ask for favors, and delegate work.

On a challenging day, you will not be open to criticism or able to critique your own project. In your mind, you make situations seem better or worse than they really are; consequently, you don't see problems until it's too late or you may unnecessarily abandon a workable project. Accurate assessments are not your forte. You can be cruel if you think it will benefit your cause. You risk too easily and lose too much.

Virgo Moon

The Moon in Virgo always involves making a choice or having to decide an issue. You must discriminate, even among subtle variations. Differences can be overemphasized and discrimination on the basis of sex, race or religion can influence your project's success. Sexual attractions are likely, and you can be intrigued by forbidden fruit. Virgo, along with Pisces, is a sign of service; volunteer your time. Virgo rules the everyday operation of any activity that can become second nature, like habits. It lends itself to tasks that are repetitious and mindless. Events might cause mental stress or physical strain. Worry, restlessness and impatience are common. Be skillful and clever while paying close attention to details. Miniatures or prototypes might assist your endeavor.

On a good day, you gain power through unity. Band together with others to achieve success. Set up tasks you want to become habitual or part of your daily routine. Let sexual intrigue work to your advantage. Learn from your mistakes. Pay attention to details and causality. Notice what does and does not work.

On a challenging day, your prejudices can affect your ability to think logically. You can make wrong decisions just because your discriminatory powers are weak, and you have not learned from your past mistakes. Sexual hang-ups cause a problem in the proceedings if there is a sexual attraction involved.

Libra Moon

When the Moon is in Libra, the emphasis is on partnerships and cooperative ventures. You don't want to act independently, so join forces. All those involved tend to be obliging. Actions are helpful and meant to stabilize or establish a union between parties. Your goal is to be fair to all concerned and to protect agreements and contracts while maintaining harmony. Cooperation in the name of the game. Approval needs are strong, and you might behave in a defensive manner. In your desire to keep things balanced, consider both sides of any issue. Learn to negotiate. You are likely to make allowances for others. All this consideration slows you down and procrastination, indecisiveness, and inactivity become a problem. However, motives tend to be sincere, uncomplicated, innocent, and lacking in ulterior motives. Others can be easily coaxed, and demands are settled fairly and in peace.

On a good day, the spirit of cooperation tends to work to your advantage. You are able to accomplish more by pooling resources and utilizing the talents of others. Even if you're indecisive, you tend to make the right decision at the right time, or your indecisiveness won't hinder success.

On a challenging day, you make poor decisions or none at all. Relationships are difficult. A lack of true cooperation hinders success and keeps you from reaching your potential. You may lose sight of your goal because you appease others to your own detriment.

Scorpio Moon

The Moon in Scorpio indicates that your intentions may not be totally honorable and things may not be on the up and up. You may be doing something you shouldn't be doing or in a way you shouldn't be doing it. Others frown on your activities. This is a time when tasks can be accomplished in secret or outside the normal channels. Do you have an inside connection? If you are in trouble, you may need assistance to get out of the mess you have gotten yourself into. Research may be important to your success, though investigations are never complete. Partial information is common. Investigations or searches of any kind are possible. Someone important to the proceedings may be absent, and if necessary, a proxy can be used. On the whole, matters are more complicated with the Moon in Scorpio. Group endeavors go well, and one has the ability to influence the masses.

On a good day, you can go around the rules and have it work out. A lot of good things can happen when you travel less-than-normal channels. Your research, though incomplete, is thorough enough for success. This is a good time to get rid of things that are worn out or are no longer useful. Clean house, throw out duplicates, and streamline business.

On a challenging day, you go too far. Crime doesn't pay and neither does dishonesty. Secrets come out. The help that you need might not be available. People are missing at an important time. Matters may be too complicated to succeed, or research may be faulty. People tend to be persistent, easily disturbed, inarticulate, or evasive. A fear of rejection might underlie your behavior. Others tend to meddle.

Sagittarius Moon

The Moon in Sagittarius indicates that your optimistic attitude will enhance the proceedings, and things naturally tend to go your way or work out well. You tend to be lucky and generous. Activities tend to formalize or legalize activities. Knowledge is disseminated easily; ideas are circulated. You seem concerned with truth and justice, but you may not practice what you preach. You can be blunt or too frank, sometimes hurting others' feelings without intention. You can say something that you should not say and end up with your foot in your mouth. You may not have a strong sense of direction, and contingency plans will be necessary. Ad-lib your way through constantly changing situations and keep a laissez faire attitude toward events. Ceremonies and social customs can influence developments. You connect with foreigners and different ethnic groups through travel. Education introduces you to new ideas, philosophies, and religious beliefs.

On a good day, your enthusiasm makes things go your way. You can succeed on optimism alone and have fun doing it. People forget your verbal blunders and hypocrisy. This is a time for grown up kids to do fun projects.

On a challenging day, you blow it in terms of etiquette and culture. You can be blunt and even insulting without realizing it. Your relaxed attitude gets you nowhere.

Capricorn Moon

When the Moon is in Capricorn you have a good plan and know when the time is right. You operate slowly, conscientiously, and cautiously. Your standing in the community or reputation is important to you. The Moon in

Capricorn indicates that you do not want to give anything up to get what you want. You endeavor to gain everything while nothing is lost. You might keep a string attached to any past proceedings. You are prone to worry and tend to be pessimistic about the future. Delays and limitations are likely, especially if someone has a grudge. This is a time for shenanigans in business and people tend to proceed without authority. You function outside limits, tap less than normal channels, or take the law into your own hands. You may not be totally honest with others. You may have to operate in enemy territory or in the face of much opposition. People tend to oppose you when the Moon is in Capricorn, and those people may be the authorities. This sign is not the best for relationships since actions tend to offend. You are hard-working, trustworthy, dependable, calculating, and self-sustaining. All activities proceed slowly and cautiously.

On a good day, you can be successful by working in secrecy or through other-than-normal channels. You gravitate toward a sneaky plan of action. You can get around those who oppose you or expectations that limit you.

On a challenging day, when you screw up, you screw up big. You get caught with your hand in the cookie jar. You lose a lot in the quest for success.

Aquarius Moon

When the Moon is in Aquarius, events tend to be disruptive and extreme. Changes come on suddenly without notice and move quickly. Activities might encompass a large scale, be universal or political, involving the masses rather than the few. When the Moon is in Aquarius, your desire to be innovative and individualistic shows. You stand out because you are different or eccentric. Activities are often humane, surprising, or inventive. The intent is to modernize or renovate. You have the ability to do things unexpectedly or in a manner which seems totally out of character or outside of normal operating procedures. This can be a time for heroic or humanitarian ventures. Regardless of the nature of the project, you will handle situations in a detached, impersonal way. Relationships might involve a break and tend to be based on friendship. Partners tend to be highly individualistic. This is not the best sign for one-on-one activities, but it does lend itself to group activities. Matters proceed with a bit of discomfort. Although you are futuristic, you can be so far ahead of your time that you have trouble relating to the present.

On a good day, you are able to buck the tide successfully. You stand out and succeed by being different or a humanitarian. Even if you are ahead of your time, ideas will be accepted. An element of surprise works to your advantage. Friends help and group activities enhance your abilities.

On a challenging day, your actions are seen as disruptive. You can be a rebel without a cause. You and your ideas can be ridiculed rather than understood or supported. Individuality becomes a liability rather than an asset.

Pisces Moon

There is something unfortunate or sad about the Pisces Moon, but misfortune can work to your advantage. People help you or support you because they feel sorry for you. Being used by others might be innate to the project, and situations involving emotional indebtedness are possible. You can be detained or forced to wait. You might feel trapped if options are limited. Misunderstandings are possible when communication is not open. You can be misinformed. Something secretive or spiritual goes on. Instability is evident so plans should be flexible. What you initiate may depend on intuitive insights or gut feelings. You tend to be timid, trusting, and possibly easily fooled. Tasks can be laborious and thankless. You are able to serve and sacrifice in order to achieve.

On a good day, your disadvantaged position works to arouse sympathy. You can make others feel so sorry they naturally want to help you. Begging works when all else fails. Others are inspired to help you, especially if you are championing a noble cause. This is a good time for experiential events and projects that help you escape reality.

On a challenging day, you lose because others see you as a wimp or a hopeless case. People are dismissive. Sacrifice gets you nowhere. Instability causes you to lose control over events. The rug is pulled out from under you.

Chapter 11
Rules

Introduction

As previously stated in the first chapters of this book, electional astrology has been based on horary astrology for eons. Horary astrology has a lot of rules which are then applied to electional astrology charts. Basically, the rules are the same for both astrological techniques. Horary rules include strictures against reading a chart which I do not always agree with. I take all rules, whether horary or electional, with a grain of salt.

Rules don't tell the story. They are individual and independent factors in an electional chart that don't add up to a complete picture; therefore, rules can be somewhat inconsequential in the broader scheme of things. No rule makes or breaks an electional chart because they are not the building blocks of an electional chart. Even if you follow all the rules, you still might not be able to create a good electional chart because rules can't tell a story. It is wise to know the rules, but to also look beyond the rules to the overall picture. Learn to see the forest and not the individual trees.

I believe electional astrology is an art form more closely aligned with storytelling than any set of hard and fast rules. The story of your success within any electional chart is written by the planets, signs, houses, aspects, and movement of the Moon. Good electional charts are built with astrological symbolism. The major problem I see as a teacher is that the student can be so focused on the rules that he or she does not relate to the entire chart and the storytelling process within an election. It is easy to create a chart with more than 3 degrees on the Ascendant or all cardinal angles. Choosing an electional chart that meets these requirements is simple, but it does not reflect your intended goal or the process by which you succeed. The election may not apply at all to the matter at hand. Even a carefully constructed chart that adheres to many rules won't make a good election if there is no cohesion. It is harder to create a chart that illustrates your success for any endeavor, and also instructs you on how best to proceed.

I will present some of the rules here. What kind of electional astrology book would this be if I did not include the rules? There may be others I do not know or have not been taught. There are many different traditions, some ancient and some modern. There will always be more rules, and if your election fails, you can find a rule to take the blame.

Though the basics rules of electional astrology are included in this chapter, remember the chart has to say what you want to happen with astrological symbolism. That is the real goal here and the gold standard in electional astrology. I will show you how to do that in subsequent chapters.

These are the rules you might pay attention to when setting up an electional chart, but do not compromise a good electional chart for the sake of a rule. The most important thing is that the chart says what you want to happen.

Rules Related to the Moon

Moon's applying aspects	The Moon is allowed all of her applying aspects before leaving the sign she is in even if the Moonsign falls across several days. The order of aspects while the Moon is in a sign is important and they tell a story. The Moon should be free of affliction from other planets. The Moon's applying aspects show you the actions you need to take or the events yet to occur. The more aspects the Moon makes, the greater the number of actions or events to expect.
Moon's separating aspects	The Moon's separating aspects reveal what has already happened.
Void of course Moon	The Moon Void of Course means nothing to worry about, or nothing will happen. If you begin a project during the VOC Moon, it may not succeed or develop. Decisions made during a Void of Course Moon may never be acted upon. Disturbing news heard during a Void of Course Moon may not be worth worrying about. You might choose this time slot to initiate an activity if you want to limit the consequences resulting from your or another's actions. For example, if you do not want new ideas to be accepted by others, choose a Void of Course Moon time to present those ideas. It is unlikely that new ideas will be accepted and anything of consequence will evolve.

Part of Fortune / VOC	To avoid a Void of Course Moon, you can choose a chart with a Void of Course Moon that makes a good aspect to the Part of Fortune indicating nothing but success, but good aspects to planets are better for storytelling.
New Moon situation	When the Moon is conjunct the Sun, either applying or separating, the person initiating the election is probably in the dark about an important piece of information. The Moon is the co-ruler of the activity and initiator unless designated elsewhere in the chart, ruling someone or something else. This time might be best for closing things down or start fresh.
Moon in Taurus, Libra, or Sagittarius	When the Moon is in a Venus or Jupiter ruled sign, things tend to go better. Pisces, a Jupiter ruled sign is not as fortunate as these three other signs.
Moon fixed & cadent	The Moon fixed and cadent cannot help itself or go unaided. Assistance may be needed in order to succeed since the person ruled by the Moon will not act in his or her own name.
Moon common (mutable) and cadent	The Moon common (or mutable) and cadent will not end up as planned either in intended destination or in finishing the matter.
Moon's final aspect	A great final aspect is the Moon in good aspect to the ruler of the sign it is in. If the Moon's final aspect is to a retrograde planet, you can recover and should try again, even if the aspect was a difficult one.

Rules Regarding the Ascendant

Ascendant rulership	The initiator is always represented by the 1st house and the Ascendant.
Ascendant unafflicted	The Ascendant should be unafflicted by not being conjunct, square, or opposition to malefics.
Ascendant at 0-3 degrees	The Ascendant should not be in too early for now degrees (less than 3 degrees) unless there is an understandable reason for being so. Sometimes the initiator is not ready or wants an electional chart for the future while preparing. In this case, it might be appropriate, or if their natal ascendant is 0-3 degrees.

Ascendant Via Combust at 15 Libra to 15 Scorpio	The Ascendant is Via Combust from 15 Libra to 15 Scorpio. It represents someone who is unfortunate, seriously disadvantaged, and not in control.
Spica at 21-23 Libra	Spica is a benefic star between 21 and 23 degrees of Libra. This is a positive placement and safe haven for the Ascendant.
Ascendant greater than 27 degrees	The Ascendant should not be in too late for now degrees (more than 27 degrees) unless there is an understandable reason for it being so. Sometimes it is already late in the game anyway.
Ascendant at 28 degrees	When the Ascendant is at 28 degrees the native "ifs" a lot (If only!).
Ascendant at 28-29 Taurus	The Ascendant should not be at 28-29 Taurus. These are degrees of sorrow ruled by the Pleiades or Weeping Sisters.
Ascendant at a critical degree, 0, 13 & 26 cardinal, 9 & 21 fixed, 4 & 21 mutable	The Ascendant should not be in a critical degree or the planet ruling the Ascendant should not be in a critical degree, and square or opposed to a malefic planet, especially if the malefic is in fall or detriment.
Ascendant same degree as the nodes	An Ascendant in the exact numerical degree as the nodes, (example, 5 Pisces node and 5 Gemini Ascendant) indicates a catastrophe, especially if the Ascendant is square, opposite, or conjunct the nodes. This is not a question of orb. Catastrophe is a bit too strong, but generally, don't choose an Ascendant in this position.
Ascendant and ruler of the 7th house	When the ruler of the 7th house applies to the Ascendant with a good aspect, that means that he or she wants what you want and there can be an agreement
Mercury ruled Ascendant	When the Ascendant is Mercury ruled, especially when the Ascendant is in Gemini, important information may be inaccurate. It is important to recheck the facts and investigate further. There is something to be corrected and the person initiating the election should be warned to research further. Ask questions. There may or may not be an issue.

Rules Regarding Planets

Many of the Ascendant rules also apply to planets or the significator of the person initiating the election or the goal.

Project significators	The planet, house, or sign ruling your project should be unafflicted & moving toward good aspects.
Planet at 0 degrees	Planets at 0 degrees are beginning a new course of action. Since 0-3 degrees are generally "too early for now," the individual might not be ready to begin immediately. Actions can be premature. It is possible that this rule doesn't apply if the native has natal planets in early degrees.
Planet Via Combust	A planet is Via Combust from 15 Libra to 15 Scorpio. It represents someone who is unfortunate and not in control. Generally, a planet in the Via Combust is weak and probably should not represent the initiator. However, you might use a planet in this position to represent the seller of a house if you wish to buy the house at a lower price. Perhaps the seller is in a tight spot and needs to sell even at a cost.
Spica 21-23 Libra	Spica is a benefic star between 21 and 23 degrees of Libra. This is a positive placement and safe haven for any significator.
Planets 28 degrees	When a significator is at 28 degrees, the native "ifs" a lot (If only this would happen, I could do that!).
27, 28, & 29 degrees	Planets at 27, 28, and 29 degrees might indicate a situation that is too late for now. Conditions have changed and perhaps you missed the boat. It is possible that these rules do not apply if the native has natal planets in late degrees.
Planet at 28-29 Taurus	28 and 29 Taurus are degrees of sorrow ruled by the Pleiades or Weeping Sisters.
Planet at 29 degrees	29 degrees shows that the person is at the end of his or her rope and about to make a definite change.
Ruler of the 7th house	When the ruler of the 7th house applies to the Ascendant or the ruler of the Ascendant with a good aspect, the person it represents wants the same thing you want and agreements are likely.

Planet same degree as the nodes	A planet in the exact numerical degree as the nodes, (example, 5 Pisces node and 5 Gemini Sun) indicates a catastrophe, especially if the planet is square, opposite, or conjunct the nodes. This is not a question of orb. Catastrophe is a bit too strong, but generally, don't choose a planet in this position.
Planet changing signs	If the planet is moving into a sign of better standing, such as rulership or exaltation, the change is more likely to be positive. If the planet is moving into a sign of detriment or fall, the change is more likely to be difficult.
Saturn in the 1st house	Saturn in the 1st house may delay matters.
Planet ruling the Ascendant	The planet ruling the Ascendant should not be afflicted. The first house rules the person initiating the election. You want that person to be well represented in the chart.
Planet in aspect to the house ruler	When a planet in a house is in bad aspect to the ruler of the house it shows someone who is at odds with the person who has authority over him or her. This afflicted planet is like an unwelcome house guest.
Planet conjunct a house cusp	A planet conjunct the cusp of the next house is on the threshold of a new activity, or situation. If the next house is more favorable, conditions can improve. The opposite is also true. If the planet has crossed the cusp and is just inside the house, someone has recently entered a new situation whether positive or negative.
Intercepted planet	Any planet in an intercepted sign is an intercepted planet, and this means interference. Something or someone is hemmed in.
Planet opposite the house it rules	A planet in the house opposite to the one it rules crosses over to the other side and can be easily influenced, especially in a mutable sign.

Rules Regarding Time Periods

The 12th house	Rules the past
The 1st house	Rules the present
The 2nd house	Rules the future
The 3rd house	Rules the distant future

Same sign on the 12th and 1st houses	When the sign on the 12th house is the same as the sign on the 1st, you bring matters and problems down on yourself. Take corrective action.
Same sign on the 1st and 2nd houses	If the sign on the 1st house is the same as the sign on the 2nd house, matters tend to stay the same and extend into the future. This can be advantageous.

Rules About Angles

Cardinal angles	Cardinal angles give you more control over the proceedings and show immediate movement forward. Cardinal signs take the lead. Things seem to start sooner and progress faster when the angles are cardinal. Consider these rules when counseling a client, but it is not something to shoot for when setting up an electional chart.
Fixed angles	Fixed angles show that matters are established, underway and sure to develop. There is no stopping the proceedings. Consider these rules when counseling a client, but it is not something to shoot for when setting up an electional chart.
Mixed Cross	A mixed cross will have intercepted signs, and this can show some kind of interference. Proceedings begin with the sign quality on the Ascendant and then proceed with the sign quality on the Midheaven.
Mutable angles	Mutable angles show that your choices are limited, and contingency plans are needed. You might have to defer to someone else and do whatever is expedient under the circumstances. Instability is common with mutable crosses. Consider these rules when counseling a client, but it is not something to shoot for when setting up an electional chart.

Rules Associated with Degrees

Planets at 0 degrees	Planets at 0 degrees are beginning a new course of action. Actions might be premature.

Via Combust - 15 Libra to 15 Scorpio	Planets between 15 Libra and 15 Scorpio are Via Combust. They represent someone who is unfortunate, not in control, and weak.
Cardinal critical degrees 0, 13, and 26	Planets that are in a critical degree represent someone who feels forced to take action as matters come to a head.
Fixed critical degrees 9 and 21	Planets that are in a critical degree represent someone who feels forced to take action as matters come to a head.
Mutable critical degrees 4 and 17	Planets that are in a critical degree represent someone who feels forced to take action as matters come to a head.
22 Leo	22 Leo is the degree of being your own worst enemy.
21-23 degrees Libra	21-23 degrees Libra is conjunct a fixed benefic star, Spica. This is a positive placement and safe haven for the Ascendant and any significator.
24 Taurus - Caput Algol	This is a malefic star associated with losing your head figuratively and unable to think straight.
27, 28, & 29 degrees	Planets at 27, 28, and 29 degrees might indicate a situation that is too late for now. Conditions have changed and perhaps you missed the boat. It is possible that these rules do not apply if the native has natal planets in late degrees.
28 Degrees	28 degrees "if's" a lot. (If only this would happen, I could do that.
28-29 degrees Taurus	28-29 Taurus is a point of sorrow ruled by the Pleiades or Weeping Sisters
29 is a critical degree	29 degrees shows that the person is at the end of his or her rope and about to make a definite change. If the planet will move into a sign of better standing, the change is likely to be positive. If the planet is moving into a sign of detriment or fall, the change is likely to be difficult. Planets in critical degree represent someone who feels forced to act as matters come to a head.

Rules About Houses

Angular houses	Angular houses are out in the open, public. Angular houses are more powerful and have the greatest effect.
Succedent houses	Succedent houses all rule money. The 2nd is your money, the 5th is the money of the home, the 8th is the money of the partner, and the 11th is the money from a job.
Cadent houses	Cadent houses are private. Things can happen in these houses, and you would never know. Things happening in the cadent houses might be unimportant.
Intercepted houses	Planets in intercepted houses can interfere with proceedings

Miscellaneous Rules

Planet on the dark side of the next house	A planet in the sign of the next house is on the dark side. This shows dissatisfaction with the affairs of the next house.

Translation of the Light Requirements

Translation of the light is a way in which two planets or significators not in aspect with one another, can become aspected through a third planet which aspects each in turn. The third planet aspect is usually a conjunction, but not always. The connection of the two out of orb planets is made by a third planet moving faster than either of the other two planets. This faster planet is usually the Moon, but there can be situations where Mercury or Venus makes the connection instead. The applying aspect is usually a conjunct or at least a good aspect. Conjunctions make for the best visuals and are the most understandable.

Here are three requirements for a translation of the light:

1. Two significators are separating from an aspect
2. They are out of orb and no longer in aspect,
3. A third planet in earlier degree and faster than either of them, can reunite them, by applying to aspect each in turn.

In this example chart, Venus and Mars are out of orb and no longer in aspect. The Moon is faster than either Venus or Mars and can conjunct them each in turn. In this way, the Moon translates the light from Mars to Venus, restoring the connection between the two planets and perfecting the aspect.

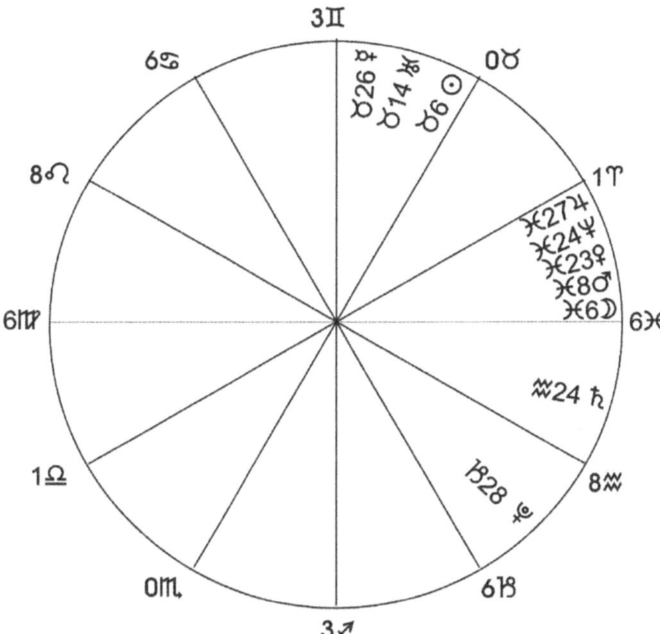

Here is a real-life scenario. Two high school sweethearts have grown apart and are totally out of touch, (not in aspect), but each has remained friends with a third schoolmate. Later in life, the schoolmate friend has a party and invites each of the sweethearts individually. They meet at the party and are reconnected.

Collection of the Light

Collection of the light is another means by which two planets not in aspect can become connected through a third planet. However, in this case, rather than a faster moving planet, collection of the light uses a slower moving planet such as Jupiter or even Saturn to make the aspect and connection. In addition, the two parties do not know each other and have never been in contact.

Here are the requirements for collection of the light aspect:

1. When two planets haven't been in aspect at all, (they're strangers),
2. And each applies to the same third planet that is slower than either of them,
3. Whose degree is later than either of them,
4. This third planet represents a person to whom they can both depend on.
5. This person collects their individual light and represents them both.
6. This can signify a third person entering the situation voluntarily to collect the light through an aspect and act as a go-between or agent for both parties and perfect the connection.

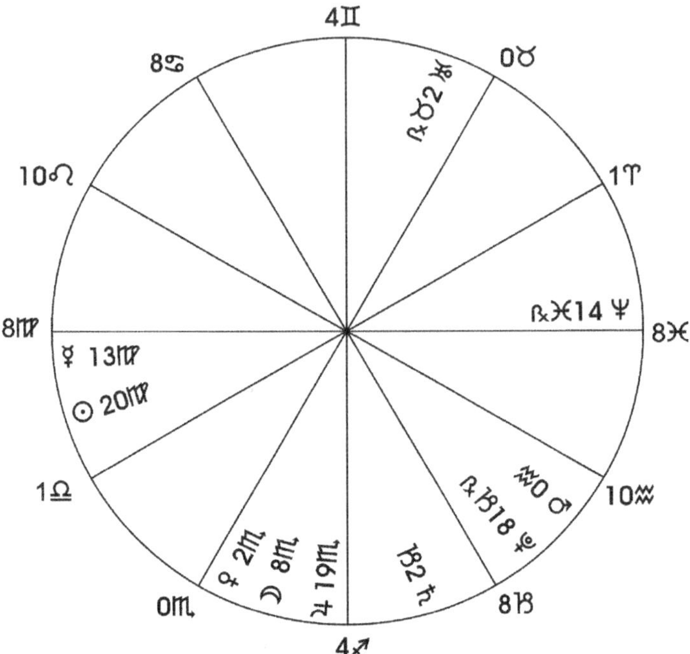

In our chart example, Mercury and Venus have not been in aspect, but they both will aspect Jupiter in the future. Mercury will sextile Jupiter, while Venus will conjunct Jupiter creating a collection of the light aspect between the two.

Here is a real-life scenario. Two individuals who have never been in contact and do not know each other are brought together by a third party. If you wish to sell your house, you would contact a real estate agent because you do not know a buyer. The agent will list your house and show it, or perhaps the real estate agent knows a buyer who is looking for a house like yours. The agent acts as a go-between, connecting the seller to the buyer to close the deal.

Mutual Reception

Planets in mutual reception get back to normal through the help of a third unnamed party. In this following chart example, Venus is in Aries, a Mars ruled sign, and Mars is in Taurus, a Venus ruled sign. They are in mutual reception, and each can be read back in the sign of rulership while retaining their respective degrees. Therefore, Venus has a secondary placement of 20 degrees Taurus in addition to the chart placement of 20 degrees Aries. Mars has a secondary placement of 5 degrees Aries in addition to its placement in the chart at 5 degrees Taurus. In this case, Venus is retrograde and this might indicate that the mutual reception is not possible, desirable, or advantageous.

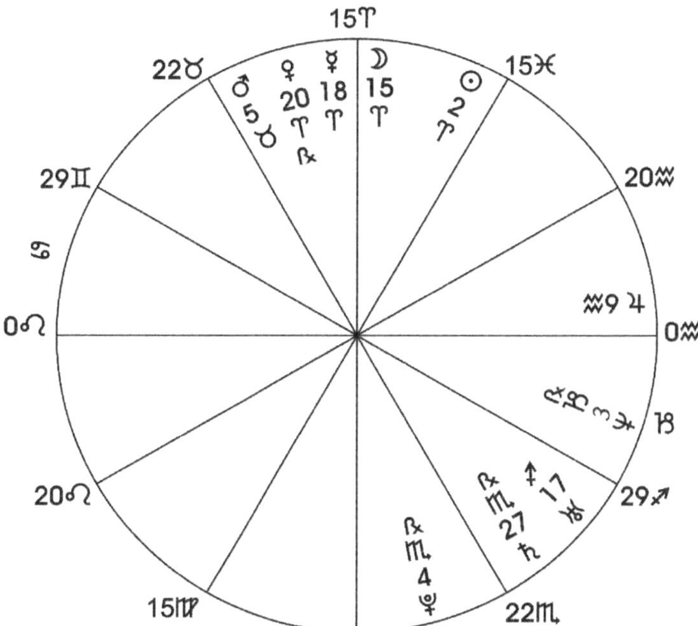

If a planet is also in exaltation such as Venus in Pisces in mutual reception with Jupiter in Taurus, it is possible that the situation will not work or that one person will not want to trade positions or lose an advantage. The same is true if one planet will be moving to a difficult position by house or aspect. The switch might not be advantageous for one or both parties. Mutual receptions can indicate an advantage, but they have to be agreed upon.

Applying and Separating Aspects and Orbs

While The Moon shows actions and events according to her applying aspects, the other personal planets such as the Sun, Mercury, Venus, and Mars can also be considered as applying or separating. But even if the planets are separating, they can still maintain an orb of influence. Planets that are mutually separating with one planet direct and the other planet retrograde, have a shorter orb of influence. This is because their backs are turned toward one another. Two planets that are mutually applying to each other have a wider orb because they are facing each other and have the ability to reach for each other.

Chapter 12

Astrological Symbolism as Language

Introduction

Rules can be pretty boring, and they should not be the first thing you think of when searching for a good electional chart. They are sometimes the last thing you think of when refining and fine-tuning a selected electional chart. What I will be teaching you about using astrological symbolism as language for storytelling goes way beyond horary and electional rules as you will see. Rules do not make or break an electional chart, and they certainly cannot tell a story. If I am not paying a lot of attention to the rules, how do I make the chart say what I want to happen?

Astrology is a symbolic language that can encode your desire or intention within an electional chart. You probably already know many interpretations for the planets, houses, and aspects. This will enable you to see planets as people or things, houses as locations or things, and aspects as actions or interactions. Planets, houses, and aspects are the building blocks for storytelling in an electional chart. They can form sentences. It is simply a matter of putting them together grammatically and coherently.

The planets, Sun, and Moon are people or actors in the electional chart. They have innate characteristics according to their sign and house placement. They are the nouns in storytelling and in sentence structure.

The houses in an electional chart can represent people, places, things or situations. This is generally where that action occurs, but they are not the action, as they are generally also nouns in the storytelling and in sentence structure.

The aspects between the planets, Sun, and Moon indicate the relationships people have with one another and the actions or interactions occurring between people or things. The aspects are the verbs in the electional chart.

The Moon is the activity in an electional chart. The Moon can be a noun, but it also shows the progress of any activity taking place in the electional chart and should be taking place with the participation of the initiator.

Think of the rules as grammar or punctuation that help you to understand astrological language.

These are the building blocks for storytelling and sentence structure. A good election chart uses astrological symbolism to reveal a story regarding your vision for the future, your desire, the process toward achievement, impediments one might encounter along the way, the nature of the final goal, and one's chances for success. A good electional chart can give you insight into how this will happen and what your role should be in the process. It is an interactive lesson plan that shows you how to be successful. That chart then facilitates an intuitive process that allows you to understand the steps needed to successfully manifest your intended goal. A good electional chart says what you want to happen. All this can be seen in the astrological symbolism of a good electional chart. Astrology is a symbolic language and never more so than in an electional chart.

A Grammar Lesson with Astrological Symbolism

Here is a short story example stated with astrological symbolism to introduce the translation technique. The planets, houses, and aspects below work together to form a coherent sentence that tells the story of what is happening. This example is purposely simple to demonstrate how to structure the various astrological elements into a meaningful statement. There are some amazing electional chart examples in the following chapters which are more complex and detailed, but this illustrates a single action and scenario.

Venus (noun) in Taurus in the 2nd house (possibly related to money) is sextile (good interaction verb aspect) to Jupiter (noun and the greater benefic) in the 11th house of salary (situation). The Moon in the 10th house (the boss) will trine (good action verb) Venus in Taurus in the 2nd house, and then sextile (good action verb) Jupiter in the 11th house of salary (positive situation) as a final aspect. The boss may decide to grant a request for a salary increase.

This astrological statement is a complete sentence and tells a simple story in astrological language. You can literally tell a detailed, multifaceted story within an electional chart, paint a picture of a successful result, and the process of attainment.

Chapter 13

Finality

What is Finality?

Before we can begin to look at some amazing example electional charts, we need to define and understand finality since finality determines the exact time of the electional chart within the chosen Moonsign.

> The elected time of any ephemeral election, whether character or activity, is the time with the greatest FINALITY you can give to the event's beginning. Finality is when you have done whatever is necessary to set an event in motion. It is the latest final time that you can control, and after that matters are out of your hands. (Gilbert Navarro)

Another way to define finality might be to go beyond the point of no return. You have crossed a crucial line in the sand and there is no going back, no rewriting of history. Things will never be the same. There is only forward movement from this time onward.

Finality is not when you sign a contract if the contract remains in your hands. Finality is when you hand over the signed contract to the other party, agency, or institution. This might occur during a meeting such as a house settlement when all pertinent individuals are present, but in other situations, there are various points of finality. If you choose to mail a contract, the point of finality is when you hand over the documents to the postal clerk to be stamped and mailed, or when you drop the stamped envelope in the blue mailbox. At that point, you cannot retrieve it. You have reached the point of finality. If you mail a document in the mailbox in front of your house, you can retrieve it at any time until it is picked up by the postal person. You have no control over the time of collection, and you might miss the time of collection. This is ill-advised.

When a couple gets married, obtaining a license to marry is not the point of finality. Nor is it the time of the wedding ceremony; it is the time of the pronouncement, "I now pronounce you husband and wife." Before that time, there is an opportunity for anyone to object to the marriage. "Should anyone present know of any reason why this couple should not be joined in holy matrimony, speak now or forever hold your peace." Once the pronouncement has occurred, the officiant needs to sign the marriage license, but this is only a formality. In other countries or localities, legalization may occur at other times. It is important to know when marriage becomes legal before attempting a marriage election.

When legalizing a business, some states allow you to walk into the local government office and choose the incorporation time. You hold your paperwork until the elected time arrives and have the clerk timestamp your documentation immediately, establishing your business as a legal entity. Some states select noon for the establishment of all businesses regardless of when the paperwork is submitted. Still, other states timestamp all paperwork when the clerk gets around to it. You are not allowed to wait and must drop off or mail your paperwork into the appropriate office. Because the procedure varies from state to state, if you intend to legalize and establish a new business, you might want to investigate the process ahead of time. This will enable you to determine the point of finality and choose the best electional time for your business. Should you have no resource other than to submit your paperwork at a chosen time, use this submission time as the birth of your business. Any paperwork with a later time stamp is either secondary or totally unimportant.

I have had clients who said they dropped off documentation at a lawyer's office, and then proceeded to tell the lawyer when to act upon the information or paperwork. This is not a good practice. You are the initiator, not the lawyer. The best elected time is when the paperwork is delivered to the lawyer. At that point, it is out of your hands. Step back and let the lawyer do his or her job. When you double up on who is doing what and when, you do not have control or clarity.

I have also heard clients suggest the same procedure for real estate actions. They choose a time and date to sign a contract to put their house on the market and give the contract to the realtor. But then they ask the realtor to not list the house for sale until further notice while they finish cleaning out the house and prepare for showings. This never works for two reasons. First, they have lost complete control over initiation as there is no longer a well-defined point of finality. Second, the realtor wants to sell their house and make money. Sellers will get a call from the realtor asking for a special showing of the house because there is this perfect buyer now who will definitely buy the house at above the asking price. Of course, that may or may not happen as there is no guarantee.

In regard to lawyers, realtors, and legal matters, if you fax or email a contract, make sure the copy will be considered legal. In some states and in some situations, the recipient must have the original signed document before moving forward. A copy or email is not considered valid. In that case, you must hand deliver, or snail mail the original signed document, and when you do so, that becomes the point of finality. In all matters, the point of finality depends on the point of legality.

When purchasing a car, the point of finality might be determined by the laws of your state, or the policy set by the dealership. Once you hand over the check to the salesperson, have you purchased the car? Can you get your check back? Is the point of finality when you sign the dealership's loan papers? Is the car legally yours only when you take possession and drive it off the lot? There is no universal answer to this question. When making a major purchase like this, ask questions to determine the best or most obvious point of finality. Use your best judgment if there are no state, dealership, or legal guidelines regarding ownership.

Determining the point finality is of the upmost importance when initiating an election because it defines the date, time, and place of the electional chart. This information is necessary for erecting any astrological chart. It is not always clear when the point of finality occurs. There are a lot of gray areas. You may be surprised that finality is not always what you think or expect, so it is important to consider the possibilities ahead of time. Know when you are truly letting go. But if you focus on the point at which you lose control over the matter at hand, or when you clearly reach and pass the point of no return, you should be able define the date, time, and place needed to erect your electional chart. Then determine the correct action you need to take to set everything in motion.

Natural Restraints

One other consideration before beginning your search for an electional time: what are the natural restraints related to any endeavor? What time periods can you use? Regarding a loan application, what are the bank's hours? Must you apply in person? Or can you apply at any time online? Regarding surgery, what days does the doctor operate and when does he start? When is his first operation of the day? Can you mail or fax the contract to the real estate agent to list your house on the market? Will the wedding be a church ceremony, or Justice of Peace? How long does the ceremony normally take? Fortunately, you can do a lot of things online nowadays so you can use off hours and even middle of the night. But before you begin looking for any electional time, you need to know what natural restraints are related to the initiation of your vision, project, or goal. When and how is it possible to realize finality?

Chapter 14
Six Steps to Creating an Electional Chart

Introduction

In the following chapters, there are a number of amazing electional charts that worked beautifully. While a chart presentation and analysis of a good election with information about the results is very insightful, the student is best served by understanding the plan of attack in getting to the best date and time. Seeing someone else's work, though inspiring, is very different from trying to find a good electional chart on your own. There are so many factors associated with elections, planets, houses, aspects, and rules. Where does one begin? It is of upmost importance for the student to understand that there are specific steps he or she should take in searching for and erecting their own electional charts. Below are the six steps needed to both create a good electional chart and then follow its instructions to a successful conclusion. In the next few chapters, these steps will be demonstrated in great detail using these exact six steps.

Steps to Create a Good Electional Chart

1. Clearly define the goal of the election chart. In many situations, this is the hardest step for many people. What do you want to be, have, do, or create? In any manifestation practice, determining what you want is the first and most vital step. State your intention as clearly as possible in real-life terms and scenarios. This step should not involve any rules or predetermined astrological factors. Rules are distracting and they have no place here at this point. You can lose sight of the big picture if you focus on rules. Keep it simple. What do you want?

2. Know which planets and houses relate to your goal. You can use the definitions in <u>Chapter Five - The Sun, Moon and Planets</u> and <u>Chapter Seven - The Houses</u>, or a rulership reference book as a guide. There are

several good ones: *The Book of Rulerships: Keywords from Classical Astrology*, by Lee Lehman, or *The Rulership Book*, by Rex E. Bills & Kris Brandt Riske. Begin to determine which astrological symbols might be important in an electional chart according to the desired result.

3. Within the chosen time search period, pick Moonsigns with the best Moon aspects and good final Moon aspect. There may be several that you want to test out. You want the best Moon aspects in addition to a good final Moon aspect because this can indicate the easiest process with the least amount of effort. Also consider planetary standing in the search area. Do you need planets in rulership or in exaltation?

4. Begin to test out the best Moonsigns. What planet is best for ruling the Ascendant? The ruler of the Ascendant is the ruler for the initiator. What are the best planets to represent the goal? What are the best planetary combinations, (ruler of the Ascendant and ruler of the goal), with the best aspects? Once you have your best Moonsigns and planetary combinations, you want to choose the best chart orientation. This involves erecting test charts and then rotating the charts through time to maximize the placements.

5. Create a chart that says what you want to happen. Does the chart tell the story of your success? Are there three confirming indications in the chart? Does the Ascendant and/or Midheaven of the final electional chart conjunct or oppose a position in the initiator's natal chart plus or minus a few degrees? The final time you pick on the day that you selected should give you a chart that says what you want to happen.

6. Follow the instructions/process seen in the chart. Do what the chart tells you to do.

Now proceed to the next chapter for a detailed demonstration and implementation of these steps in a real-life situation.

Chapter 15
Swim Chart Example

Introduction

There are no perfect charts. There are good charts, even great charts, but no perfect ones. Some of the charts I will be presenting might "look" perfect to you, but they are not. They are only perfect in the eyes of the beholder who sees the goal clearly represented in the chart and understands exactly what must be done to successfully accomplish the mission and attain the goal. Impediments or challenges exist in every electional chart, but everything that is negative tends to fall away and become extraneous once you understand how to deal with any issues. It is the goal that draws you and the necessary steps to success that are key. Near perfection comes from what is important and relevant. This is what draws your attention, informs you, inspires you, and gives you the confidence to succeed.

My Electional Problem

I had lived in Baltimore City for ten years. In 1984, we temporarily relocated to New Jersey and in the spring of 1986, my family is relocating from New Jersey back to Maryland. Because I did the electional chart to sell our New Jersey home, it sold in a matter of days for more than the asking price. But we could not find a house to buy in Maryland, and we were forced to build a home. The house would not be ready until mid-August. In the meantime, we would be living with my mother-in-law in a Baltimore "rowhouse" with little to no front or backyard. The house was filled with crystal, china, and antiques. I had three active boys, ages thirteen, nine, and three. This was not a good situation, and we needed an activity and some place to go during the summer months.

Before we moved to NJ, we belonged to a swim club. Many of our friends and our children's friends attended the same pool. Joining the club again would be perfect. There was only one problem. When I called for an application, I was told there were twenty-two families ahead of us on a two-year waiting list.

Acceptance for the coming summer was impossible. I did not have two years to wait; I needed to join the pool that summer. I requested an application anyway. This called for a good electional chart that would determine when I mailed in the application, and the chart would have to say what I wanted to happen.

Step 1 - Clearly Define the Goal

It is important to have a clearly stated goal before looking for a good election time. Here is my clearly defined goal: I want to rejoin the swim club this summer. I want to be accepted despite a long waiting list.

The Chart Has to Say What You Want to Happen

The most important thing to remember when you are choosing an elected time is that the chart has to say what you want to happen. At this point, I had no idea how I would do that. The only thing I had to go on was my clearly defined goal. The planets, aspects, and signs will need to reflect my intention and process moving forward in time to a successful conclusion. Don't start out with a preconceived notion of what the chart should look like. This becomes a creative project when you look in the ephemeris and aspectarian to see what is available.

Natural Restraints

For any electional chart, you need to know what natural restraints exist and what time of day you can use. For this chart, there are no natural restraints. I can mail the application at a local post office blue box any time of day or night.

Step 2 - Know which House or Houses Relate to Your Goal

The 2nd step is to know what house or houses relate to your goal. There may be more than one house, and there may be several to choose from. Perhaps you are not certain and need to test houses out as you go along. It is not unheard of to try a house placement and chart orientation, then reach a dead end, having to move on to a different approach and another house. This is where electional astrology becomes a creative and intuitive art form. There is no standard or one size that fits all.

The 1st house in any electional chart rules the "here" position. In other words, this is where you are now. It is the house of remaining. The 7th house in an electional chart rules the "there" position, or where you wish to go. It is the house of removing. In some charts it can represent where your wish to go, as in "I don't want to be here" (1st house), but "I want to go there (7th house). For this reason, the 7th house will play an important role in this election. I and my family want to go "there" to the pool. We do not want to be stuck "here" in my mother-in-law's rowhouse. The 1st house to 7th house dynamic was the easiest set of houses to consider, and I chose to work with them.

Step 3 - Choose a Good Moonsign

Looking at Moonsigns in an aspectarian gives one an understanding of the astrological weather for any given time period. It is important to familiarize yourself with the ephemeris and the aspectarian. This helps in discovering what is a good day, a great day, or the best day within the search parameters. Remember, the Moon is allowed all of her applying aspects until leaving the sign, and the final Moon aspect is very important. I frequently track what is going on in the future in the aspectarian. I constantly know what is the best day in the coming month. The Moonsign I picked for this election was a great day and you will soon see why.

Step 4 - Choose the Best Planets to Represent You and Your Goal

It is important what planets you pick to represent you and your goal. This involves standing: rulership, exaltation, detriment, and fall. Standing might be the secret to good electional astrology. The person or people initiating the election are ruled by the 1st house, any 1st house planets that are not intercepted, and the rulers of the 1st house cusp. The 7th house is ruled by planets in the 7th house not assigned elsewhere, and the rulers of the house cusp.

In this Moonsign, there are three planets in rulership, Venus in Taurus, Jupiter in Pisces, and Pluto in Scorpio. What is so great about planets in rulership? They belong!! They are in the right place at the right time doing what is correct. They have rights in the matter at hand or membership. They only encounter expected problems. I am hoping to have one of those planets represent me in my electional chart.

Planets in Rulership

☉♌ ☽♋ ☿♊♍ ♀♉♎ ♂♈♏
♃♐♓ ♄♑♒ ♅♒ ♆♓ ♇♏

- **Belong**
- Are capable
- Are doing what they should be doing
- Have rights in the matter at hand - **membership**
- Healthy
- Encounter only expected problems

There are also three planets in exaltation, the Moon in Taurus, the Sun in Aries, and Mars in Capricorn. Planets in exaltation are welcomed and treated as the honored guest. They have clout. But most importantly, planets in exaltation can represent someone who can rise to a higher position. It is my hope that I can use one or more of the exalted planets to rise higher on the waiting list. I want to be welcomed as an honored guest at the pool. These are just some of the keywords associated with a planet in exaltation.

Only Mercury is in detriment in this Moonsign. I do not want to be represented by a planet in detriment. I would have no rights, I would not be welcomed, and I would not be accepted into the pool.

Planets in fall are in signs opposite the signs of exaltation. This is worse than being in detriment because you are at fault and should be to blame. There is one planet in fall, Mercury, which is both in detriment and in fall in Pisces. You might be thinking Mercury in Pisces represents children swimming, but this is not a good significator.

Planets in Fall

☉♎ ☽♏ ☿♌♓ ♀♍ ♂♋
♃♑ ♄♈ ♅♉ ♆♐ ♇♌

- Aren't welcomed
- Unhealthy
- Are at fault and should apologize
- Are incapable and unqualified
- Experience a fall from grace
- They do something they should not do

Finally, there are three peregrine planets that are not lucky enough to be in a sign or element that they rule. They have a roving, aimless, and pointless vibration in the matter at hand. Saturn in Sagittarius, Uranus in Sagittarius, and Neptune in Capricorn are peregrine in this Moonsign.

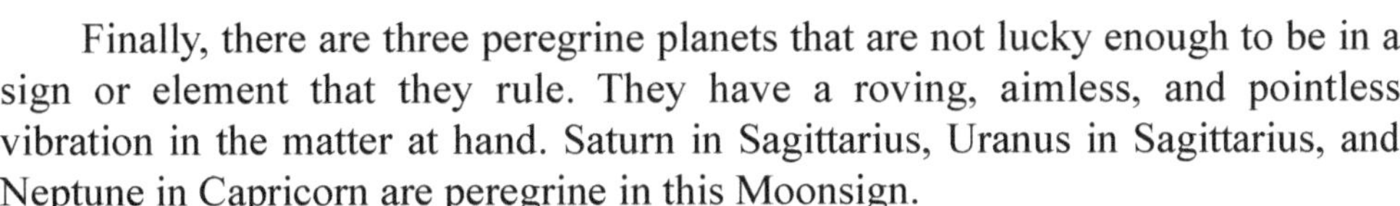

Peregrine Planets

Are not lucky enough to be in
a sign or element that they rule.
They have a roving, aimless, and pointless
vibration in the matter at hand.

Obviously, I would not want to be ruled by a peregrine planet and end up wandering aimlessly through the streets of Baltimore City with my three children in tow. Since I want to belong at the pool, a planet in rulership would indicate acceptance. A planet in exaltation could indicate that I rose to a higher position on the waiting list and became an honored guest. I need to focus on Venus, Jupiter, Pluto, Moon, Sun and Mars as planets to represent me.

Planets in Rulership	• Venus in Taurus • Jupiter in Pisces • Pluto in Scorpio
Planets in Exaltation	• Moon in Taurus • Sun in Aries • Mars in Capricorn
Peregrine Planets	• Saturn in Sagittarius • Uranus in Sagittarius • Neptune in Capricorn
Detriment & in Fall	• Mercury in Pisces

This is the scoreboard for the Moonsign I have picked. There are three planets in rulership, three planets in exaltation, three peregrine planets, and Mercury in detriment and also fall.

In addition to picking strong and appropriate planets, you want the planet or planets ruling you or your goal to have good aspects. Do not pick a planet to rule you that is being assault by numerous bad aspects or is hemmed in between two encroaching malefics. Here is a look at the rulership and exalted planets individually according to the aspects they have.

Venus

Venus is in rulership in Taurus, a sign of comfort. Venus is the lesser benefic. It has only one difficult aspect, an opposition to Pluto.

$\triangle$ ♇

$\triangle$ ♂

✶ ♃

☌ ☽

☍ ♀

Jupiter

Jupiter is in rulership in the water sign Pisces. It is the greater benefic. Rulership can show the right to belong. It has all good aspects.

⚹ ♀
△ ♇
⚹ ☽
⚹ ♆
⚹ ♂

Pluto

Pluto is in rulership in Scorpio and shows the right to belong, but at night? There is an after 5:00 pm option that I don't want. Nor do I want to sneak into the pool. Pluto rules complicated matters. I do not want to be ruled by Pluto, and I believe I have much better choices with Venus and Jupiter also in rulership.

☍ ♀
☍ ☽
△ ♃
⚹ ♆
⚹ ♂

The Sun

The Sun is in Exaltation in Aries. I want to be the honored guest and rise to a higher position on the waiting list. This is fun in the summer Sun, but definitely not a "wet" planet.

△ ♅

Mars

Mars is exalted in Capricorn and shows the ability to rise on the waiting list, but is Mars in Capricorn a fun planet or more suitable for career and business?

☌ ♆
⚹ ♇
⚹ ♃
△ ♀
△ ☽

The Moon

The Moon is exalted in Taurus. This feels like the Nobel Prize. It is possible to climb higher on the waiting list. I tend to favor the Moon in Taurus as it comes around once every month, not like Venus which is exalted once a year or Jupiter once every twelve years. The Moon might not have good aspects in any given month, but when it does, it can be very useful.

Note that the Moon will oppose Pluto. I do not want complications, so I will want a time after the opposition to Pluto, and hopefully before the conjunction to Venus. Only applying Moon aspects are important to the activity in the electional chart. The rest of the Moon's aspects are all good including the contra-parallel to Neptune Retrograde. As an aside, the final aspect retrograde can indicate my return, in this case, a return to the pool.

☍ ♇
☌ ♀
⚹ ♃
∥ ♄
⚹ ☿
♆℞

Step 5 - The Chart Has to Say What You Want to Happen

The chart has to say what I want to happen. I want the ruler of the Ascendant, which is my significator, placed in the 7th house indicating that I can go "there" to the pool. I want the planet representing me to be in rulership or exaltation showing that I have rights in the matter at hand, I belong, and I have membership, or that I am the welcomed guest. I need to choose a planet that rules the Ascendant yet appears in the 7th house. I will focus on Pluto, Mars, Sun, Jupiter, Venus, and Moon.

- Pluto is in Scorpio and could not fall into the 7th house with a Scorpio Ascendant. It would land in the 1st house. Pluto is not a good choice.

- Mars is in Capricorn and could not fall into the 7th house with an Aries Ascendant. It would fall into the 10th house. With a Scorpio Ascendant, Mars would fall into the third house. Mars will not work for this chart.

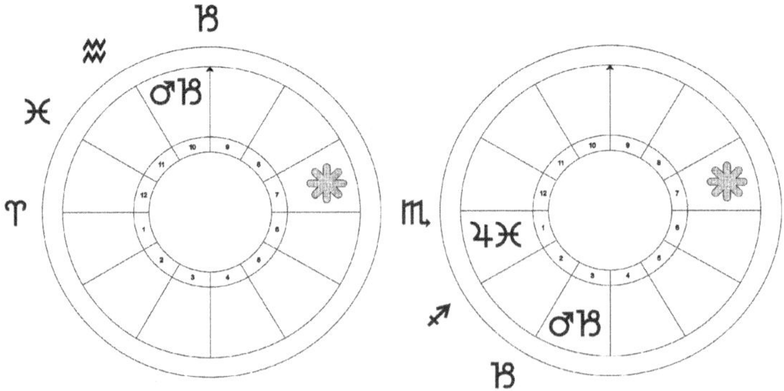

- The Aries Sun would not fall into the 7th house with a Leo Ascendant. It would fall into the 9th house.

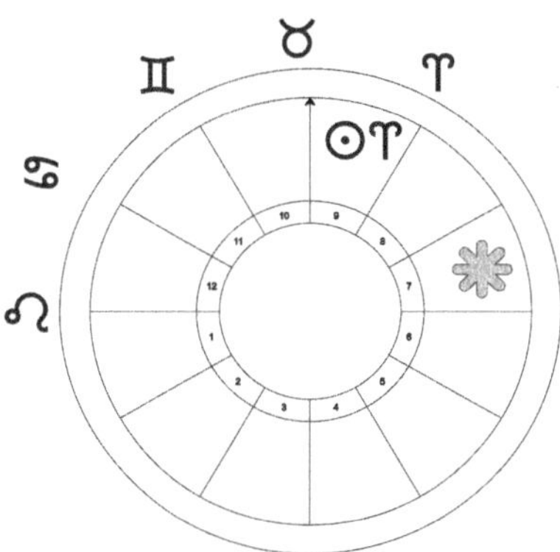

- Jupiter in Pisces will not fall into the 7th house. With a Sagittarius Ascendant, Jupiter would fall into the 4th house. With a Pisces Ascendant, Jupiter would fall into the 1st house.

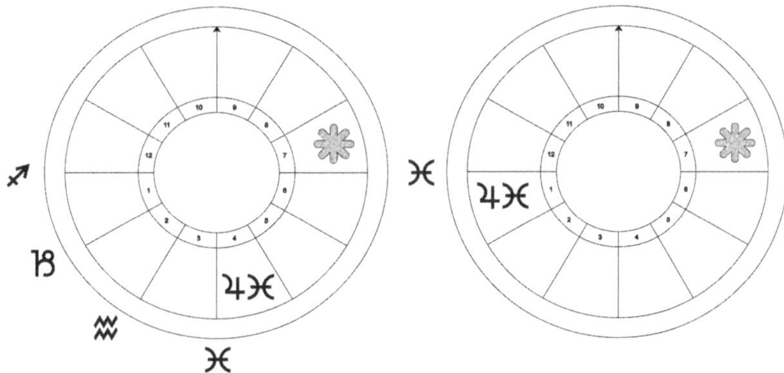

- The Taurus Moon would not fall into the 7th house with a Cancer Ascendant. The Moon would fall into the 11th house.

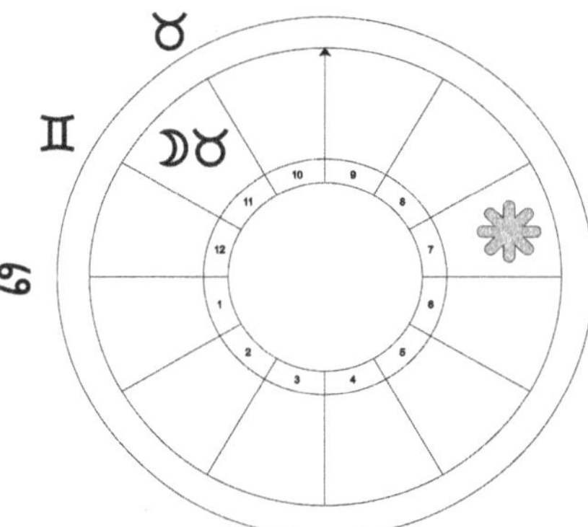

- Venus in Taurus would not fall into the 7th house with a Taurus Ascendant. It would fall into the 1st house.

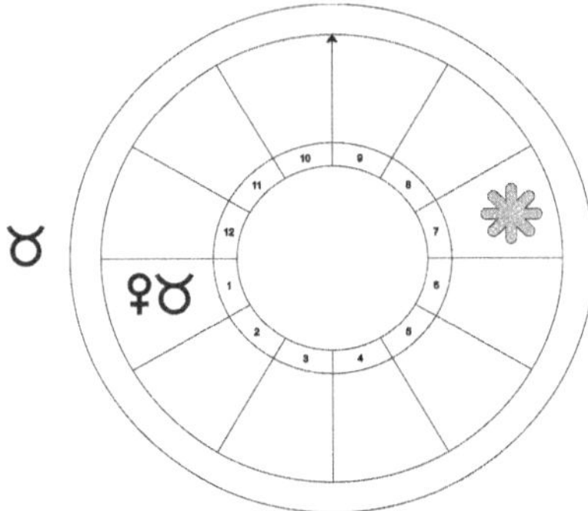

- But, using a Libra Ascendant, it might be possible for Venus in Taurus to fall into the 7th house. I will be looking for a time after the Moon opposes Pluto, but applying to a conjunction to Venus.

I have decided to put Venus, ruler of the Ascendant, in the 7th house showing my significator "there" at the pool. I have decided that the Taurus Moon should be separating from Pluto as I do not want complications. I also want the exalted Moon to apply to a conjunction to Venus in Taurus, my significator, indicating that I am accepted and welcomed at the pool. While working with the timing of the chart, I discovered that the exalted Aries Sun can also fall into the 7th house.

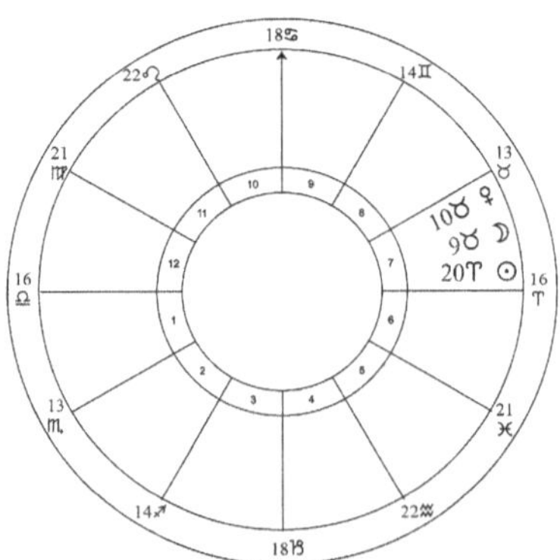

Planets in exaltation rise to a higher position and are the honored guests. In any election chart, the Moon rules the activity and tends to work for the initiator as a co-significator. To place the Moon in the 7th house is another indication that my family may rise higher on the waiting list. The Sun exalted in the 7th house in Aries represents the pool owners and membership board. Since exalted planets tend to indicate someone who does the honorable thing, we can expect that they will be more than fair with us and our request for membership.

Even though the chart is falling into place with all the planets in the 7th house, there might still be room to make minor improvements. In this case, it is to my benefit to also have Jupiter fall into the 5th house. The 5th house rules my children. Jupiter in rulership Pisces, a water sign, in the 5th house of children indicates that they have a right to swim. Not only do I belong at the pool, but they also belong in the water. Planets in rulership have rights. My children have the right to be there.

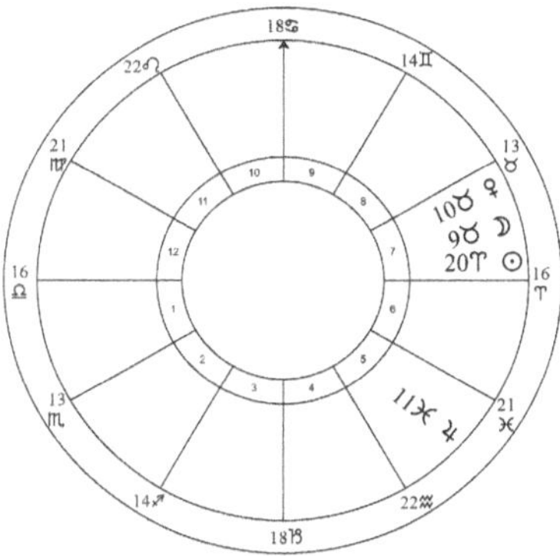

The chart has to say what I want to happen, and I believe this chart does. I am left wondering how this will come about when I focus on the 3rd house. Their bylaws are vague. Perhaps they have never addressed the issue of admitting a returning member to the pool. Certainly, a member who paid on time and was never a problem at the pool is a better bet than an unknown new member.

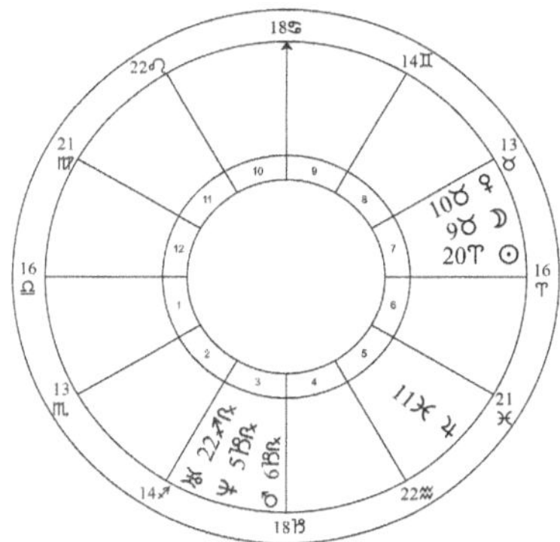

Step 6 - Follow Instructions and Do What the Chart Tells You to Do

Once you have finalized the chart, intuitive insights into the path for success can arise. The chart dynamic, (planets, houses, signs, and aspects), helps you understand the steps needed to successfully manifest your intended goal. In regard to this chart, I knew what to do.

Neptune rules confusion or matters undefined. Uranus rules change. The 3rd house rules bylaws. The bylaws of the pool are unclear in some way and subject to change. This is information I can use to my advantage. I know from the chart that I should not just submit my application. I should write a complementary letter (Libra Ascendant and Venus in Taurus as my ruler) stating that we were past members for many years and how much we had enjoyed the pool. I also mentioned our difficult situation and asked if there are any considerations given to returning members. This might bring the bylaws into question, triggering a change and allowing us to move higher on the waiting list. This is exactly what happened. Here is the complete electional chart. I mailed the application with my letter in a blue post office box at the appointed time.

Activity Electional Chart

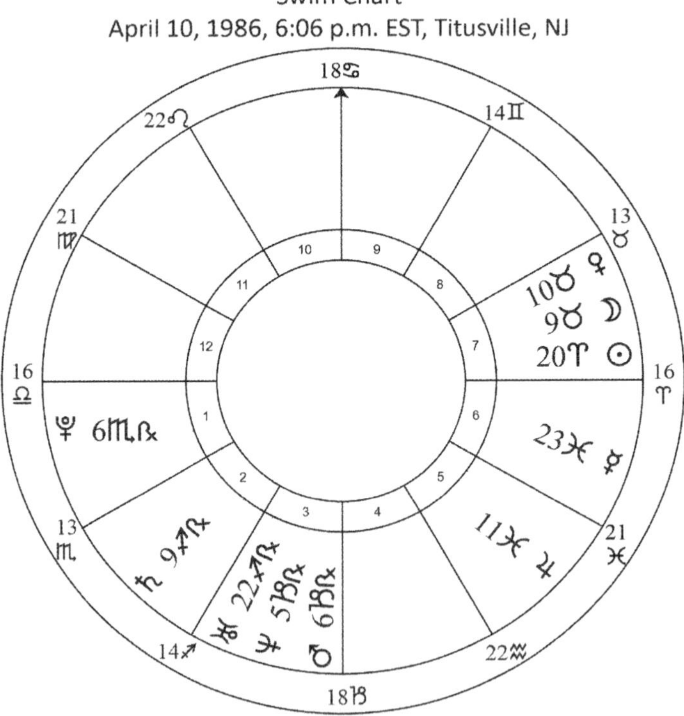

Moon Aspects: (△♂) ☽♂♀ ☽⚹♃ ☽♯♄ ☽⚹♀ ☽♯♆℞

Note the Moon's aspects below the chart. The Moon moves to conjunct Venus, my significator, then sextile Jupiter in water Pisces in the 5th house of children, parallel retrograde Saturn in the 3rd house of bylaws, sextile Mercury, and the final aspect is a contra-parallel to retrograde Neptune in the 3rd house of confusing bylaws. These are all good aspects.

I was subsequently accepted into the pool. They changed the bylaws to move all returning members to the top of the waiting list. I was number two on the list. There was one other returning member ahead of me.

Admittedly, this is an exceptional chart and an exceptional turn of events, but it is an excellent illustration of what an election can do and how one would work with the chart intuitively to increase your odds and create the most positive outcome.

Confirming Aspects

In many traditions, both spiritual and psychological, interpretation rests on three confirming aspects. I believe this is a good practice for electional astrology. When seeking to have the chart say what you want to happen, look for aspects that support your interpretation. The greater the number of confirming aspect, or the greater the consistency in your interpretation, the better. In this chart, there are a number of confirmations. Here are just a few.

1. My ruler is in the "there" 7th house.

2. Exalted Moon is in the 7th applying to my ruler Venus.

3. Exalted Sun in the 7th house.

4. Jupiter in Pisces is in the 5th house of children.

5. Neptune of confusion and Uranus of change are in the bylaws 3rd house.

Relationship to the Natal Chart

The electional chart frequently relates back to the initiator's natal chart. The Ascendant or the Midheaven of the electional chart is usually conjunct or opposed to a planet in the initiator's natal chart. This is one way to tell if the individual will use the election. In this case, the 16 Libra Ascendant of the swim chart is opposite my natal Sun at 17 Aries.

I do not normally look at the natal chart when choosing an electional chart. It is the last thing I do. I want the chart to tell me the best time and orientation without being influenced by the natal chart. It is a last step. I compare the election Ascendant and Midheaven to the client's natal chart. In all cases, there should be a relationship.

Chapter 16
Computer Service Complaint

Introduction

I had purchased a top-of-the-line laptop computer directly from Dell's website. I had owned it for ten months. This computer was my baby, and I named her Bella. I took excellent care of her, but at ten months the touch pad began to left click on its own. This was an infrequent problem, but after making all possible touchpad adjustments with the assistance of Dell tech support, it was recommended that I send the computer in for repair. I would only lose a few days of work as the turn-around time was 24 hours. I removed the hard drive, put Bella in her original shipping container and sent her off to Dell. I decided to send the computer in for repair on March 8, 2000, a great day even though Mercury was retrograde.

The UPS man bought a computer back two days later. Before I even opened the box, energetically, I knew it was not Bella. The computer I received was scratched, dusty, and dirty. It looked like someone had licked their hand and then used it to wipe the sticky screen. The latch was broken, and the computer would not stay closed. The service tag was falling off from being transferred from my computer to this trashed imposter. I was devastated. This was not my Bella.

I immediately called Dell tech support to report the error. They were no help. As far as they were concerned, if a service tag was on the computer, it was my computer. They refused to believe that the computer service tag had been switched. I was given three choices:

1. Keep this abused impostor

2. Send it back in for repair

3. Send it in for exchange

Instead, I decided to complain directly to Michael Dell.

Step 1 -Clearly Define the Goal of the Electional Chart

I want a new, free computer as good as or better than Bella.

Step 2 - Know Which House or Houses Relate to Your Goal

The 3rd house rules computers so I will start by focusing on that house.

Step 3 - Pick a Moonsign with the Best Moon Aspects

I chose a Moon in Pisces with the following placements:

Planets in Rulership	Uranus in Aquarius
Planets in Exaltation	Sun in Aries Venus in Pisces
Planets in Detriment	Mercury in Pisces
Planets in Fall	Mercury in Pisces Mars in Taurus
Peregrine Planets	Saturn in Taurus Neptune in Aquarius Pluto in Sagittarius

These are the planets on the day I chose. Rulership planets show I have rights in the matter at hand. I may or may not use Uranus. Planets in exaltation can show an upgrade from this trashed computer. I will probably use either or both exalted planets, the Sun in Aries and Venus in Pisces. Planets in exaltation are also honorable. I may use one of these planets to represent Michael Dell as an honorable business owner who will respond positively to my complaint. Planets in detriment and fall indicate blame. I need to choose planets that show the service department was to blame for this trashed computer switch. This is a lot to consider, but the bottom-line, simplified goal is that I want an upgraded computer and that is exalted planets in the third house of computers.

Step 4 - Choose the Best Planets to Represent You or Your Goal

I began to build the chart with two exalted planets, Venus in Pisces and Sun in Aries in the 3rd house of computers. I also decided to have the Pisces Moon in the 3rd house applying to a conjunction to Venus and parallel to the Sun.

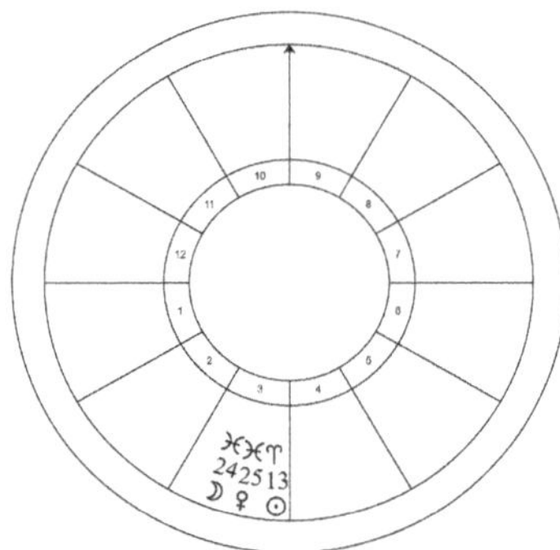

But there are two other components to my goal. First, I needed someone to blame for this mistake. In any complaint election or lawsuit, you want the other person to be as wrong as you can make them in the chart. This means that their ruler needs to be in detriment, or even better, in fall. Planets in fall indicate someone who has something to apologize for. In this chart I want someone, a 6th (service department) and/or 7th house (unknown person), to have done something he or she should not have done. They were supposed to repair my computer, not switch services tags with a dirty imposter. My ability to acquire a new computer depends on someone being at fault. Looking at the planets of the day, Mercury and Mars are in fall, while Mercury is also in detriment.

If the 3rd house contains Pisces and Aries planets, Mars in Taurus cannot be in the 6th or 7th house or rule either house. Aries will be on the 4th house cusp. Scorpio will be on the 11th. I decided to use Mercury in fall and detriment as representative of someone to blame. Mercury in Pisces lands in the 3rd house because it is close to Venus in Pisces, but I am able to make it the ruler of the 6th house of service employees and also the 7th house of the unknown person. I had someone to blame.

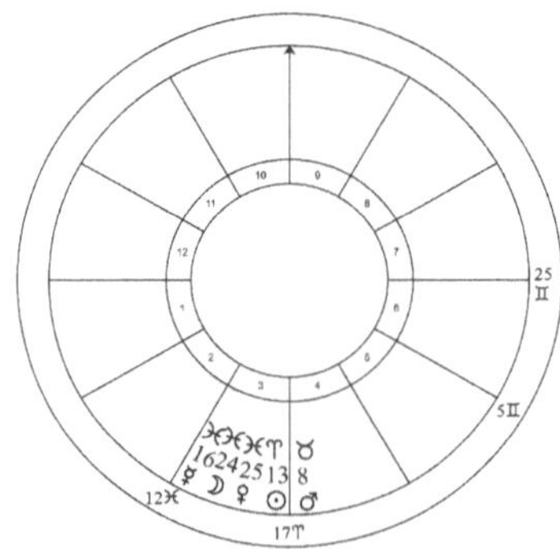

But I still want Michael Dell and his company to do the honorable thing and correct this error. by replacing my computer. For this I will need a planet in rulership or exaltation associated with the 10th house of companies and CEOs. If I put Libra on the Midheaven, the ruler is now Venus in Pisces exaltation. This shows that the company will respond in an honorable manner.

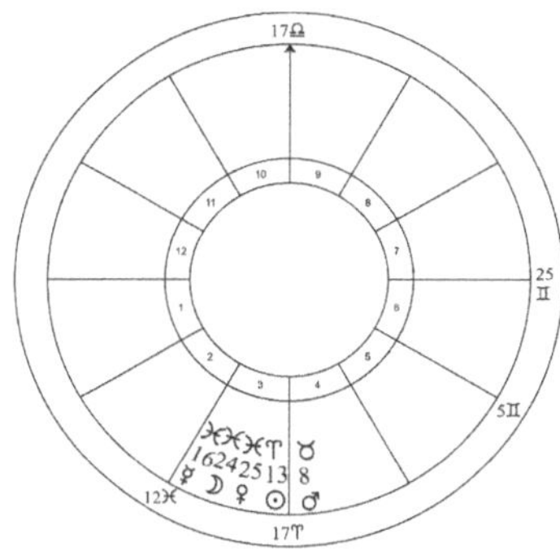

Step 5 - The Chart has to Say What You Want to Happen

These are the three things I am looking for in this electional chart:

1. An upgraded computer
2. Someone to blame
3. Dell to be honorable and remedy the situation

The Elected Time

The time of this chart was in the wee hours of the morning on April 3, 2000, still within the time of the April 2nd great day. This chart is simple, and the purpose is clear. More than anything, I want a new computer. It is not possible to find and return Bella once the service tag was removed.

I chose this day, almost a month after receiving the trashed imposter computer as it was a great day. It has several planets in exaltation and rulership, and many of the aspects were good. I chose a time when the activity Moon in Pisces was applying to a conjunction to an exalted Venus in Pisces in the 3rd house and then a contra-parallel to the exalted Sun in Aries as the final aspect. I believed that this electional chart indicated that I would receive a new, upgraded computer because this chart said what I wanted to happen.

Step 6 - Do What the Chart Tells You to Do

I wrote a complaint letter directly to Michael Dell. I did not ask for a new computer. That is understood in the chart. I combined left brain logic & astrological knowledge with right brain insight & intuition. This is a co-creative process & now I must do my part. I believe the chart says what I want to happen, and I have my confirming aspects.

Activity Electional Chart

Computer Service Complaint
April 3, 2000, 00:25 a.m. EST, Glenelg, MD

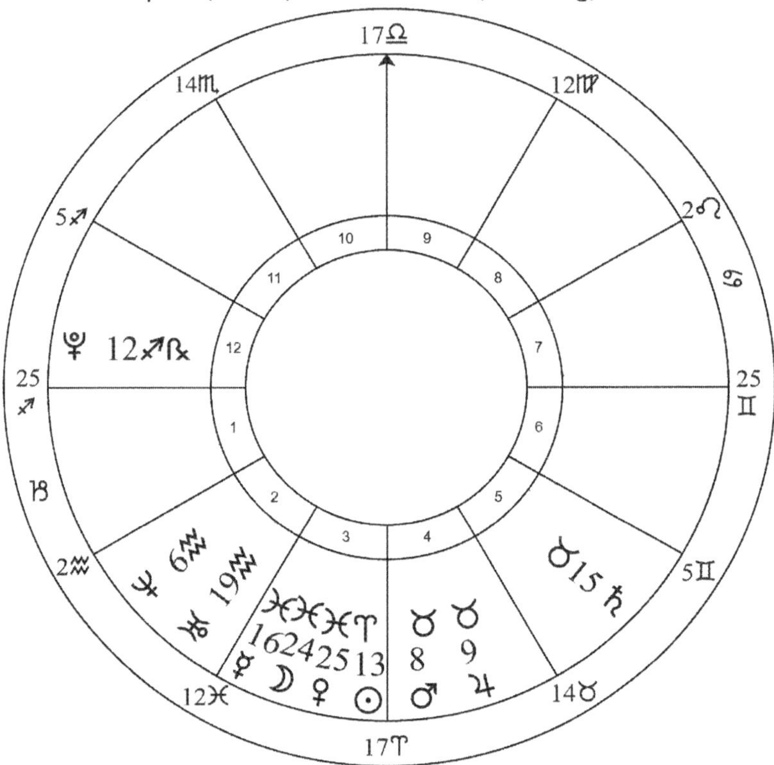

Moon's Aspects: (∥☿) ☽♂♀ ☽⚹☉

Confirming aspects

1. I have my upgrade with Venus in Pisces and Sun in Aries, both exalted in the 3rd house of computers.

2. I have my person to blame with Mercury in detriment and fall ruling the 6th house of service employees and 7th house of the unknown person.

3. I have Michael Dell and his company listening to my complaint and responding honorably with Libra on the Midheaven and the ruler Venus in Pisces exaltation.

4. With Sagittarius on the Ascendant, I am ruled by Jupiter in exaltation by house being in the end of the matter 4th. Jupiter rules the 3rd house of computers, and it is in mutual reception with Venus indicating that I can get back to normal through the help of a 3rd person, Matters will turn out well in the end and in my favor.

5. The Pisces Moon is moving to conjunct Venus in Pisces exaltation, then contra-parallel the exalted Sun in Aries as a final aspect.

Outcome: It took over a month for Dell to respond. On May 22, 2000, Michael Dell's personal assistant called me to ask me about my lost computer and the computer I received in return. Given the information I provided, I was sent a brand new, upgraded computer that was twice as powerful as Bella with a larger hard drive. Dell went on to investigate their outsourced service provider and ultimately changed to in-house Dell repair. My new, upgraded computer arrived June 10th.

Chapter 17
Publishing

Introduction

Unless you are self-publishing, you have no control over the publication date. This is set by the publisher. You do have control when you submit the book to a literary agent or editor. None of the charts in this chapter are self-published.

If you want to sell or publish a book, the manuscript should be ruled by a strong planet such as Mercury in exaltation or rulership with positive aspects that indicate publication. There are other planets in exaltation or rulership you can use depending on the genre or personal choice, but first and foremost, the book should be well represented in the chart and favorably aspected to the ruler of the editor or agent, (7th house), and/or the ruler of the publisher, (9th house). The chart can also show payment to the author.

The Ascendant, which rules the author is not so important, though you would not want the author's ruler to be seriously deficient or afflicted. In the case of publishing most elections, the book is the most important element in the electional chart.

Election to Submit a Book Larger than Expected

Melissat is a well-known author. She was under contract to write a three-hundred-page romance novel. If you know anything about the publishing industry, you sign a contract for a book that is a certain number of pages, and then the book is scheduled for printing and advertising at some date in the future. The schedule is not flexible. You need to hand in the manuscript on time with the correct number of pages, give or take a few. She had actually written a four-hundred-page book. She did not want her book cut down or edited to the required size and asked for a time to submit the manuscript when it will be accepted as it is at four hundred pages.

The Goal

The goal of this chart is to make the book and storyline so good as to prevent cutting, and for the editor to have a favorable response while the publisher accepts the oversized novel as is. The goal is focused on the book and not the author.

Know What Houses are Important

Books are ruled by the 3rd house; publishers are ruled by the 9th house. An editor or agent might be seen in the 7th house of the other or unknown person. These are the houses to focus on for this election.

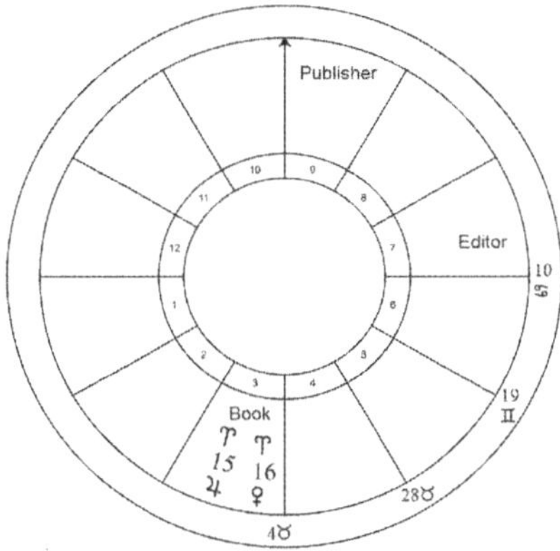

Choose a Good Moonsign

I have picked a Leo Moonsign that makes good aspects. In this Moonsign and at this time, there are no exalted planets and only Pluto is in rulership, not a good choice. When doing an electional chart, you must be flexible and work with what is in the ephemeris and aspectarian.

I chose Jupiter in Aries to represent the book since Jupiter rules big things. Jupiter is in a fire sign, so it is not peregrine, and Jupiter is the greater benefic. Jupiter is conjunct Venus, the lesser benefic. I am giving the book the best planets available. I include Venus in the 3rd house that rules the book. This seems fitting as Jupiter is out of place in the third house. It is the house of detriment and therefore does not qualify or fit into expectations.

The ruler of the 9th house of publishers is Venus which is in the 3rd house of books conjunct Jupiter, the ruler for the oversized book. This indicates that the publisher has crossed over to the other side or has come over to the author's way of thinking and likes the book. Since Venus is in detriment, the publisher is doing something he or she should not and would not normally do in accepting the oversized book.

The Leo Moon in the 7th house of the editor is applying to a trine to Venus showing the editor agrees with the publisher. Leo Moon shows someone in authority. The Moon is newly separating from a trine to Jupiter. The orb is still less than one degree. Since the Moon is allowed all of her aspects until leaving the sign, she will also trine Saturn, ruler of the Ascendant, and Uranus creating a Grand Trine in fire. This shows that the editor will also accept the manuscript as is, and no changes will be made. The Moon's final aspect is a trine to Uranus retrograde.

Activity Election Chart

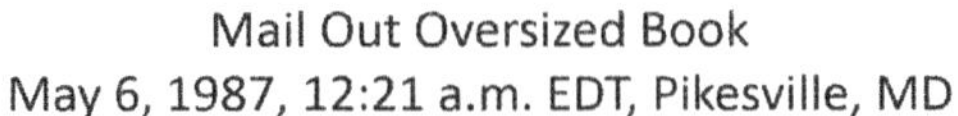

Mail Out Oversized Book
May 6, 1987, 12:21 a.m. EDT, Pikesville, MD

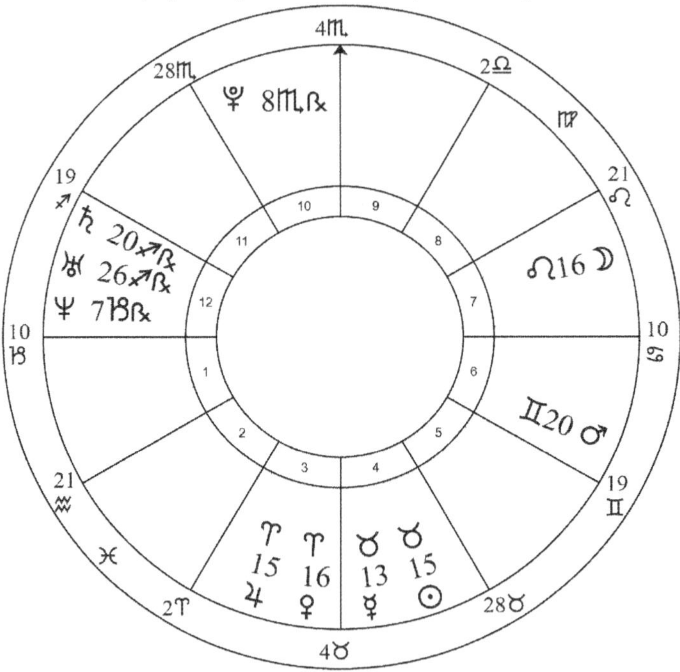

Moon's Aspects: (△♃) ☽△♀ △♄ ✶♂ ∥☉ ∥☿ △♅℞

Sun and Mercury in the 4th house show that things end well and since Mercury is in a fixed sign, the book was not edited. Mars is in the 6th house, kept out of the creative 5th so the work would not be cut.

Outcome: When the manuscript arrived on the editor's desk, a letter also arrived from another author saying she could not meet her 400-page book deadline. Melissa's book fits perfectly into the vacant slot.

Confirming Aspects

1. Venus, ruler of the publisher, is conjunct Jupiter, the ruler of the book.
2. Publisher's Venus in detriment Aries has crossed over to the 3rd house.
3. The Leo Moon, representing the editor is applying to a trine to Venus.
4. The Leo Moon is newly separating from Jupiter, ruler of the book, but is still within a tight orb.

5. The Moon forms a fire Grand Trine with Jupiter, Venus, Uranus, and Saturn.

6. The Moon's final aspect, trine Uranus, indicates changed expectations and the book acceptance as is.

An Election to Sell a Book

Jack is a bestselling author of numerous mystery books. He is currently on contract with a major publishing house. Jack is a highly creative individual and wanted to crossover from mysteries to adventure fiction. He wrote an action book and presented it to his current editor who rejected the manuscript as it was and requested numerous rewrites and story changes. For over a year, Jack tried to please the editor, but each revision was rejected. The situation was not only demoralizing to Jack, but also threw him into financial chaos. When the manuscript was released by the editor for sale to another publishing house, Jack wanted to elect a time to sell the story as quickly as possible.

The goal of this electional chart is to sell the book to a different publisher. One of the easiest ways to show that the book is a good one is to make the ruler of the 3rd house (written material) an exalted planet. Leo is on the 3rd house cusp which is ruled by the Sun. The Sun is exalted in Aries, elevated in the chart, accidentally dignified by being angular, and placed in the success 10th house.

Activity Election Chart

Sell a Book for Publication
April 14, 1999, 11:05 a.m. EDT, Baltimore, MD

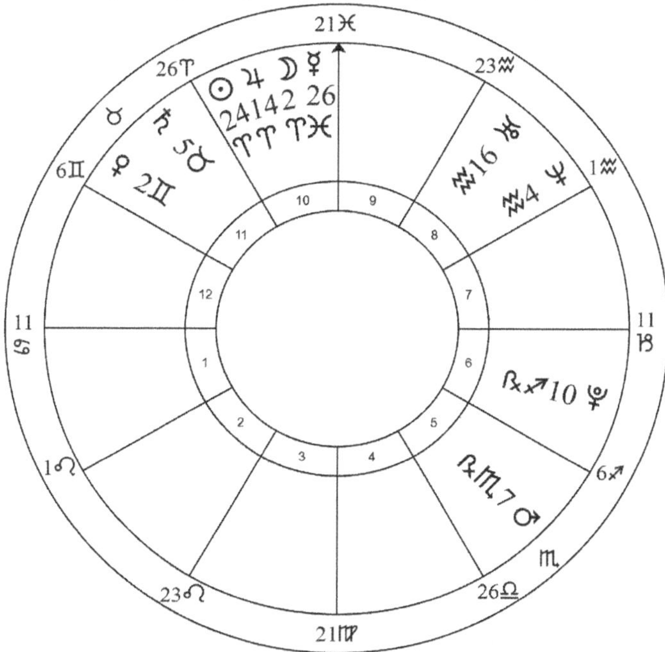

Moon's Aspects: (✶♀) ☽✶♆ △♀ ♂♃ ✶♅ ♯♀ //♃ ♂☉

The publisher will like the book because Jupiter, the natural ruler of publishers, is in the 10th house, widely conjunct the Sun. Uranus, ruler of the 9th house of publishers, is also widely sextile the Sun from the 8th house of royalty payments and advances. The Moon will translate (or carry) the light of Jupiter and Uranus to the Sun, completing those aspects despite the wide orbs.

Money matters are shown in the 2nd and 8th houses. The 2nd house cusp is Leo, also ruled by the exalted Sun. The activity Moon, Jack's ruler (co-ruler of the person initiating the election) will move to conjunct the Sun as a final aspect, bringing Jack together with money for an advance on his book. Uranus in the 8th will also be sextiled by the Moon. The chart confirms that the book will be sold, and the author will receive a much-needed advance.

Outcome: The book sold in ten days, included within a three-book contract for a large sum of money. The sale also established Jack as a multifaceted writer, capable of more than one genre of writing.

Election to Return Book Rights to the Author

This is another publishing election. In this case, Christine has asked several times that the rights to her earlier books be returned to her. She has been a writer since the 1980s and back then, contracts did not include digital rights. There were no ebooks or kindle books at that time, and no provisions for future media alternatives were written into the contracts.

The publishing company cannot create an ebook from Christine's earlier books since it is not in the contract. Publishing contracts were written with the clause that as long as the book was in paperback print, the contract was in effect, and the publishing house had exclusive rights to the book. This meant Christine did not own the publishing rights to her own books, and she could not publish the books in newer formats either. The author's earlier books were not selling well, but they were still in print. My client's oldest books were in limbo and though my client had been recovering the rights to many of her books, this particular publisher refused.

The goal is to return the book rights to my client. In this chart, the first house will be important as I will need to show that my client has rights in the matter at hand. I will need the planet ruling the Ascendant to be in rulership. The 3rd house will be important as it rules books. The 9th house rules the publisher, and I will need the publisher to be represented by a planet in detriment or fall. This will indicate that the publisher is wrongfully denying my client's request. I will also consider the 7th house as the undesignated person who might be making the decision regarding the rights. Retrograde planets can indicate the return of lost objects, and any retrograde planets might be helpful in the 3rd, 7th or 9th house.

The author had requested the reversion of rights several times without a positive response. For this attempt, she was willing to email a written request at the appointed time, even though it was in the early hours of the morning.

All the angles are mutable which indicates that change is possible. The Ascendant of the chart is Virgo. The ruler of Virgo is Mercury in exaltation and rulership. Mercury is the ruler of the author as she is the one initiating the election and request. Since her ruler Mercury is in a sign that it rules, the author has rights in the matter at hand. Because Mercury is in exaltation, the author can "rise to a higher position." The author has plans to convert these older books to the Kindle format and sell them herself on Amazon. Mercury is also the ruler of anything written including books. Mercury is in the author's 1st house indicating that she will be in possession of the rights to her books.

Activity Election Chart

Request to Return Book Rights to the Author
September 13, 2018. 5:25 a.m. EDT, Newport, RI

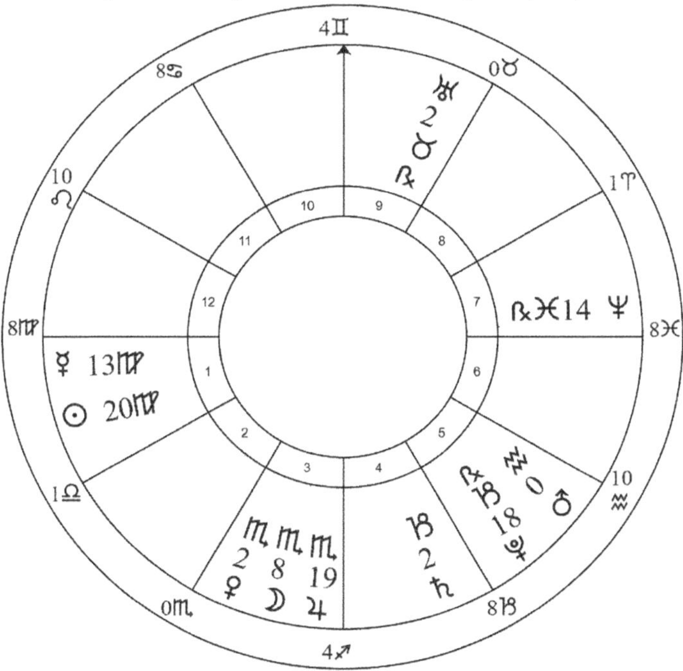

Moon's Aspects: (∥☿) ⚹☿ △♆ ⚹♅ ⚹♇ ☌♃ ⚹☉

The 7th house of the undesignated person or perhaps editor has Pisces on the cusp. Neptune is in the 7th house in a mutable sign. Perhaps the publisher can be easily swayed. Jupiter is the other ruler of Pisces, and it is the natural ruler of publishers. Jupiter is in your 3rd house showing that the author should have possession of her own books.

The 9th house rules publishers. In this case, Taurus is on the 9th house cusp and the ruler of Taurus, Venus, is in the 3rd house indicating that the publisher will come over to the author's way of thinking. This is especially true as Venus is in a fixed sign and in detriment. The publisher is doing something he/she should not be doing. In the 9th house, Uranus is retrograde and in fall in Taurus indicating the publisher is at fault and to blame. He or she should apologize. The publisher is likely to change position abruptly and for unknown reasons.

The Moon is the activity of the chart and co-ruler of my client. The Moon is in the 3rd house of books moving to sextile Mercury in Virgo in the 1st house. Then it will trine Neptune in the 7th house, ruling the editor, showing agreement. Next it will contra-parallel Uranus retrograde in the 9th house of publishers showing a change of mind. The Moon will conjunct Jupiter indicating the book rights are returned to Christine who should own the rights to her own books, while the publisher is in the wrong. The Moon's final aspect is a sextile to the 1st house Sun showing success in the matter at hand. These are the noted confirming aspects.

Outcome: In October, Melissa was notified that the rights to her books were reverted to her. They were converted to the Kindle format and earned $100,000 the next year.

Chapter 18

Buying, Selling, or Renting a House

Introduction

When buying or selling a home, a change in residence should be reflected in the transits. progressions, and solar arc aspects as they relate to the natal chart. There is no one-size-fits-all formula. Interpretation becomes a matter of synthesis because it depends somewhat on the reasons for buying or selling a home. It is important to investigate the circumstances associated with moving. Is it a planned and welcomed event, or a forced change under duress? Is it related to a job transfer or a search for new employment? Does it involve a lifestyle change? Is it a relocation cross town or cross country? What will be the financial impact? Is the expectation and hope to sell high and buy low, or will there be losses related to the move? There are a number of reasons and considerations, and it would be impossible to cover all the astrological notations, but the main indication of a sale or move is a notable increase in the number of aspects to the natal and their significance as seen in the transits, progressions, solar arcs, and possibly, the solar return. Below are the most common, straight forward indications of a move related to either buying or selling a home, but there are others depending on the reasons for moving and the circumstances around that transition. However, check the natal, transits & progressions for buying or selling a home and this will help you determine timing.

Transits

1. Major transits or aspects to the MC and/or the IC such as a conjunction, sextile or trine from Jupiter if the move is welcomed, but you can have stressful aspects from Saturn, Uranus, Neptune, or Pluto. The move might be sudden (Uranus), or the individual might be facing great uncertainty (Neptune). Perhaps the move is because a relationship is either beginning or ending. Endings can be associated with Pluto. A transit from Mars alone with an outer planet aspect might indicate the timing of a major transition.

2. Aspects to the MC would also be important if the move involved a job or career change. In this case, there might be aspects to planets in the 10th house or the Sun indicating one job ending or another beginning.
3. Major transits to the 4th house cusp, to 4th house planets, or to the 4th house ruler.
4. Major transits to the Moon.
5. When the move is over a great distance, there may be transits to the Ascendant indicating relationships are changing. Similar aspects are likely when a relationship is ending.
6. Financial changes related to a windfall occur when selling a home. A large expense might be seen in the transits when buying a home. These changes, whether positive or negative, might be noted in the 2nd house (funds), the 8th house (mortgage), or in regard to Venus or Jupiter.
7. Transits from Saturn might delay a move or sale.
8. Sometimes matters are not settled while Mercury is retrograde.

Progressions

1. Progressed Moon aspects to the MC, IC, Ascendant, or any of the planets
2. Progressed MC or IC aspects.
3. Progressed Ascendant aspect to the natal chart or progressed planets.

Solar Arcs

1. Arc aspects to the MC, IC, or Moon
2. Arc Moon aspects to the MC, IC, or any of the planets

Solar Return

1. Solar return Sun in the solar return 8th house can indicate a major change like a move across country.
2. Pluto in the solar return 4th house is the single strongest indication of a move unless you are doing major home renovations.
3. Uranus in the solar return 4th house can indicate a move, yearlong renovations, or someone moving in or out.
4. Neptune in the solar return 4th house can indicate uncertainty in regard to a move or domestic situations.
5. Saturn in the solar return 4th house can indicate a delay because of a need to make repairs before selling.

As presented in <u>Chapter 3, Two Approaches to Electional Astrology</u>, a Transitmaster that lists all the transits, progressions, and Solar Arcs in sequential order, can be most helpful in pinpointing times when a home might sell or an individual might be moving.

Buying a House or Property

An electional chart is a planetary picture of the client's vision. Within the elected chart are seen the challenges and opportunities that the individual will face during the quest for success. When selecting an elected time, the most important thing to remember is that the chart should say what one wants to happen.

To buy a house, the individual must submit the signed bid to the realtor at the elected time. The bid then goes to the seller for review and either acceptance, rejection, or counteroffer. The electional chart for the bid is meant to connect the buyer with the desired home or property. The **buyer** is represented in the electional chart by:

- the Ascendant
- the Ascendant ruler,
- any planets in the 1st house that are not intercepted
- possibly the Moon

The **home**, building, property, or land that the buyer wishes to purchase is represented in the electional chart by:

- the 4th house
- the ruler of the 4th house cusp
- any planets in the 4th house that are not significators for the buyer

The **seller** is represented in the electional chart by:

- the 7th house
- the 7th house cusp rulers
- any planets in the 7th house

There are a number of ways to connect the buyer, ruled by the 1st house to the home that the buyer wishes to purchase, ruled by the 4th house.

- The buyer's ruler might be in the 4th showing residency.
- The ruler of the 4th house might be in the 1st indicating the buyer's ownership.
- The Ascendant and the 4th house cusp could be ruled by the same planet indicating commonality.
- A good aspect, such as a conjunction, sextile, or trine between the ruler for the buyer and the ruler for the seller indicates agreement in regard to the price of the house and the transfer of ownership.

The 5th house can indicate the selling price of the home. Some planets in the 5th house could indicate a cut in the price, especially Uranus, Saturn, and Mars. Other planets might indicate a price increase such as Sun, Venus, or Jupiter.

Submit a Bid to Buy a House for Less

This is the first electional chart I ever did back in 1984. I hand calculated this chart with an ephemeris and table of houses in a hotel room before we bid on a house. The house was listed for $124, 900, after having just been reduced from $130,000 a few days before. We couldn't afford the house and needed the price to drop even more. The house went on the market the previous summer or fall.

Jupiter is a planet that will meet you more than halfway, especially when it is in the 7th house. In this chart, Jupiter is in fall in Capricorn in the 7th house of the seller. The seller is at a disadvantage and likely to do something against her best interest. We bid $110,000 figuring we would eventually agree on $117,000, a halfway point. This we could afford. Instead, the seller simply accepted our offer without attempting to counter. The 5th house is the price of the home. Note Saturn and Pluto in the 5th house indicating a lower selling price.

We are the buyers and our ruler is Mercury. The home is ruled by the 4th house, and also ruled by Mercury, connecting us as the buyers to the home. The seller is ruled by the 7th house. Her ruler, Jupiter, is square to Mercury, disconnecting the seller from the home. The Moon's final aspect is a trine to Mercury showing agreement. The activity Moon, our co-ruler, will parallel Jupiter also showing agreement. Venus is in the success 10th house.

Activity Election Chart

Offer to Buy a House for Less
March 22, 1984, 10:20 a.m. EST, Pennington, NJ

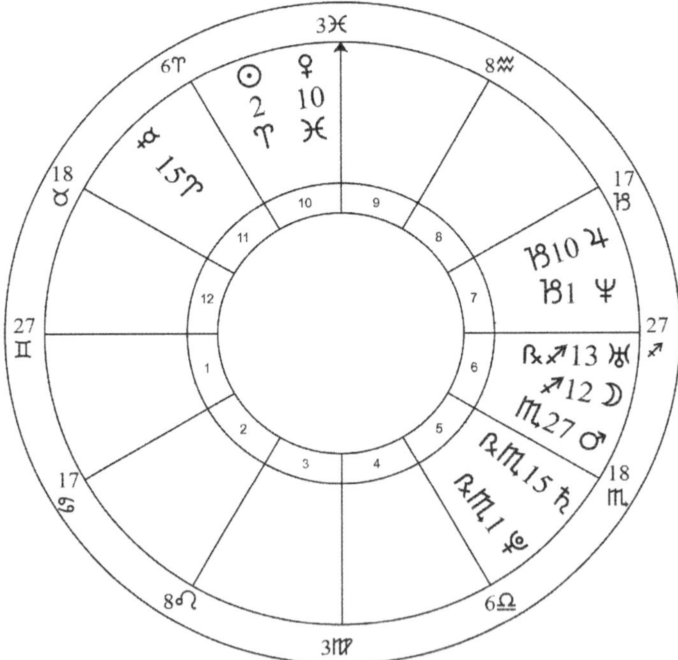

Moon's Aspects: (∥⚸) ∥♃ ☌⚸ △☿

Note the Moon's applying conjunction to Uranus after the parallel to Jupiter and before the trine to Mercury. This aspect is actually an occultation. The Moon will eclipse Uranus. Beneficial occultations, (to Venus or Jupiter), are never as good as they are expected to be, and difficult occultations, (to a malefic), are never as bad as they could be. In this case, there was a six-week old New Jersey garbage strike at the time of the purchase. The garage was filled with trash since the dumps were all closed during the strike and there was no place to put the garbage.

In addition, there was two feet of water in the basement when we bought the house and moved in. When the firemen arrived to drain the basement water, the wooden steps for the basement hatch collapsed from rot. The flooding problem had plagued the previous owner even after the installation of a $5000 sump pump and French drain. We soon discovered that the contractors never connected the sump pump to the drainage pipe that went out to the street. A simple $40 plumbing repair fixed the problem, the French drain began to work properly, and the basement never flooded again.

Contract to build a house

If you have ever signed with a contractor to build a house, you know there are many decisions to be made and numerous forms to be completed before the final and most important document is signed, and the deposit check handed over. This is a problem when trying to choose an electional chart to build the house of your dreams. Sometimes the best you can do is choose a good Moonsign and a good period within the Moonsign. That is what I did for this event.

The planets were lined up, one after another, and they moved through the 4th house which ruled the home. I wanted a nice planet in the 4th house to indicate a well-constructed, beautiful home. I would have been happy with either the Moon, Jupiter, Sun, or Venus in the 4th house. There was only one time period when no planet would be in the 4th house and that was between 10:05 pm and 10:20 pm on April 3rd, after Jupiter had left the 4th and before the Sun entered.

Here is the breakdown of the planets moving through the 4th house.

- From 6:00 pm on April 3, 1986, (the time of the meeting with the builder), until 8:20 pm, the Pisces Moon was in the 4th house

- From 8:00 pm until 10:05 pm, Jupiter in Pisces was in the 4th house.

- From 10:20 pm until 12:10 am on April 4, 1986, the Aries Sun was in the 4th house

- From 11:30 pm 4/3 until past my bedtime, Venus in Taurus was in the 4th house

Activity Election Chart

Contract to Build a House
April 3, 1986, 9:43 p.m. EST, Ellicott City, MD

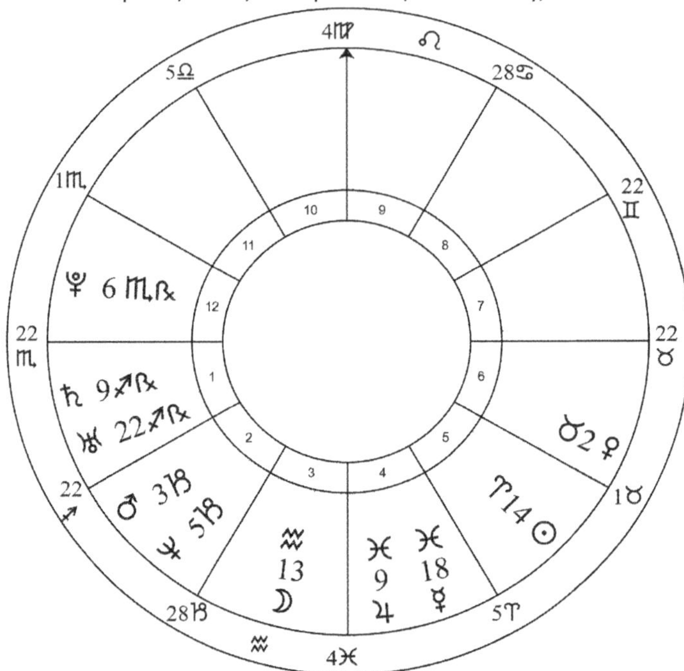

Moon's Aspects: (∥♆) ⚹☉ ∥♄ ⚹♅

This is the final chart for the signing of the important papers and handing over the deposit check to the builder. Building the house took longer than expected. That Spring was very cold and rainy. Note Saturn of delays retrograde in the 1st house. We had thought we might be able to negotiate a lower price for the house, but that was not possible. Note the Sun exalted in Aries in the 5th house of the price of the home holding strong. There were five buyers waiting to bid higher on the house should our deal fall through. The builder is ruled by the 7th house, (house of the undesignated person), and 6th house (contractor). He is ruled by Venus is rulership in Taurus. He was very honest and honorable. In many ways the house was better than we expected. Every time we drove down from New Jersey to see the progress on the house, we were surprised by the quality of the workmanship and the materials being used. After nineteen years, we sold our home for three-and-a-half times the purchase price.

Sell a Home or Property

To sell a home, the seller must meet with a realtor to completely fill out a real estate contract, (except for the signature), to put the house on the market. The seller must request that the realtor leave the prepped and ready contract to be signed and delivered at a later date and time. This creates an opportunity for the seller to choose a specific time and electional chart to submit the signed contract to the realtor. It can be dropped off at the realtor's office, mailed at the post office, or emailed, (assuming an emailed copy is considered legal). Flexibility is important. In many cases, the best electional time is around midnight when the Sun and personal planets are at the nadir or in the 4th house.

The electional chart to list a house for sale is meant to connect the buyer, ruled by the 7th house, with the home being sold, ruled by the 4th house. In the electional chart, the **buyer** is represented by:

- the 7th house
- the 7th house ruler
- any planets in the 7th house that are not intercepted

The **home**, building, property, or land that the buyer wishes to purchase is represented in the electional chart by:

- the 4th house
- the ruler of the 4th house
- any planets in the 4th house
- possibly the Moon

The **seller** is represented in the electional chart by:

- the Ascendant
- the 1st house cusp rulers
- any planets in the 1st house

There are a number of ways to connect the buyer, ruled by the 7th house, to the home that the buyer wishes to purchase, ruled by the 4th house.

- The buyer's ruler might be in the 4th showing residency.
- The ruler of the 4th house might be in the 7th house indicating the buyer has ownership.
- The 7th house cusp and the 4th house cusp might be ruled by the same planet indicating commonality.
- A good aspect, such as a conjunction, sextile, or trine aspect between the ruler for the buyer and the ruler for the seller might indicate agreement in regard to the price of the house and the transfer of ownership.

The home, ruled by the 4th should not be connected to the seller, or at least more closely connected to the buyer than the seller. In the electional chart, the 5th house is indicative of the selling price of the property. Some planets in the 5th house might indicate an increased selling price such as Sun, Venus, and Jupiter. Planets like Uranus, Mars, and Saturn in the 5th house might indicate a cut in the selling price of the house.

Planets like Pluto and Uranus in the 4th house of the electional chart for the home being sold, might indicate major problems with the home. With Neptune, these problems might be hidden. A good quality, structurally sound, and upscale home might be represented by Sun, Moon, Venus, or Jupiter in the 4th house, in rulership or exaltation with good aspects and unafflicted,

You can define the nature of the home sale in the electional chart. Perhaps you wish to sell your house quickly. Maybe you want to sell your house but then rent it back while you build your new home. Or you want to sell the home in "as is" condition without the hassle of inspections or repairs. You can be specific about your concerns or wishes in your electional chart.

Contract to Sell a Home

Situation: Dave and his family had already moved to their new home. The old home was being cleaned up to go on the market. Dave wanted to sell the old house quickly so he would not be carrying two mortgages for any length of time.

Activity Election Chart

Contract to Sell a House Quickly
January 28, 2001, 00:30 a.m. EST, Chantilly, VA

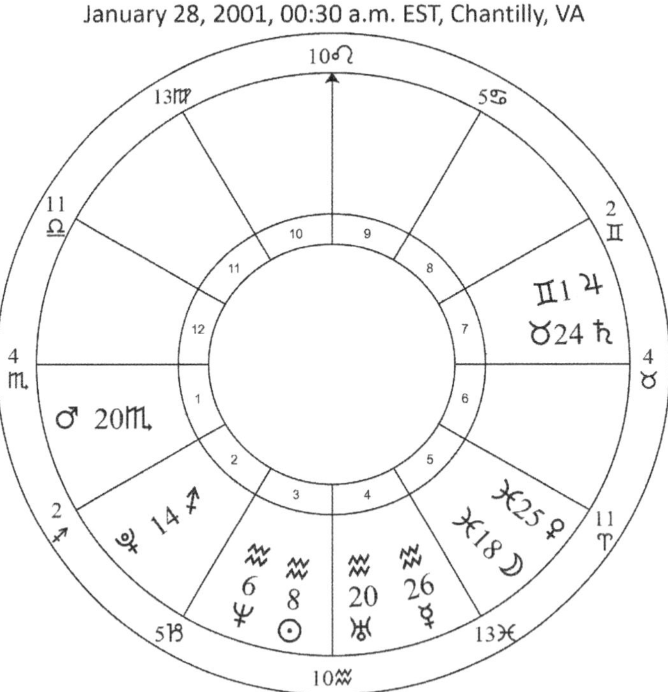

Moon's Aspects: (□♀) △♂ ⚹♄ ☌♀

This is an election to put a house on the market and to sell it at a good price. Since Venus will be going into Aries detriment soon, and then Venus will remain in Aries and retrograde for several months, it was decided to list the house while Venus was in Pisces. The Moon's final aspect is a conjunction to Venus in Pisces. In this chart, we need to connect the house for sale with the buyer.

- The buyer is ruled by Venus, ruler of the 7th house Taurus cusp, and Jupiter and Saturn in the 7th.
- The 4th house is ruled by Uranus and Saturn, ruler of the Aquarius cusp, and Mercury in the 4th.
- The seller is ruled by Mars and Pluto, rulers of the Scorpio Ascendant.

Saturn, ruler of the 4th is placed in the 7th house of the buyer, signaling future ownership. The Moon, natural ruler of any home, is moving to sextile Saturn, ruler for the buyer, and applying to a conjunction to Venus, ruler of the 7th house cusp. These are all indications that connect the home with the buyer. The Moon will also trine Mars, ruler for the seller who is happy to let the house go. The ruler for the seller trines Venus, ruler for the buyer, showing agreement regarding the transfer of ownership. The fact that Uranus is in the 4th house indicates a transfer of ownership and a quick sale.

The price of the house is ruled by the 5th or the money house of the 4th. The Moon might indicate a change in the price, but Venus in exaltation will tend toward a higher price. The house should show well and sell high, especially if more than one person is bidding. The seller will be happy with the offer once all the bids are in. Mars, ruler for the seller, is trine Venus, ruler for the buyer and the selling price of the home. Jupiter is in the 7th house, but conjunct the 8th house cusp of the buyer's money showing that the buyer has sufficient funds to purchase the home.

Outcome: The client sent the real estate contract to the agent at the elected time. The house never went into multi-listing because it sold by Thursday of the same week. Settlement followed quickly and without any hassle.

Election to Sell a House Quickly and Rent it Back

My clients wanted to sell their house, but then rent it back for a year while they built their new home. This is an unusual request that needed some extra consideration beyond the normal home-selling election.

- The seller is ruled by the Leo Ascendant and the Sun exalted in Aries.
- The home is ruled by Venus, in detriment in Aries.
- The buyer is represented by the rulers of the 7th house Aquarius cusp, Uranus and Saturn, and Jupiter in the 7th.
- In this chart, the Moon would be considered the activity of the chart and probably not a significator for the seller or buyer.

Activity Election Chart

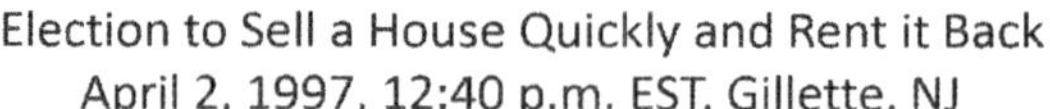

Election to Sell a House Quickly and Rent it Back
April 2, 1997, 12:40 p.m. EST, Gillette, NJ

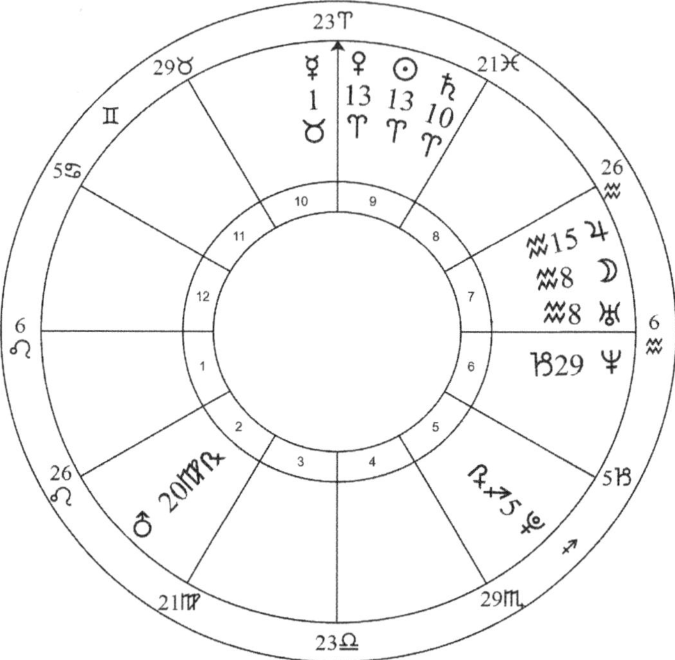

Moon's Aspects: (♂⛢) ☽□☿ ✶♄ ✶☉ ✶♀ ♂♃

The seller is making a strong showing in the chart being represented by an exalted planet and therefore might be able to set the terms for sale. The buyer is ruled by Saturn in fall in Aries and weakened by being combust the Sun. In this chart, the exalted Sun and the seller are seen as much stronger than the buyer. Because the seller is so strong in the chart, while the buyer is so weak, the buyer will need to bend to the sellers' wishes in regard to the contract and terms. It is unlikely that the buyer will be able to set any terms of the sale. The seller will have the upper hand.

The 4th house representing the home is ruled by Venus, which is conjunct and Cazimi the sellers' Sun, being only 3 minutes apart. This signals the sellers' intention to hold on to the house after the sale. Venus has separated from the buyer's ruler Saturn, and the Sun is between the two. The strength of the Sun-Venus conjunction shows that the seller still has an interest in the home and is keeping a string attached.

Twenty-three Libra on the 4th house cusp is a benefic star, Spica, indicating luck in this matter. The sign on the first house is Leo, a fixed sign that is also on the 2nd house indicating that the present extends into the future.

The Moon is last over Uranus meaning matters should move quickly. A quick sale is indicated. But then the Moon will sextile Saturn and things will slow down when the sellers rent the house back for a year. After sextiling Saturn, the Moon will go on to sextile the sellers' Sun, sextile Venus, ruler for the home, and finally conjunct Jupiter is the 7th house as the buyer takes possession. People ruled by Jupiter, and especially when Jupiter is in the 7th house, tend to meet you more than half-way in any agreement which is exactly what this buyer did.

Outcome: Everything went according to plan. The house sold quickly, and the sellers were able to rent the home back for a year.

Election to Sell a Fixer-Upper Without Making Repairs

Situation: George wanted to sell a rental house at a good price without having to fix it up. The house needed a new roof, siding, and gutters. These problems were very obvious. He interviewed a number of realtors who suggested he should list the house for no more than $290,000, but would probably sell it for between $280,000 and $285,000. Against the realtor's advice, the owner decided to list it for $295,500, figuring he could come down if necessary.

Activity Election Chart

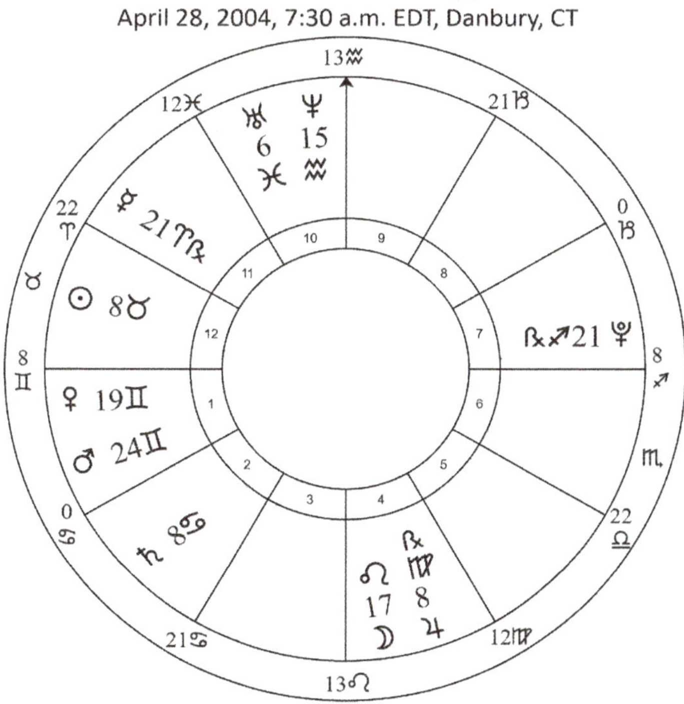

Moon's Aspects: (☌♆) ☽⚹♀ △♀ △♇ ⚹♂ □♆

There were two back-to-back great days in 2004, one on April 28th and then on May 2nd. It was decided to sign the contract and list the house on Wednesday, April 28th, at 7:30 A.M. The open house was scheduled for the following great day, Sunday, May 2nd.

What makes April 28th a great day is the number of good, strong Moon aspects, and Jupiter trine to the Sun. The Moon is the activity of the election chart, and when the Moon makes all good aspects before leaving the sign, it means matters progress with ease. Jupiter trine to the Sun can indicate great benefit.

- The seller is ruled by Mercury, Venus, and Mars.
- The buyer is ruled by Jupiter and Pluto
- The home for sale is ruled by the Sun and Moon.

In this electional chart, Jupiter rules the 7th house and is in the 4th house connecting the home to the buyer. The chart literally shows the buyer, (ruled by Jupiter), in residence in the home (Jupiter in the 4th house). Jupiter is a benefic, and indicates someone who will meet you more than halfway, so it is expected that the much-needed, major repairs will not be an issue in the sale of this house. Mercury, the ruler of the Ascendant and seller is retrograde (retreating), trine the Moon in the 4th house, (change in the home), for an easy sell. The man had tried to sell this house years before and failed. Since this was a second or repeat attempt, Mercury retrograde was not a problem. The Moon in the 4th house will move to sextile Venus and Mars in the 1st house of the seller showing benefit. The Moon will also move to trine Pluto in the 7th house of the buyer showing agreement. The Moon's final aspect is a contra-parallel to Neptune, so there might be some confusion in the process.

Initial results: George received a bid on the house for $292,000 the day after listing. I advised him that this was too soon and there was another contract coming. This advice was discerned from the transits to the seller's natal chart which showed Saturn transiting the Moon on May 8th. I suggested he stall until after the open house on Sunday, May 2nd.

Outcome: A second buyer saw the house while it was open on Sunday and decided to make an offer. But for reasons not fully known, she was working with several realtors. The listing agent heard from each of the buyer's realtors about an offer coming in and responded, "We have one contract on the table, (the original contract for $292,00), and another coming in. Your client had better bid high if she wants the house." What no one knew at the time was that the second buyer was bidding against herself and raising her offer. This was the lucky break expected with the May 2nd great electional day. It also relates back to the Moon's final aspect, (contra-parallel Neptune), in the April 28th election to put the house on the market.

The buyer finally placed her bid at $297,000. The house was inspected and despite the obvious problems, the buyer only asked for a few electrical repairs totaling less than $400. George was thrilled! He commented, "I spent $150 for an electional chart, and I got my money back tenfold with an offer $1,500 over list." He also gained $5000 over the first bid and even more than that over what the agents had suggested as a listing price.

Election to Raise the Rent but Retain the Tenants

Karen owns a condo and she has long-term tenants. They have been good tenants. They mow the lawn, shovel the snow, and take good care of her property. She wants to raise the rent significantly to be in line with other rental properties in her area. She is afraid they might leave and asks for an elected time to notify them of the rent increase. Karen wants them to accept the increase without objection and continue to live in the condo.

Activity Election Chart

Election to Raise the Rent but Retain Tenants
May 1, 2022, 9:45 p.m. EDT, Danbury, CT

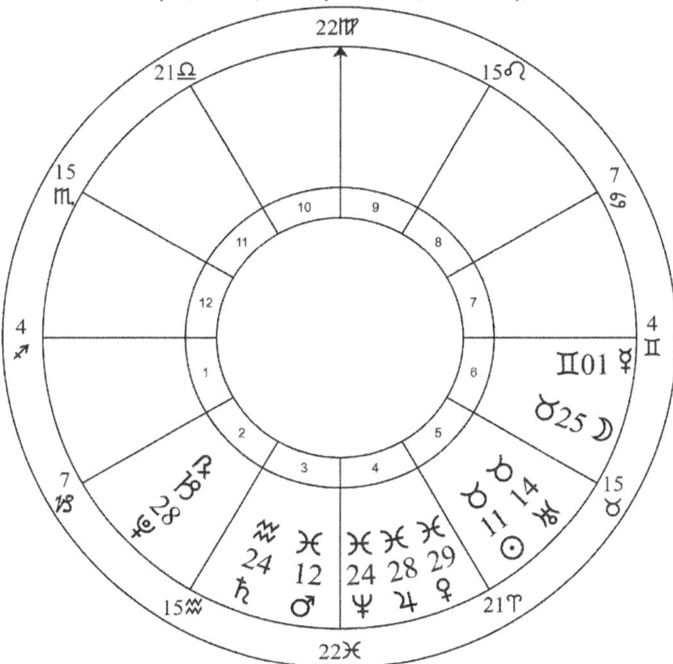

Moon's Aspects: (□♄) ☽⚹♆ ⚹♃ △♇ ⚹♀

My client, Karen, is ruled by Jupiter and the Sagittarius Ascendant. Her ruler is in the 4th house showing that she owns the condo. Jupiter is in rulership indicating that she has every right to raise the rent.

The tenants are ruled by Venus and the 6th house of tenants. The fixed sign Taurus is on the cusp of the 6th house indicating that the tenants will stay. Venus is in the 4th house showing that they live in the condo. Venus is exalted indicating that they are very good tenants who always pay the rent on time. The tenants are also ruled by the exalted Moon in the fixed sign of Taurus in the 6th house confirming that they are valued tenants and that they will stay.

Venus, ruler of the tenants, and Jupiter, ruler of my landlord client, are conjunct in the 4th house of the condo residence. There will be agreement about the rental increase. The Moon is moving to sextile Jupiter, trine Pluto in the 2nd house of the owner's money, and then sextile Venus as a final aspect.

Outcome: Karen did raise the rent, and the tenants accepted the increase and stayed.

Chapter 19
Diets and Health

Introduction

There are several things to consider when electing a diet chart. If the individual is interested in making a major change for personal or health reasons, the change should be reflected in the transits, progressions, or solar arcs to the natal chart. Consider doing a radical search first to determine the most appropriate timing.

Important Factors Related to Diet Charts

- The 1st house rules the body, personal change, and any change in appearance.
- The 6th house rules health and health habits including exercise.
- The Sun rules health in general.
- The Moon rules gradual change and emotional eating.
- Mercury rules nutritional and health related information.
- Venus is associated with improving health and breaking sugar addictions.
- Mars rules exercise.
- Jupiter rules improvement and helpful, supportive people
- Saturn rules any decrease or loss including weight loss, smaller clothing size, portion control, and structured health plans or routines.
- Uranus rules rapid and/or major change.
- Neptune rules any addiction, and philosophies that aim to overcome addictions such as Overeaters Anonymous.
- Pluto rules dramatic changes and psychological reasons for weight gain.

Election to Start a Diet

Judy was interested in starting a weight loss diet that included a healthy lifestyle that she could live with long term. Although weight loss was the initial goal, a sustainable lifestyle was the ultimate objective. She wanted to know the best foods to eat and how to curb emotional eating. Judy felt out of control due to stress which led her to consume a lot of high calorie, processed foods. She did not feel that she could diet and change her lifestyle on her own. She was looking for professional help and support. Judy hired a nutritionist with the help of her doctor. Judy also discussed her intentions with her therapist, spiritual director, roommates, and friends.

Activity Election Chart

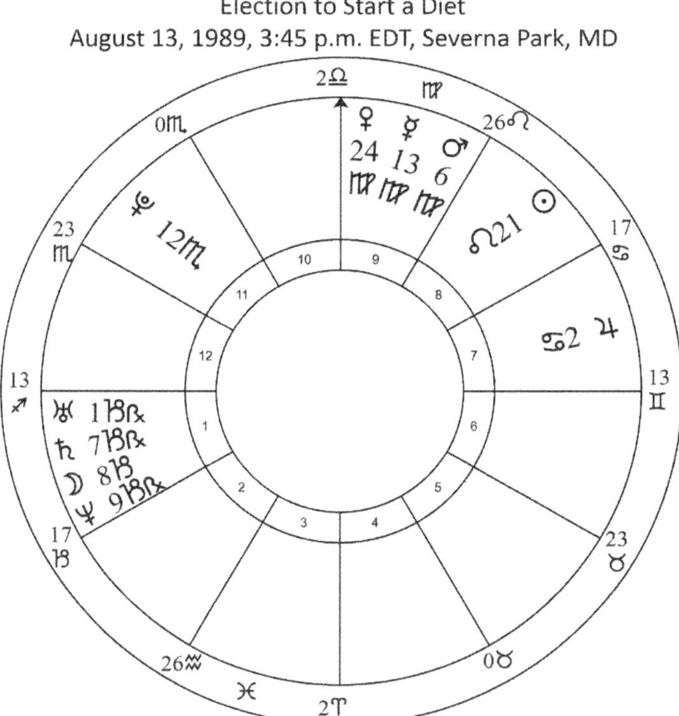

Election to Start a Diet
August 13, 1989, 3:45 p.m. EDT, Severna Park, MD

Moon's Aspects: (♂♄) ♂♇ ☽⚹♇ △☿ //♅ △♀ ⚹♃ //♄

The 1st house rules the body, and she wished to change conditions in this house. Change occurs wherever the Moon is, and in this case, the Moon is in the 1st house. Uranus, the planet of major change, and Saturn the planet of planning and control are also in the 1st house. Saturn rules decrease, or in this case, weight loss. Saturn is in rulership, so she has the strength to do this. Neptune in the 1st house indicates that there is much that is unknown. Judy admitted that she was clueless when it came to healthy eating and a healthy lifestyle. This was something she had never practiced or learned.

The ruler of the Ascendant is Jupiter exalted in Cancer and in the 7th house of helpful professionals. Jupiter shows that others are very supportive and helpful in this matter. They will meet her more than halfway. Through the professionals' help and the support of others, my client can rise to a healthier position.

The Moon is moving to trine Mercury in Virgo exaltation and rulership in the 9th house of philosophy and higher learning. Judy needs to acquire knowledge about good nutrition and adopt a healthier belief system in regard to food.

Venus is in fall in Virgo indicating a problem with sugar. Judy admitted that sugary snacks were her downfall. Venus is intercepted to help limit this problem. The Sun is at 21 Leo, a critical degree where one can feel forced to act, or in her case, eat. This critical degree is followed by 22 Leo which is a degree of being your own worst enemy. She has done this to herself. Judy was a compulsive eater.

To initiate the diet, Judy decided to compose a detailed statement regarding her plans and signed it at the appropriate time. She was essentially writing a vision statement to herself. Here is her contract for a new body image which she wrote and sent to me after receiving the electional chart and its interpretation.

- I will use no sugars in my body.

- I will cleanse my body of any impurities and harmful additives.

- I will drink Slimfast two times a day.

- I will eat a balanced dinner.

- I will begin an exercise program of walking, swimming, etc.

- I will share this program with the people I live with, my therapist, and my spiritual director.

- I will compose affirmations to recite before meals and during the day when they are needed.

- At the end of each month, I will take an inventory of my progress with a positive approach.

- I will include affirmations in my meditation.

- At the end of each day, I will affirm my progress. I will not berate myself if I've not fulfilled my contract.

- I will include in my journal my feelings about my body image, including dialogues about hidden anger.

- I will, in seeing my therapist, see this as an opportunity to work on self-image and begin that work.

- I will continue this program until I feel I am happy with myself and my body and no longer need to hide behind fat.

Outcome: Judy stuck with her program and lost thirty-two pounds over six months. She became healthier and more active as the weight came off.

An Election to Sign up for Weight Watchers

My client, Beth, was interested in starting a weight loss diet that included a healthy lifestyle. She had investigated various weight loss and healthy lifestyle plans and felt that the Weight Watchers program fit her best. Beth was looking for nutritional education, psychological counseling, and professional support.

She wanted to know the best foods to eat, and how to curb emotional eating. Beth felt out of control due to stress which resulted in her consumption of a lot of high calorie, processed foods. She did not feel that she could lose weight and change her lifestyle on her own. She was looking for professional help and supportive meetings. Beth requested an electional time to sign up for Weight Watchers online.

Activity Election Chart

Election to Join Weight Watchers and Start a Diet
Seprember 3, 2018, 7:35 p.m. EDT, Killingworth, CT

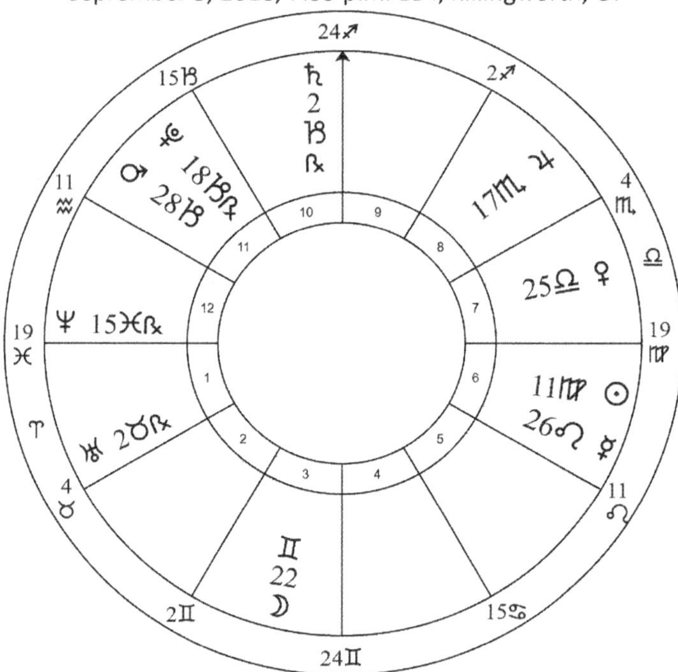

Moon's Aspects: (⚻♇) △♀ ⚹☿ ⚻♂

Nutritional Education: The Sun is in Virgo; the sign associated with health in the 6th house of healthy habits along with Mercury. Virgo is an intellectual sign with an emphasis on practical applications. Virgo focuses on what works. I think of it as the "karma busting" sign. Mercury is the planet of knowledge, but it is in fall in Leo. Beth's present understanding of how to lose weight and what to eat is limited. The Moon in Gemini in the 3rd house of communication is moving to sextile Mercury showing the introduction of new information.

Psychological Counseling: Beth is pretty introspective as noted by Neptune conjunct the Ascendant, so light counseling in a group setting would be all that was needed. She felt she was dealing with present-day stress, not trauma from the past. Jupiter is in Scorpio, the sign of in-depth investigation in the 8th house of psychological awareness. Jupiter is sextile Pluto in the 11th house of groups and trine to both Neptune and the Ascendant showing a more lighthearted form of counseling would be sufficient. The Moon is in Gemini to promote intelligent insights into the reasons for emotional eating.

Professional Support: Venus is in rulership in Libra in the 7th house of the other person. Venus is strong by sign, house, and is accidentally dignified by being angular. The Moon in Gemini is moving to trine Venus showing good communication with a professional. Venus is also sextile to Mercury in the 6th house. Venus is square to Mars in the 11th house of groups. My client will be challenged by helpful hints from the other group members and will have to make adjustments as the Moon's final aspect is a quincunx to Mars. Key phrase for the Moon's final aspect a quincunx is "change your mind and settle for less." In this case, my client had to change her response to anger, emotional eating, and health habits. Beth started walking to alleviate anger. This had the added benefit that between healthy eating and walking, she became pain free over time.

All the angles of this chart are mutable showing that she must have contingency plans as she progresses and customizes the diet to suit her needs, ultimately making it a sustainable lifestyle change. She will make necessary adjustments along the way while progressing toward her goal. Uranus, the planet of change, is in the 1st house which rules the body.

Outcome: Beth joined weight Watchers online at the elected time to get the support she needed. She did not compose a contract. Beth went to meetings for two years and lost 40 pounds. She kept the weight off during the pandemic when she did not attend. She continues to use the Weight Watchers app.

Chapter 20

Legal Issues

Introduction

In any election that involves a legal matter, and especially if there is a lawsuit, the plaintiff or the person who initiates the action or lawsuit is ruled by the 1st house. The other party, or person being sued is generally shown in the 7th house. If the other entity is a business, it might also be ruled by the 10th house.

In these situations, the rulers of the initiator or plaintiff are usually placed in rulership, exaltation, or elevated in some way over the astrological standing of the other party or defendant to show that the plaintiff has an advantage or strong case. The rulers for the other party, or the defendant's rulers in this type of electional chart are usually placed in detriment or fall to show fault or disadvantage. In this way, the chart will indicate that the scales are tipped in favor of the plaintiff.

An Election to File a Lawsuit in Small Claims Court

This is an election to file a lawsuit against the distributor of my book, *Planets in Solar Returns: Yearly Cycles of Transformation and Growth*. I initiated this lawsuit for $2,675.40 in small claims court in Kansas City, Kansas. For many years, I thought the distributor of my book was cheating me on royalty payments. I could not prove this until the print run of several thousand books stored in the distributor's warehouse ran out and I could audit my account.

I negotiated with the company through 2018. I am a document freak, and I sent them a notebook of all the report copies they had given me over the years since 2008 proving that I was owed money. They did their own audit which showed the same discrepancy I had noted. At that point, they claimed that I never sent them the claimed number of books. I had the book printer and the freight company send them documentation showing delivery and receipt of the appropriate number of books. They said they would send a check; they never did. I threatened to sue. They stopped taking my calls.

I called the town court in Kansas City and asked for the paperwork to file a lawsuit in small claims court, which they did mail to me. I was prepared to fly to Kansas City, if need be, with my documentation.

Activity Election Chart

Lawsuit Filed Against My Book Distributor
January 1, 2019, 5:06 a.m. EST, Higganum, CT

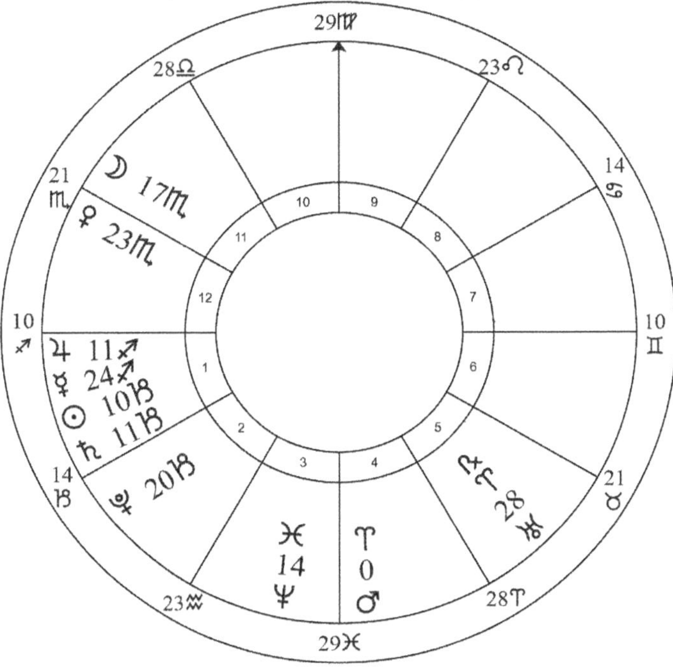

Moon's Aspects: (△♇) ⚹♇ ☌♀ //♀

You might be wondering how I managed to mail a copy of the paperwork with two-day tracking on New Year's Day at 5:06 am. I live in a small town and know the postmaster well. I brought the paperwork into the post office several days before the holiday and got everything stamped ahead of time. Then I mailed it in the blue post box at the appointed time.

As you probably already suspect, I am going to be the person with a planet in rulership. I have rights. The distributor is going to be in detriment and to blame. I am ruled by Jupiter in rulership Sagittarius conjunct the Ascendant and accidentally dignified by being angular. The 1st house also shows Saturn in rulership Capricorn. Saturn and Capricorn rule the court system, and this puts the courts on my side.

The distributor, ruled by either the 10th house of business or the 7th house of the other person, is ruled by Mercury in detriment in Sagittarius. This shows that the distributor is in the wrong. Since Mercury has come over to my 1st house and Mercury is in a mutable sign, the distributor will cave and send me a check. A secondary ruler for the distributor is the 9th house. Since the cusp is Leo, the ruler is the Sun, and the Sun can also be found in the first house. The Moon in Scorpio will move to sextile Pluto in the 2nd house of my money and then conjunct and parallel Venus.

Outcome: The distributor called me as soon as he was served. He said, "I thought we had a deal?" I replied, "We did! You agreed to send me a check, and you didn't!" He immediately cut a check for the exact amount missing from the audit for my books. He also paid for the court filing and mailing. I waited until the checks cleared and then cancelled the court case. Settling out of court can be reflected in the Moon aspects. In this case, the Moon's final aspect is a conjunction to Venus showing agreement over money and the likelihood of settling out of court. When the litigants' rulers are in good aspect, settling out of court is also likely.

Election Related to Property Lines

I live in a lake community that was formed in 1929. At that time, the properties were surveyed and all the lots were 100 by 50 feet. Over time, various surveys were done, lots were combined, property monuments were lost, and most people had no idea where their property started or ended. There is a stone wall around more than three-fourths of my property. Before the purchase, I asked the realtor, who was also the property owner, where the property line lay on the eastern side of my house. She replied, "Somewhere between here and the wall," which was technically correct, but very deceptive.

In 2015, my neighbor to the east had his property surveyed for the installation of a new septic system. It was at that time that I discovered that although there was a stone wall equidistant between our properties, his property line was past the stone wall by twenty-five feet and actually six inches from my house. My eastern bay window was on my property, but the bird feeders that hung from that window were not.

I did research at the town hall and discovered that there was actually a 100 by 50 foot vacant lot between our two houses which was bisected by the stone wall. Unfortunately, the entire vacant lot was owned by my neighbor. Neither of us were aware of this. Because of the stone wall and the height difference between our properties, they always assumed I owned the land west of the stone wall while they owned the property east of the stone wall. I had lived here for ten years and had maintained the disputed land on my side of the wall. Various other individuals living in my home had also maintained the property west of the stone wall for over fifty years. The boundary line issue was created in the 1960s and was a problem for both of us.

I was on friendly terms with my neighbors, and they joked about installing a picnic table next to my bay window. When we all learned of this boundary issue they said, "Don't worry! We will figure something out." I consulted a lawyer on what to do about the situation. He suggested I offer to pay all survey and transfer fees if they would give me land west of the stone wall for free. Since my neighbors' children were grown, they had plans to sell their cottage. They could not sell until this issue was settled. I followed the lawyer's suggestion and made them an offer. This would solve all of our problems and they readily agreed. This is the electional chart set for time that I mailed a letter to my neighbor with the terms.

Activity Election Chart

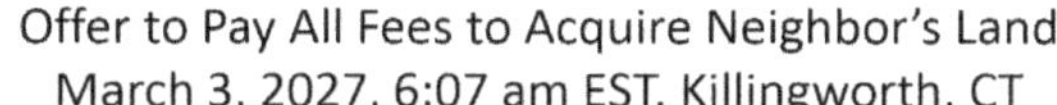

Offer to Pay All Fees to Acquire Neighbor's Land
March 3, 2027, 6:07 am EST, Killingworth, CT

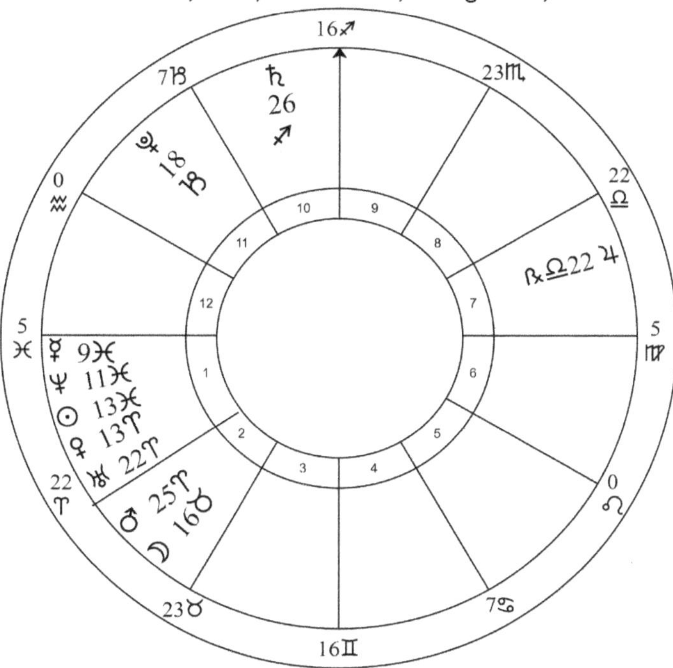

Moon's Aspects: (∥♀) △♆ ♀℞

Jupiter is in the 7th house indicating my neighbors will be generous and meet me more than halfway in this agreement. My neighbor's other ruler is Mercury in detriment and fall in Pisces and conjunct Neptune. They were as surprised and confused as I was. Mercury is in the 1st house indicating that they will come over to my way of thinking especially since Mercury is in a mutable sign. Mercury is also the ruler of the 4th house, indicating that some of the land will come into my possession.

Venus is turning retrograde in the 1st house. The Moon in Taurus is honorable, and indicates that this is a beneficial deal for all parties. The Moon's previous aspect is a parallel to Venus.

Mercury can sometimes indicate something to be corrected, especially when Mercury is in detriment or fall, and an important ruler in the chart. We had to go to the town zoning commission to get approval for the transfer. The town has very strict rules regarding property size and shape. In this case, they waved all objections since the transfer corrected an abnormal property line issue and created a more uniform lot for both parties.

Outcome: I paid all the lawyer and transfer fees. My neighbors gave me footage west of the wall for free. They sold their property shortly thereafter.

Chapter 21
Business and Job Charts

Introduction

Business elections, whether founding a new business, expanding an existing business, or selling an established business, should be reflected in the transits, progressions, and solar arcs pertinent to the native's chart. At some point you will need to do a radical search to ascertain the best time period. This is generally a major event and just like buying and selling a home, the event has astrological significance that should be reflected in the native's chart.

Step One - Ask Questions

Before you can begin any work on an election for the establishment of a business election, you must ask questions and gather information about the person or people you are making the election for, and what their vision or intention is for the business.

1. Is the election for a new business or an existing one? If the election is for an existing business, is there a pre-exisitng horoscope chart for the business? What is the hoped for change for this established business?

2. What type of business is this? Does it involve sales or service? What is the product or service being offered? Will the business be domestic, foreign, multinational, or international?

3. Will the business take the form of a sole proprietorship, partnership, limited liability corporation, "C" or "S" corporation? If the business is a corporation, will it be privately owned or publicly traded with stockholders either now or in the future?

4. What are the restraints related to any incorporation plans? Where will the incorporation take place? Must paperwork be submitted in person? Can everything be done through the internet or snail mail? Will a third party, such as a lawyer, be involved?

5. If the business is not being incorporated, what method will be used to launch or change the business?

6. What is the financial situation? Are there startup funds or will the business incur personal or investment debt?

7. Are there any anticipated problems involving legal issues, trademarks, pattens, copyrights, personnel, or competition?

8. What is the birth information, including birth date, time, and place (if available) for any owners or founders?

9. Finally, what is the time frame for this election?

Endeavor to understand the business plan. Ask questions until you get a feel for the chart factors that will be most appropriate. These questions are not just to create a good 10th house business chart. You cannot build a chart just on the 10th house of success, or on the 2nd house of moneymaking. When the emphasis is on success or money first with little concern for the nature of the business, the chart is shallow. A quality product and a strong vision should be reflected in the chart. When the business is good and strong, money and success will follow. Research into the nature of the business can also help you decide where to put the less desirable planets.

Step Two - Do a Radical Search

Sometimes the client has a specific, narrow time period in mind that you must work within. Sometimes the time period is very large, and you are left to choose the most propitious weeks or months. Occasionally, the client's intentions seem off. Their expectations are too ambitious and their plans too disorganized for an immediate launch. Make recommendations and explain what you see or don't see in the immediate future astrologically. Counseling the client is part of the process of erecting a good electional chart.

It is important to check the individual's natal chart, transits, progressions, and solar arcs to discover the most propitious and successful time period. When you do a radical electional search as described in <u>Chapter 3: Two Approaches to Electional Astrology</u>, you should see changes or aspects related to the Midheaven, its ruler/s and any planets in the 10th house, rulers for the 6th house cusp, and any planets in the 6th house. The 10th house rules career, ambition, and self-employment. The 6th house is more closely associated with the daily running and organization of the business, its efficiency, and the office environment. You can also check for changes related to the 2nd house of money, or the 11th house of salary or money generated by the business (2nd of the 10th house). How do future finances look for the owners? Check the transits and progressions for the coming year. Can you counsel the business client about expenditures, income, and how best to proceed?

Step Three - Develop a Good Electional Chart

An electional chart is an astrological picture of the business plan moving forward. Develop an election that speaks to the owner's vision and complements the owner's natal chart. Then interpret the electional chart for the client, giving positive guidance as seen in the chart that is relevant to the business. Counsel him, her, or them regarding problems that might arise and what to avoid, keeping in mind that there are no perfect charts. Provide whatever timing is seen in the electional chart, and in the transits and progressions relative to the owners' natal charts.

The client will live with the business electional chart for as long as the business exists. Business charts are character elections, and they endure over time so make it the best chart you can. A business chart is an astrological picture of the process, nature, and vision conveyed to you by the client. The chart needs to reflect the business owners' vision and be compatible with the business owner/s natal charts so that a strong connection and bond is formed between the two.

Incorporation or Finality

If the business is being incorporated, the procedure differs from state to state. In some states, you can walk into the state office, and they will immediately stamp your incorporation papers in front of you. In other states, you mail in the paperwork or drop it off, and the state will either register all incorporations at noon on the day of receipt or whenever they get around to it. You will not have any control over this time.

I prefer the time when the paperwork leaves your hands as the point of finality and the chart of the business, however, I do also look at the state time-stamped chart. I see that chart as secondary since it may or may not reflect the characteristics of your business and your choices. Fortunately, at this time, many states allow you to apply online for incorporation and that gives you the greatest amount of freedom.

Business Website Launch

There are a number of things to consider for this election. The website is for feed and supplements for cats, dogs and horses. Pets, small animals, and health are ruled by Virgo and the 6th house. Horses are ruled by Jupiter. Large animals are ruled by the 12th house. There should be a connection between the 10th house of business and these signs and/or planets. I believe the ruler of the 6th house should also be strong as this rules the daily running of the business, organization, animals, and their health. The 2nd house of money and the 11th house of money from the business should be fortified to increase income.

1.   The 10th house of career and business for this election has 4 rulers. The ruler of the 10th house cusp is Mercury. Mercury is both exalted and in rulership in Virgo. Planets that are exalted show an element of the chart that will rise to a higher position. The client wants the business to thrive, so it should be ruled by a strong planet. Mercury also rules health, nutrition, small animals, and pets.

2.   Jupiter, the ruler of horses, is also the planet of expansion. It is in the 10th house of business and career. The client wants the business to expand and prosper.

3.   The Sun is the light of any chart, and when it is in the 10th house of success it reflects a strong business. In most states, businesses are incorporated at noon. That always puts the Sun in the 10th house.

4.   Mars in the 10th shows ambition, innovation, and originality. This business owner is promoting her own mixes of products she creates. The 10th house of career and business is set up to reflect a progressive, prosperous, and expanding business that promotes her products.

Character Election Chart

Election to Launch a Website Selling Animal Supplements
September 18, 2004, 11:58 a.m. PDT

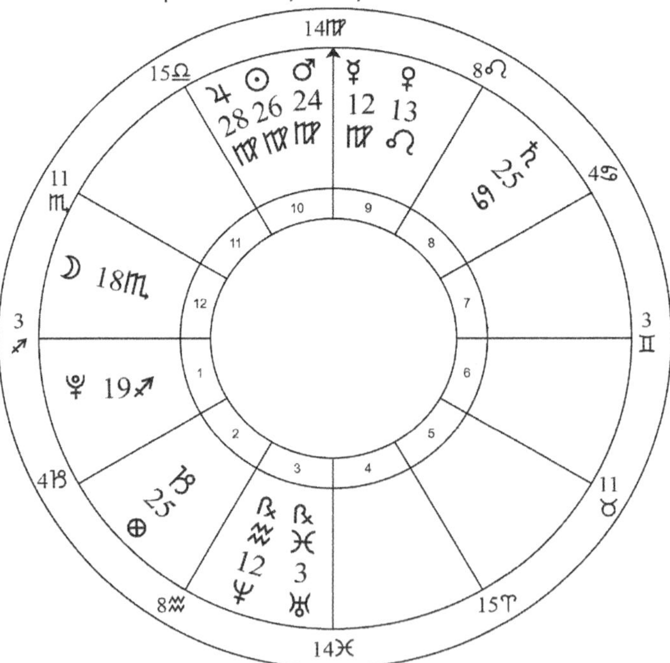

Moon's Aspects: (∥♆) ☽⚹♄ △♄ ⚹♂ ⚹☉ ⚹♃
I have withheld the business location to protect my client's privacy.

5. Venus is the ruler of the 11th house which is the money from the business or salary. Venus is the natural ruler of money. The Part of Fortune is in the 2nd house which rules the client's money. The Part of Fortune is a benefic Part. It is trine or in good aspect to Mars, Sun and Jupiter in the 10th house. This lends support. Venus is the ruler of the 6th house of small animals, organizational ability, and daily business routine. Venus shows the love and care she has for animals, and in a fixed sign indicates a stable routine and a pleasant work environment.

6. The Moon in the election is in Scorpio. The client will want to keep the formulas she develops secret. Scorpio rules secrecy, research, and intuition. The electional Moon is waxing, growing in light, and makes all good aspects, moving to trine Saturn and then sextile 10th house Mars, Sun and Jupiter. Careful planning leads to success and a prosperous business expanding over time.

The election chart has to have strengths on its own, but it must also connect strongly to the client's natal chart and complement the business owner. In this case, the election Moon is conjunct the native's natal Ascendant. This shows that the client is emotionally involved with this business. The election chart 4th house cusp which shows the root of the business path is conjunct to the client's natal Venus. The client has a sense of purpose. This is what she is here to do on the planet at this time.

As with all election charts, there are things I do not care for in the chart. No electional chart is perfect. There is only the best chart within the given time period. This is the best chart in September of that year. It is a chart of empowerment with Pluto in the first house. My client can transform her life with this chart and business if she stays on target. Note that there are 6 mutable planets in this chart. Her personality must support the business by staying organized and consistent. With Pluto in the first square to the 10th house planets, Neptune in the 3rd opposing Venus, and Uranus in the 3rd, she might have a tendency at times to be erratic, confused, indecisive, fearful, controlling, and obsessive. It is important to stay out of debt as it will bind her. If she takes care of the business, the business will take care of her.

Update: This business is still going strong. The owner recently told me in 2023 that she is now running $350,000 in sales.

Request for an External Buyer's Position at Nordstrom

This is an election to affect a job change. My client is presently employed at Nordstrom in the women's couture-fashion department. She is on her feet for an 8-hour shift. She wants to become an outside sales representative and buyer for Nordstrom's gift department. This will give her more freedom, less time standing, and allow her to be creative with the choices she makes for the store.

Taurus is on the ascendant of the chart, and the ruler Venus is in exaltation in Pisces and accidentally dignified by being in the 10th house of career and success. This shows great strength, and she is sure to rise to a higher position.

The 10th house also holds three other planets. Uranus is in rulership in Aquarius and accidentally dignified in the 10th house. It is the ruler for the 10th house cusp, and Nordstrom, her employer. Since Uranus rules change, this is a good indication that her job description or position will be changing. Neptune in the 10th shows that there is some uncertainty in the proposal as a similar change has never been done before. The Sun in the 10th shows that this is an area in which my client wishes to grow and shine. These four planets together strengthen the career house, and confirm that good things should flow from it.

Activity Election Chart

Election to Request an External Buyers Position at Nordstrom
February 15, 2002, 11:04 a.m. EST, Mclean, VA

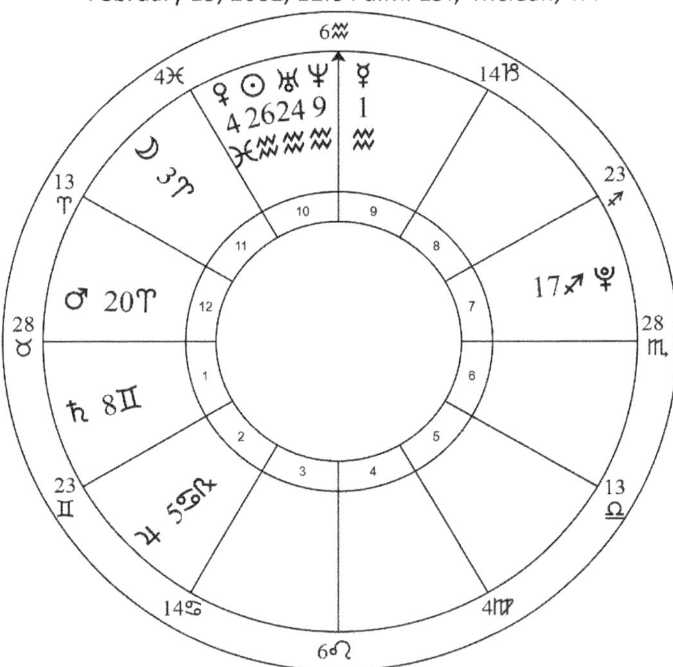

Moon's Aspects: (⚹☿) ☽□♃ ⚹♄ ⚹♆ △♇ ☌♂ ⚹♅ ⚹☉

Outcome: The chart was set for 11:00 a.m. EST with the Ascendant at 26 Taurus which is a positive degree, but the meeting was delayed until the manager was available. The problem with many job electional charts is that you have little control over meeting times. Regardless, my client got the new position as a gift buyer for Nordstrom. She worked at this job for many years and loved the work.

Job Application versus Job Interview

One of the fine points related to career and job change is the distinction between submitting a job application and scheduling a job interview. In my experience, they are two totally separate things. Submitting a job application, whether online or in person, is a request for an interview. It is to help you get noticed and secure a positive response in the form of an interview. It is only step one in the process. It does not secure a job. You do have a lot of control over when a job application is submitted, and this is the most appropriate time to use an electional chart. The chart can help you better understand the position, and what assets or skills you wish to highlight in your application and during any subsequent interview.

Step two is the job interview which is generally set by the interviewer. Many times you cannot even choose a particular day. Sometimes there are several interviews with various department heads before you are hired. The higher the salary or position, the greater the number of interviews especially for technical, executive, or managerial positions. You have little control over the timing of an interview other than being available or not.

At that point, the acceptance of a job offer, or the start date and time for a new job might provide clues to the nature of the work, its characterization, and your experience. Frequently, you have little to no control over your start date and time.

Job Application Submitted for an Executive Position

This election is to submit an application for an executive position. Georgia had a prominent position at Macy's and J.C. Penney and is now looking for a more advanced position in retail. The ruler of the 1st house cusp is Mars. Mars is in the 10th house of career and executive positions. This is where she wants to go. Mars is exalted by sign in Capricorn, exalted by house in the 10th of success, and accidentally dignified by being angular, denoting her value as an executive employee.

Georgia is also ruled by the Moon which is exalted in Taurus. This is because the Moon is in the 1st house along with Jupiter and Uranus, which are all accidentally dignified by being angular. Jupiter in Taurus is in mutual reception with Venus in Sagittarius. Jupiter has a secondary position of 6 degrees Sagittarius in the 8th house. Venus has a secondary position of 25 degrees Taurus in the 2nd house. Uranus is in fall on the cusp of the 2nd house.

Georgia is hoping to make a positive change. It is interesting to note that the Sun surpasses Pluto to become the Moon's final aspect. Whatever complications might arise can later be surpassed by a more favorable outcome. One should stay positive!

Georgia submitted two applications during the time period around this chart and subsequently had two interviews. The time period I suggested was between 11:00 a.m. and 11:20. This was to keep Mars in the 10th house.

Activity Election Chart

Job Application for an Executive Position
January 19, 2024, 11:10 a.m. CST, Richardson, TX

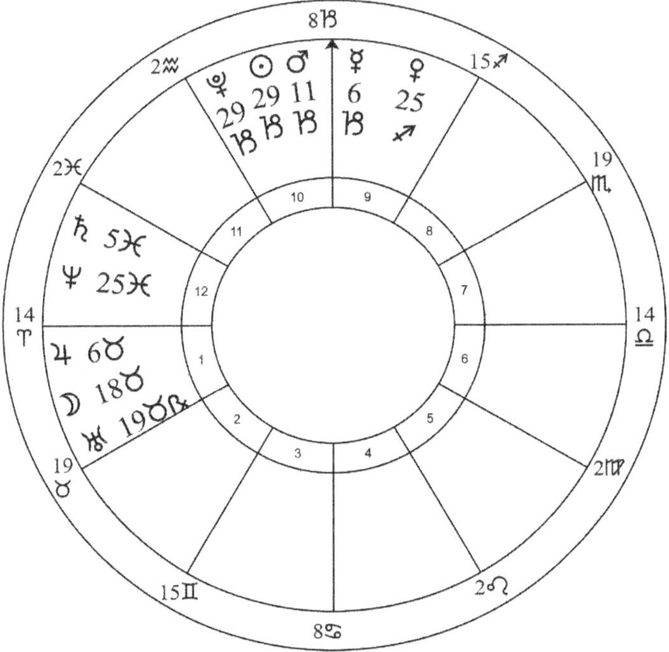

Moon's Aspects: (∥♅) ☽☌♅ ∦☉ ⚹♆ ∦♀ ∦☿ ∦♇ △♆ △☉

Outcome: Note the Moon moving to conjunct Uranus. There was a surprise. Neither of the jobs were as advertised, and Georgia was not interested in either position once she was interviewed, but this led to an interview with a much larger company for a job she had not known about. Sometimes when a good election does not work out, it leads to or fosters a new and sometimes better option.

Job Application Submission for a Technical Position

This is a job application submission election erected for the same time period and Moonsign as the previous chart, however, the orientation is different. The focus is on a 6th house technical position rather than a 10th house executive one. Even though the emphasis is on the 6th house, exalted planets are still in the 10th.

Most notably, the ruler of the Ascendant and my client, Caroline, is the Moon in the 10th house. It is exalted in Taurus and accidentally dignified by being angular in the 10th house of success. Mars is the ruler of the Aries Midheaven, and it is exalted in Capricorn in the 6th house of office and technical work.

Activity Election Chart

Job Application for a Technical Position
January 18, 2024, 5:00 p.m. CST, Carrollton, TX

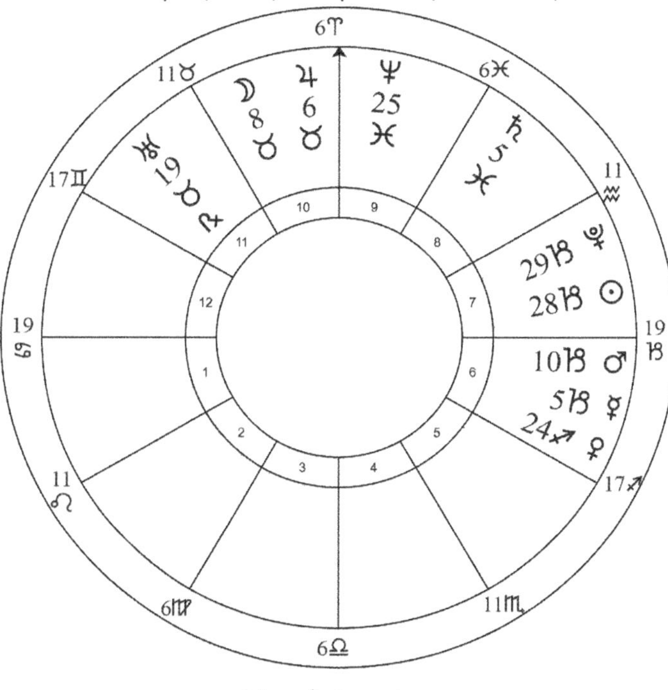

Moon's Aspects:
(♂♃) △♂ //♅ ♂♅ #⊙ ⚹♆ #♀ #☿ #♇ △♆ △⊙

The Moon's first aspect is a trine to Mars. If you are creating an election to submit a job application, you want quality planets to represent you. Choose planets in exaltation to rise to a higher position, or planets in rulership to showcase your qualifications and expertise.

Many of the aspects in these two charts are the same. Venus in Sagittarius is still in mutual reception with Jupiter in Taurus. Venus has a secondary position at 24 Taurus in the 11th house. Jupiter has a secondary position of 6 Sagittarius in the 5th house. The Moon makes all good aspects. The Moon's final aspect is a trine to the Sun, even though the Sun is in earlier degree than Pluto. The Sun surpasses Pluto, and this makes endings even better.

Caroline is an independent technician doing computer work. She was let go from her previous position when her contract ended. She believes age discrimination played a role in her employment situation. She is finding the job search difficult, and is taking courses to expand her skills.

This is the electional chart that I created for Caroline, however, she did not use it to submit an application. Instead, she scheduled a job interview for as close as she could get to the elected time. The interview started at 4 p.m. and was the last interview of the day. The company closed at 5 p.m. Near the end of the interview at 4:45 p.m., my client was offered a position with the company. She immediately accepted. She told me later that this was her dream job, a position she had always wanted.

The chart of her acceptance is below. The aspects at the start of the interview were the same as the 5 p.m. chart, only the orientation of the chart and the house placements differed slightly over time. By the end of the interview, the electional chart I created and the job acceptance chart were very similar. As far as I know, there were no issues with the Moon conjunction to Uranus aspect other than she is an independent contractor and not a full employee.

Update: One year later, Caroline is still employed by this company. She enjoys the work and is able to work from home.

Activity Election Chart

Job Acceptance for a Technical Position
January 18, 2024, 4:45 p.m. CST, Carrollton, TX

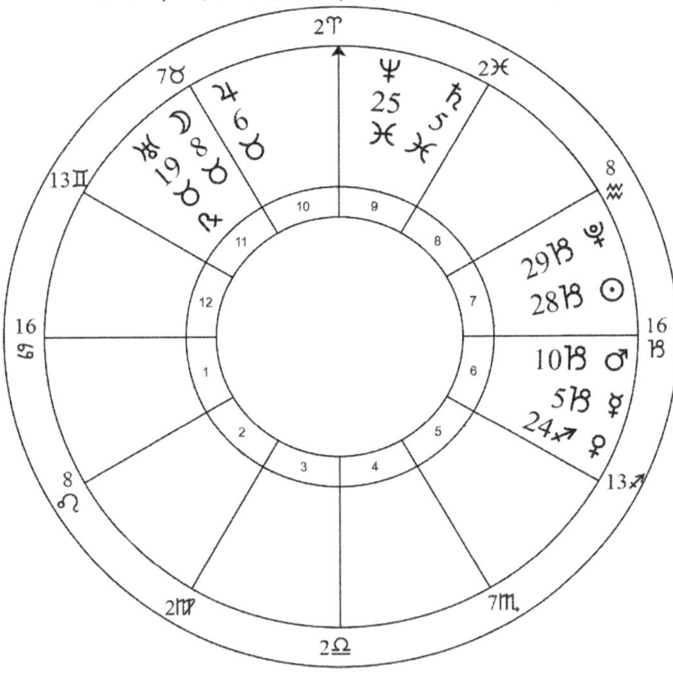

Moon's Aspects:
(♂♃) △♂ ∥♅ ♂♅ ♯☉ ⚹♆ ♯♀ ♯☿ ♯♇ △♇ △☉

Chapter 22
Home Improvement Charts

Introduction

I have used electional astrology for various home repairs and purchases. It makes home improvements easier and less expensive. I learned my lesson in 1984 with a disastrous siding job. You will see what I mean with the "bad home improvement" chart in this chapter. The wallpaper chart which follows is probably the simplest election I have ever done. If you are just starting to create your own electional charts, this can be a good place to start.

Election to Successfully Reorder Wallpaper

We temporarily relocated to New Jersey and bought a fixer-upper. I redid the kitchen among other things. I wallpapered an accent wall and the area between the cupboard and counters to cover horrible, dated Formica. I ran out of wallpaper. I was short by one foot. I reordered it twice. I reordered twice more with samples. Nothing matched.

The 10th house in an electional chart is often referred to as "the success tenth." This might apply to any type of electional chart you might choose as the purpose of electing a specific time is to be successful in an endeavor.

Retrograde Mercury, Venus, and Mars represent changing circumstances that may be reversed. For example, Mercury retrograde can rule anything that begins with an "R" including reply, return, replace, redo, renovate, rework, recondition, and repair. Using retrograde planets in an electional chart can be advantageous, especially when you wish to successfully repeat a task you failed at the first time around.

My electional goal is to successfully reorder wallpaper. This is what the chart has to say, and this is how the chart will say what I want to happen:

- Success = 10th
- Reorder = Retrograde
- Wallpaper = Venus
- Activity = Moon applying to a conjunction to Venus retrograde

I actually waited three more months until Venus went retrograde to try once again to reorder matching wallpaper. I waited outside the store until I knew the Ascendant was in Leo and the ruler the exalted Sun. But then, the clerk took me right away, thus the "too early for now" degrees on the Ascendant.

Activity Election Chart

Election to Reorder Wallpaper
March 22, 1985, 12:57 p.m. EST, Lawrenceville, NJ

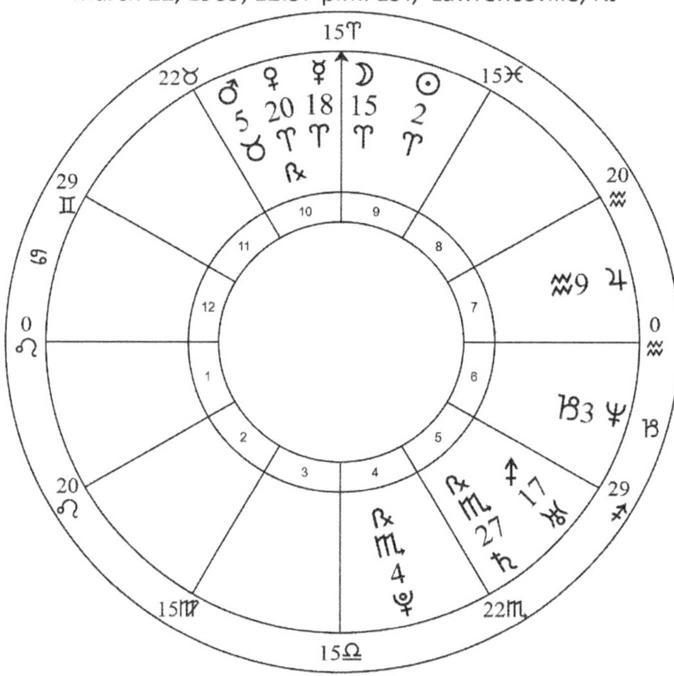

Moon's Aspects: (∥♀) ⛢℞ ☽△⛢ ♂☿ ♂♀℞

Outcome: This time I was successful. The wallpaper matched perfectly even though it was a different dye lot, and I had not sent in a sample. I placed Venus retrograde in the success 10th house with the Moon applying to a conjunction to retrograde Venus as a final aspect.

Bad Home Improvement

What were they thinking? This is a bad home improvement project that went completely off the rails and wrong. As previously mentioned, we bought a fixer-upper in New Jersey. The siding was pressed sawdust and was crumbling when they purchased the home. We planned to sell the house after two years in 1986. We contacted a major national company for an estimate. The company was a well-known department store that also did home repairs. We ended up with a high-pressure salesman who insisted we sign a contract immediately to qualify for a limited-time offer. It was late at night and we were tired. We buckled under pressure. The chart shows the time of the signing.

Activity Election Chart

Bad Home Improvement
June 15, 1984, 10:53 p.m. EDT, Titusville, NJ

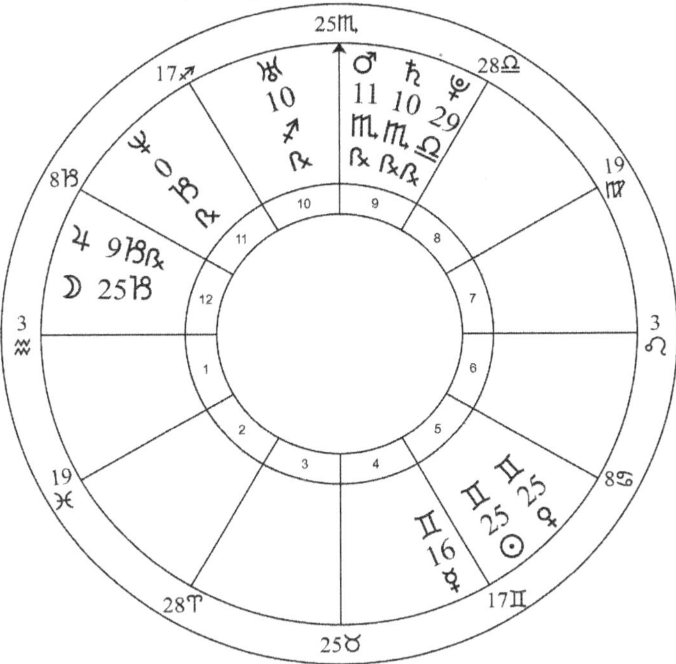

Moon's Aspects: (⚹♀) □♇℞

The Moon has only one major aspect to make, a square to Pluto retrograde. Fortunately, Pluto is retrograde in a cardinal sign meaning that even though we regret the course of action taken, we have a chance to redo the project. It is tougher to redo when the final aspect is to a fixed retrograde malefic. It becomes less likely that one will attempt a do-over. Negative results might be permanent.

Before the Moon makes the final aspect to Pluto, it had quincunx Venus which was combust the Sun. The Sun rules success in general, and Venus rules all beautification projects. In this chart, it is also the ruler of the 4th house of home and the end of the matter. The quincunx is an aspect calling for adjustment. You might change your mind and settle for less.

There were major problems right from the start as the company had hired a lot of unskilled labor to meet consumer orders. It was obvious that the crew was inexperienced and untrained.

So how bad was the siding?

1. The siding itself looked like shiny tinfoil.

2. The crew never removed the old crumbling siding leading to an uneven ripple effect on all the walls both vertically and horizontally.

3. The crew never removed any fixtures including outside lights, preferring to just cut a bigger hole in the siding to fit it over the light fixture. They would then fill in the huge hole with up to 4 inches of white caulk.

I called the salesman within the first 30 minutes of the project because it was obviously so bad right from the start. He never returned the call. He was never seen again. After three days of continuing horrible workmanship, and no response to numerous calls to the salesman and the project manager, I ordered the crew off my property by threatening to call the police. Only then did the manager show up, and in less than 30 minutes. He offered the siding job at half price. Knowing that we had plans to sell the house in less than two years, I was aware of the problems this horrid siding job would cause. I told the manager, "You could give the siding job to me for free, and I would still tell you to take it down."

Outcome: The siding was removed and our deposit was returned.

Good Home Improvement

So now the house looks like it is covered in bullet holes, and we need a good siding contractor. The following chart is the redo of the bad home improvement project. Since we were flipping the house, we desperately needed new siding. For this next attempt, we hired a local siding contractor recommended by our realtor. We met with the siding contractor and inspected some of his previous work. Then I picked the best time to meet with the contractor to sign the paperwork and turn over a deposit. We were not able to choose the best day to begin residing the house and this is generally not possible with contractors. They start whenever they finish a previous job.

Mercury is the ruler of the 4th house of home and Mercury is in exaltation and rulership in the 6th house of people you hire. Virgo is also on the cusp of the 7th house of the other person or contractor, and he was an excellent siding contractor. Planets that are in exaltation indicate something that rises to a higher position. The Moon is past the square to Uranus and Mars at the time of the contract signing.

This chart is proof positive that parallels are good final aspects. Note the opposition Sun and square Neptune in the Moon's aspects. I knew I had a personality problem with this contractor. He was probably the most chauvinist person I ever met, but I knew I needed to get over it and do what the chart told me to do. The Moon's last aspect is a parallel to Venus in rulership Libra in the 7th house of the contractor. I needed to make a connection with this contractor while he was working on the house for several weeks and I did that through hospitality.

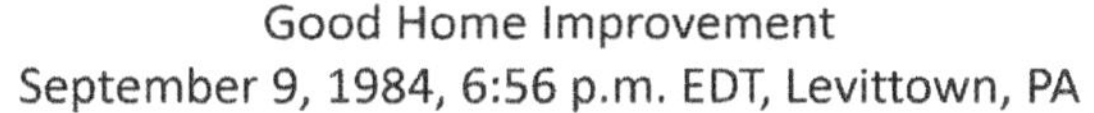

Activity Election Chart

Good Home Improvement
September 9, 1984, 6:56 p.m. EDT, Levittown, PA

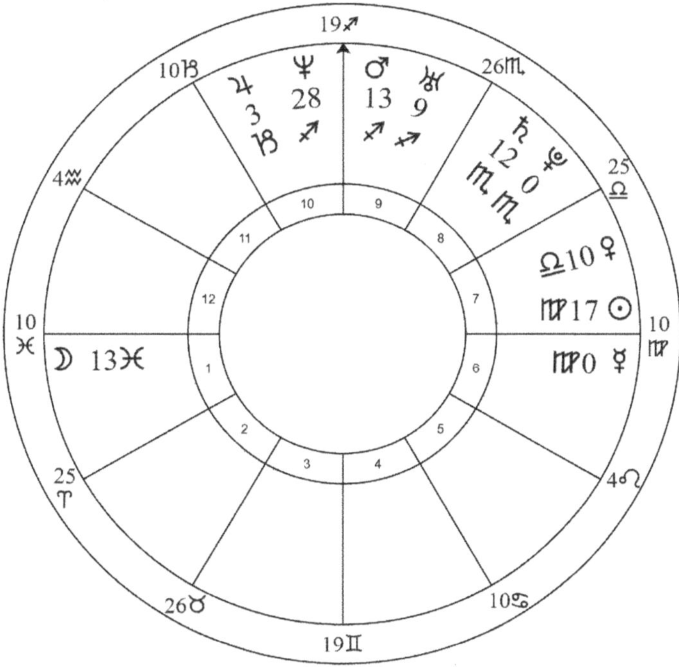

Moon's Aspects: (□♂) ∦☿ ☍☉ □♆ ∦☉ ∥♀

The rulers of the Ascendant are Jupiter and Neptune and they both trine Mercury ruling the contractor. We, as the homeowners, and the contractor want the same thing - a good result. This was an alchemical process where I aligned myself with the contractor by becoming the personification of the little woman and gracious host. I did what the chart told me to do. Every day at 10:30 a.m., I would roll out fresh baked Sarah Lee, coffee, and cream. I felt a cordial relationship was key and I treated the contractor as a guest at my home. Every morning the crew consumed everything I put out, including the pint of cream.

Outcome: Most mornings, the contractor would say, "You know that doorway or window needs some trim. Let me fix that for free." And that is how we got a fabulous siding job for the house, plus a few extra free window and door trims for $50 of Sara Lee, coffee, and daily pints of half-and-half. I turned an opposition Sun into a parallel Sun followed by a parallel Venus in Libra in the 7th house. I did what the chart told me to do.

Chapter 23
Surgery Charts

Difficulties Associated with Surgery Charts

I think some of the hardest charts to do are surgery charts, not only because there is so much on the line, but also because there are major restraints. Doctors only operate on certain days of the week. If the doctor only does this surgery on Tuesdays, you can hit a string of bad aspects on every Tuesday for several months before the Moonsigns shift. In addition, surgeons generally preform one surgery after another so if you are not first in line when the surgeon starts, you have no idea of when the surgery will be. In that case, you can only pick the best day. Generally, you have very limited time frames to choose from.

In addition, there are many different kinds of surgery, and they may require different kinds of electional charts. Some surgeries are to cut things off or out. Bleeding might be a major issue. Other surgeries involve implants and the addition of life saving innovations. Some surgeries are exploratory, looking to uncover the source of a problem. If you are having a biopsy for cancer, you do not want any findings of consequence. In this case, you might choose a Void of Course Moon time slot.

Step one - Ask Questions

Here are a number of questions that are essential to beginning the process. An astrologer needs to fully understand the situation before searching for an appropriate electional time. Gather information.

- What type of surgery is being performed?
- Was the need for surgery caused by an injury?
- What is the possible diagnosis related to surgery?
- On what days does the doctor perform surgery?
- Where is the surgery performed, (city and state)?
- What time does the doctor start the first surgery?

- What "first surgery of the day" appointments are currently open?
- What is the expected recovery time?

Step Two - Do a Radical Search to Find a Good Time Period

The second step would be to do a radical search of the individual's transits, progressions, and solar arcs to find the most appropriate time period. Knowing the expected recovery length is relevant to your search. Will the individual require physical therapy or need to enter a rehabilitation facility?

Step Three - Choose a Best Chart Within the Defined Time Period

Here are a few extra definitions and considerations when setting up a surgery electional chart. I offer these for added information, but as with all rules, the most important thing is that the chart has to say what you want to happen. As always you want to choose a Moonsign with a good final Moon aspect, and limit or eliminate the number of interim negative aspects.

- Pluto rules complications.
- Neptune rules anesthesia.
- Uranus rules unexpected findings and sudden events.
- Saturn rules obstructions, calcifications, bones in general, and the spine.
- Jupiter rules issues associated with diet that can be corrected.
- Mars rules cutting. Good aspects can indicate the surgeon cuts the right amount of tissue, not too much and not too little, and bleeding was limited.
- Venus can indicate an improvement, or problems caused by overindulgence and social disease.
- Mercury rules the nervous system and microsurgery.
- The Moon rules the activity during surgery. The Moon should not be in the sign of the organ being operated on.
- There may be more bleeding during a full Moon.
- The Sun rules the patient's constitution and general health.
- The doctor is ruled by the 7th house. The ruler should be in good standing and unafflicted.
- Surgery is ruled by the 8th house. The ruler should be in good standing and unafflicted.
- For an improvement, the ruler of the Ascendant should be in rulership or exaltation with good aspects.
- Consider the rulership for the body part being worked on.
- No surgery chart can have all of these things right.

Spinal Surgery

This is the chart of a 14-hour surgery to correct a spinal deformity. The Moon is rising in the 1st house which rules the body, and will first sextile Mars and then conjunct Venus as a final aspect. In this chart, both Mars and Venus are in fall which would not be my choice, but this is the time period I had to work with and the best Moonsign in that time period. Remember, the best you can do is to choose the best Moonsign within the given time period, and then choose the best time in that Moonsign given any restraints imposed by the surgeon.

Activity Election Chart

Spinal Surgery for Scoliosis
August 9, 2013, 8:30 a.m. EDT, Manhattan, NY

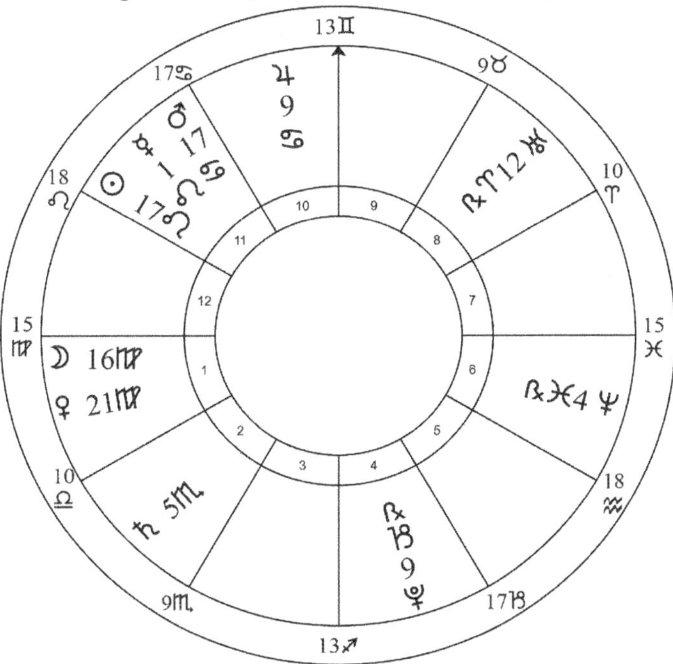

Moon's Aspects: (✶♃) ✶♂ ♂♀

The surgeon starts surgery at 8:30 am and the surgery is expected to last all day. There are no later times. Mercury, the ruler of the Ascendant, is in fall in Leo. Two other planets are in fall or detriment, (Venus and Mars). This might be a reflection of the extent of the spinal deformity and limitations in regard to correction. Fortunately, the Sun, which is the natural ruler of the individual is in rulership. Neptune is also in rulership while Jupiter is exalted. When dealing with a situation like this, you can fortify the planets through house placement. Mercury is exalted by house in the 11th house. Venus is accidentally dignified by being angular. The conjunction to Venus, the lesser benefic, is the Virgo Moon's final aspect indicating an improvement in the end.

Jupiter, the greater benefic, rules the doctor 7th house and is exalted in Cancer. It is in the success 10th. Neptune, the other ruler of the 7th house is in rulership. The surgeon is highly skilled, even gifted. There was some uncertainty as to how much correction the surgeon could do to straighten the spine. Uncertainty shows with Neptune in the 6th house of health. Saturn and Capricorn rule spines. Saturn is in a Grand Trine with Neptune and Jupiter. Recovery was expected to be long at six weeks.

In the days immediately before surgery, Leslie was selling her vacation home with all its furniture. She called me to say that everything was too stressful, and she was going to kill the deal. The buyer had become difficult to deal with. I counseled Leslie and explained that before any major change, stress and energy will rise. It was particularly stressful at this time since settlement of the house sale was scheduled the day before surgery. Leslie calmed down and went through with the sale of her house. During settlement she learned that the buyer was also scheduled for surgery the day after settlement. This added stress had caused both women to be reactionary. My client was glad the sale was finalized so she could focus on healing after the surgery.

Outcome: My client was pleased with the results of the surgery and called it a success. She did have physical therapy for several months after the surgery.

Knee Replacement Surgery

This is a knee replacement surgery that had to be done on a Tuesday during a time when the Moon's final aspect was consistently negative. During this time period, Pluto was in late degree Capricorn, Neptune was in late degree Pisces, and Saturn was in late degree of Aquarius. This meant that all Moonsigns, whether cardinal, fixed, or mutable, had a high chance of a negative final aspect. It was difficult to find a good final aspect on a string of Tuesdays for several months. My client's main concern was the risk of having drop foot as a result of the surgery.

There is uncertainty as the Moon will conjunct Neptune, however, then the Moon will parallel Neptune afterwards indicating that issues associated with Neptune might be resolved with time. Parallels are the good side of a conjunction. A parallel or contra-parallel following a stressful aspect involving the same planet is usually a hopeful sign.

Patricia had the first surgery of the day time slot at 7:00 am. She did not want to rely on following any previous surgeries on that day. Pluto is rising, but did not present any complications. The Moon's first aspect was a sextile to Uranus, and the surgery went better than expected. She handled the anesthesia well. Neptune rules anesthesia and the Moon parallels Neptune after the conjunction. The Capricorn Ascendant is ruled by Saturn which is in rulership in Aquarius.

Activity Election Chart

Knee Replacement Surgery
January 24, 2023, 7:00 a.m. CST, Corpus Christi, TX

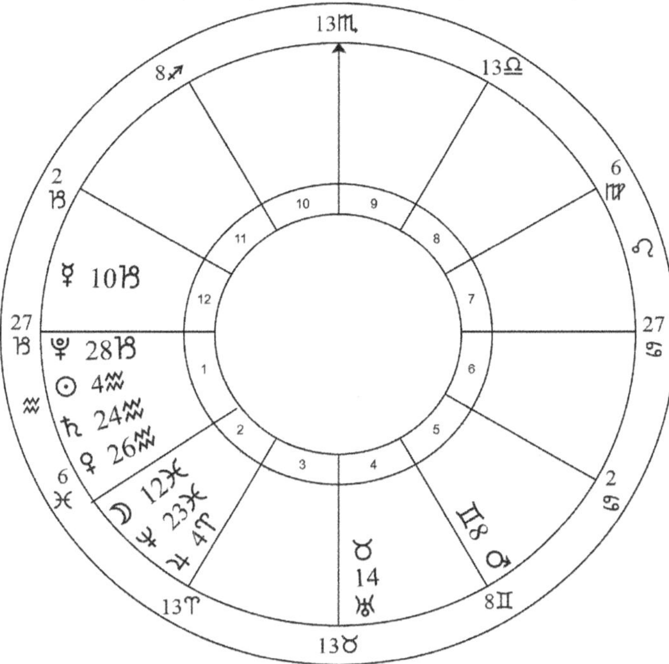

Moon's Aspects: (⚹☿) ⚹♅ ☌♆ ∥♆ ⚹♇

Outcome: The unexpected event related to Neptune turned out to be Covid which Patricia developed shortly after arriving home. Fortunately, it was a very mild case. The Moon is in Pisces which rules feet, but the foot was not the part of the body being worked on: this was a knee replacement. Patricia was pleased with the result of the surgery and her recovery. She did not develop drop foot.

Chapter 24
Insurance

Introduction

When filing an insurance claim or appeal, you want your ruler to be in rulership. This would indicate that you have a valid claim and the right to compensation. If compensation involves a cash settlement, you might focus on Venus or Jupiter. If compensation involves restoration after an accident or weather-related event, you might want an appropriate planet in exaltation showing that conditions are improved or returned to normal. Rulers should be strong by sign and making good aspects, especially to the Moon.

An Election to File an Insurance Claim

Situation: A violent thunderstorm producing horizontal rain caused water damage to the kitchen floor in our home. A claim needed to be filed quickly with the insurance company, but there were possible problems. The gutter on the back of the house was discovered to be substandard causing an overflow of water by the kitchen doors. The builder should have installed a wider gutter and downspout, or have added a second downspout to handle the heavy rain pouring off the roof.

The kitchen doors themselves were aging. Rain leaked around, through, and under the door. It also came through the door locks and keyholes due to the force of the wind. The kitchen linoleum was soaked and discolored, but only damaged directly in front of the doors. However, the same flooring extended throughout the kitchen, down a long hallway, and into a laundry room. We wanted the insurance company to honor a claim to replace all the flooring despite limited damage, the faulty gutter, and aging doors. We contacted the insurance company by phone at the appointed time and officially filed a claim. This was less than a week after the storm.

To receive money from an insurance claim, an individual must have a right to financial compensation or restoration. In other words, the ruler of the Ascendant should be in rulership, (having rights in the matter at hand), or in exaltation (able to rise to a higher or improved position). In addition, the ruler for the house in which the damage occurred should also be in rulership or exaltation. Since the damage occurred in a home, the 4th house will be important. If the damage occurred at a business, one might consider the 6th or 10th house.

In this chart, the ruler of the Ascendant is Venus in rulership Taurus. We have rights in the matter at hand. Uranus is both the ruler of the 4th house cusp and resides in the 4th house. Uranus rules disruption or change, reflecting the damage. Uranus is in rulership in Aquarius. Clearly, we have the right to file an insurance claim and seek restoration. Note that Neptune is also in the 4th house. Neptune rules water and in this case water damage which occurred for a number of reasons, the violent storm, faulty gutter, and aging doors. It is left to the insurance agent to determine the nature of the claim and the extent of the repair.

Activity Election Chart

Insurance Claim
June 28, 2001, 2:54 p.m. EDT, Glenelg, MD

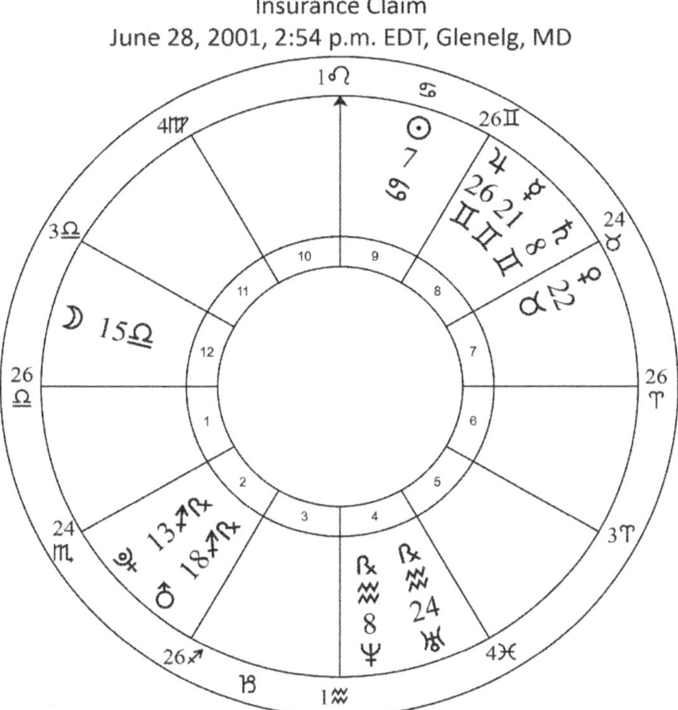

Moon's Aspects: (⚹♀) ⚹♂ △☿ ⚻♀ △♅ △♃

The ruler of the insurance company (9th house) is Mercury in rulership in Gemini. This indicates that the insurance company has reasonable standards that will be honored. The activity Moon in Libra will transit to trine Mercury, then Uranus creating a Grand Trine in air. The Moon's final aspect is a trine to Jupiter in the 8th house of others' money and insurance claims. Jupiter becomes part of the Grand Trine formation before the Moon leaves the Moonsign. Jupiter is a natural ruler for insurance. This connects the home (Uranus), with the insurance company (Mercury), and the claim funds (Jupiter in the 8th house) needed for repairs. We did not mention the problems with the gutter and the doors during the agent's inspection, and our flooring claim was approved.

Outcome: The insurance company paid to have all the flooring replaced and there was enough money to upgrade from linoleum to a better type of flooring. Settlement of the claim took almost a year because we paid to have the gutter, downspout, and French doors replaced before installing new flooring. There was a slight disagreement over the amount of money to be paid for water damage to an upstairs bedroom. Note Mars and Pluto oppose Saturn in the 8th house. We did the bedroom repairs ourselves as this damage was minimal and involved repainting a wall.

An Election to Appeal Medicare Coverage Denial

I have original Medicare with a supplemental Medigap policy. I had an annual appointment with a new primary physician. I am in good health, but given my family history, she ordered routine blood tests for electrolytes, blood glucose, vitamin D, anemia, thyroid issues, cholesterol, and lipids. These are common blood tests that any doctor might run for a yearly checkup. The cost for the blood work was $383 which the medical practice submitted to Medicare for reimbursement. Six months later I received a bill for the full amount. Medicare had denied the claim.

I contacted Medicare directly only to learn that they do not pay for routine blood work even though it had been part of every physical I had ever had before Medicare. According to Medicare literature, routine physical exams are not covered either. You meet annually with your primary physician for a "yearly wellness visit." During the appointment, you are asked to fill out a "Health Risk Assessment." It is meant to determine if you are developing dementia as you age, or have physical disabilities that require intervention such as an inability to walk, drive, hear, see, and care for yourself. The focus is on care planning for the future. Blood work screenings for cardiovascular disease are allowed once every five years. Diabetes screenings are given to those who are at risk. All blood work associated with the annual wellness visit needs to be justified or follow a set schedule. I was unaware of these limitations and perhaps my doctor was uninformed also.

I decided to appeal the denial by filling out the Medicare form provided on the Medicare website and listing all the reasons why these blood tests were appropriate based on my family history and past blood work. The form was submitted at the time shown on the electional chart.

Activity Election Chart

Medicare Insurance Appeal
February 7, 2024, 1:58 p.m. EST, Killingworth, CT

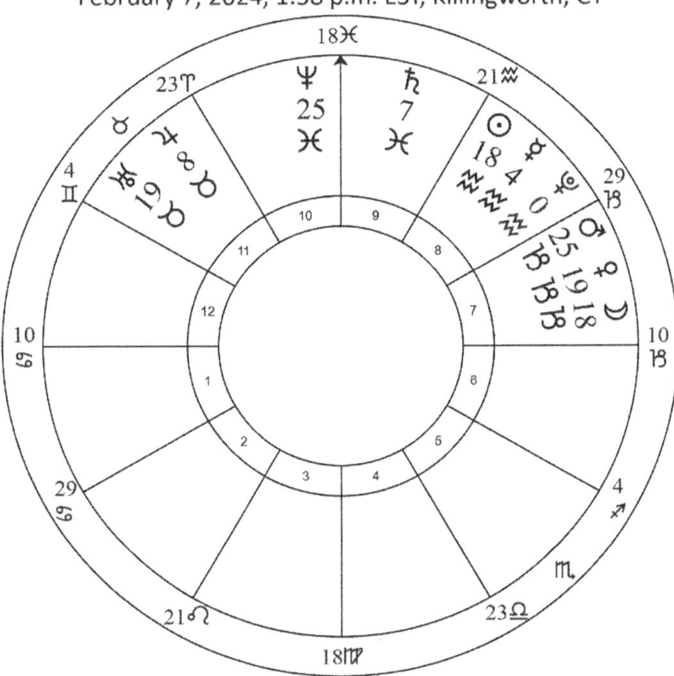

Moon's Aspects: (△♃) ♂♀ △♅ ✶♆ ♂♂

The ruler of the Ascendant is the Moon in fall in Capricorn. I misunderstood what Medicare would cover. I am at fault to a certain extent, but remember it is possible to succeed even when you are not qualified. In this case, I want Medicare to cover the expense for blood work. I am interested in a financial return, so I like the Moon moving to conjunct Venus in the 7th house. The Moon rules the activity of the chart and my 2nd house of money. The fact that the Moon in fall is in the 7th house indicates that either Medicare misrepresented what they will and will not cover, (perhaps they are flexible about this), or they may choose to cover expenses even if they normally would not.

Outcome: Medicare wrote back and further explained their policy, however, they agreed to cover part of the expense given my reasons for justifying most of the blood tests. I received a check for $321. They also admonished me not to expect this result in the future.

Chapter 25

Purchasing a Car

Introduction

When purchasing a car or making a significant purchase such as an appliance, furniture, recreational vehicle, or boat, it is important to consider the qualities that the item should have, what it will be used for, and how it will enhance your life. If dependability is a factor, planets in fixed signs and good aspects to Saturn might be appropriate. If you are purchasing a luxury item like jewelry, should it increase in value over time? Will it be an heirloom? Consider Venus, Jupiter and the Moon increasing in light. If you have small children, should furniture be durable and easy to clean? Before making a significant purchase, think about the most important characteristics you want and need, and translate those attributes into astrological language for incorporation into the most appropriate electional chart for the time of purchase.

Purchasing a Car

This was the electional chart for the purchase of my car. This was the time when I handed over the personal and cashier's checks to the salesman. My car was a 2007 Toyota Prius that I bought new. I drove it for seventeen years and 222,000 miles. Other than routine maintenance, (oil changes, new tires, and one set of brake pads), I had only one repair. I treated my car like a truck, hauling bags of leaves to the dump every fall, but she always cleaned up. She was still in good shape, inside and out, and mechanically sound when thieves cut off and stole her catalytic converter one night while I was on vacation at a rental property. The insurance company considered my car a total loss.

The ruler of cars is Mercury. I would have preferred a Mercury in Virgo, but could not wait four or five months. My 19-year-old Mazda Protégé with 186,000 miles on it was failing. So, I did the next best thing, I chose a strong stable Mercury in Taurus and made it the ruler of the 3rd house of cars. Beyond that, I chose a good Moonsign with a good final aspect. The Moon's previous aspect was a sextile to Jupiter. This meant that the car was well-built. I had researched the car, considered incentives, gas mileage, and tax breaks. The Moon was moving to trine Venus and Neptune creating a Grand Trine in air. Mercury in Taurus was in mutual reception with Venus in Gemini.

Activity Election Chart

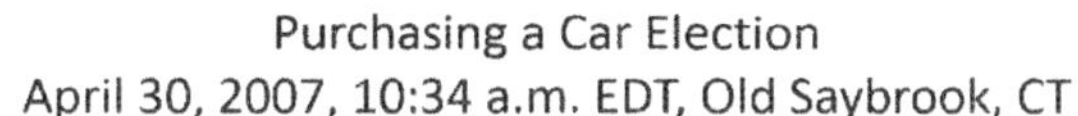

Purchasing a Car Election
April 30, 2007, 10:34 a.m. EDT, Old Saybrook, CT

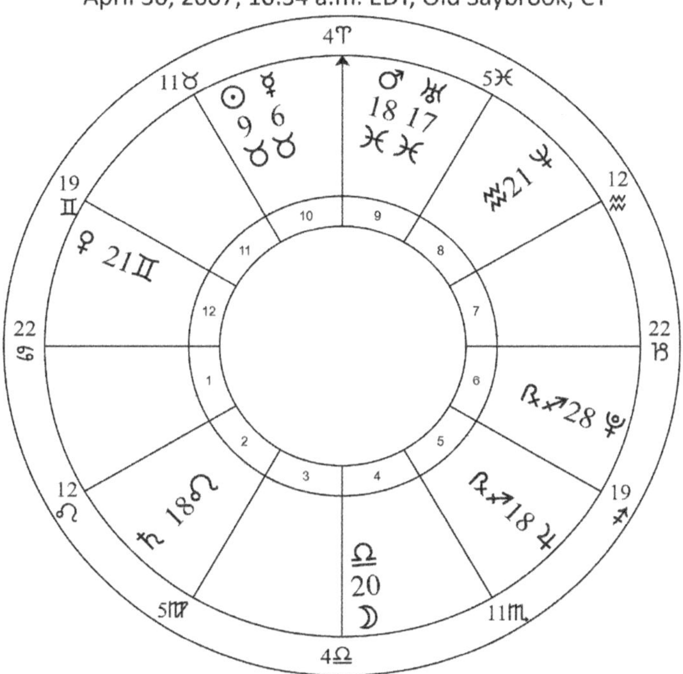

Moon's Aspects: (✶♃) ☽△♀ △♆ ⚹☿ ✶♇ //♆

I do not see the theft in the electional chart, and because the car was so dependable, I would have driven it forever. But I frequently make long trips through New York City, and I had wondered if the car would eventually breakdown on such a trip. It was probably time for a new car. I put the insurance money toward the purchase of a new Toyota Prius which has numerous safety features the old car did not have. I consider this a good thing.

I treat my car and all of my possessions with great respect and gratitude. They serve me and I appreciate their presence. I name my cars like we have a personal relationship. My new Prius is called, "Red." When I arrive home, I thank Red for a safe journey.

Chapter 26
Financial Issues

Introduction

When creating an electional chart to apply for a scholarship, loan, or grant, focus on the benefics, Venus and Jupiter. Venus is the natural ruler of money and is known as the lesser benefic, while Jupiter is known as the greater benefic and the ruler of generosity. Hopefully, the ruler of the Ascendant in the application chart is strong by sign and aspect, but sometimes the applicant does not have the best credit history and rating. In this situation, good aspects showing approval are especially important. You can succeed from a poor starting position with a strong chart. Planets in detriment can represent someone who receives even when not qualified.

The two most important houses in the application chart are generally the 2nd and 8th houses. The 2nd house rules money which might be yours when the application is approved. The 8th house rules money belonging to another, bank, or institution. Sufficient funds could be made available to you. These are options and placements you might use.

- Venus and/or Jupiter are important financial significators.
- Consider placing the Sun, Jupiter, Venus, exalted planets, or well-aspected planets in the 2nd house of your money.
- Consider placing the Sun, Jupiter, Venus, exalted, or well-aspected planets in the 8th house of the bank , institution, or other's money.
- The activity Moon's applying aspects should show the approval of your request or the transfer of funds.

Applying for a College Scholarship

My son was in college, and while my husband and I were together, he did not qualify for financial assistance. All forms for scholarships, loans, and financial assistance had to be submitted by March 1st. When my husband moved out, my ability to pay for my son's education changed dramatically. Even though it was way past the deadline, I decided to submit an application with my new financial situation and chose an elected time to do so.

My son is ruled by the 5th house. The money house for a child is the 6th house, (in other words, the 2nd of the 5th). The Moon, ruler of the 8th house of other's money, loans, and grants is exalted in Taurus in my son's money house. This shows that the money of others transfers and becomes the child's money. As the Moon is exalted in Taurus, it will be a sizable financial package. The Moon is moving to conjunct Venus in Taurus rulership also in the 6th house of my son's money. Venus in rulership shows that he qualified for major financial assistance. Taurus and Venus are natural rulers for money.

Activity Election Chart

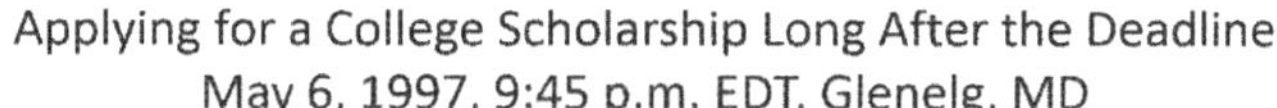

Applying for a College Scholarship Long After the Deadline
May 6, 1997, 9:45 p.m. EDT, Glenelg, MD

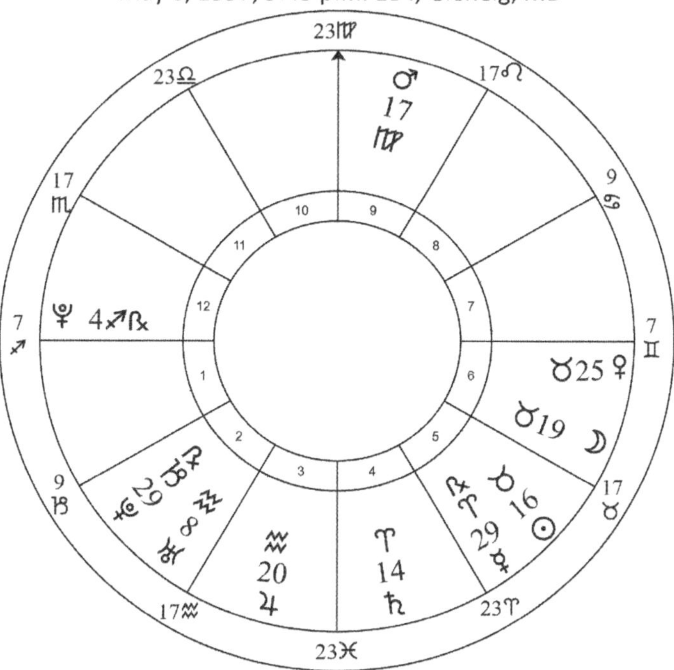

Moon's Aspects: (△♂) ☽□♃ ♂♀ ⚹♃ △♆℞

The rulers for my son are Mars, Sun, and Mercury. Mars is the ruler of the 5th house cusp, and resides in the 9th house, the natural house of universities and higher education. My son is already enrolled in school. He is a sophomore in good standing. This is confirmed by the Moon separating from a trine to Mars as the previous aspect.

This is further confirmed by the Sun in the 5th house, but ruling the 9th house of universities. He is at school and intends to finish his degree and graduate in two years.

My son's third ruler is Mercury, retrograde and peregrine in Aries. This is appropriate as my husband and I have just separated, and I am submitting an updated and drastically different financial statement with reduced income. I hope to correct inaccurate information submitted months earlier when we were together. Mercury retrograde rules anything that begins with an "R." When Mercury is retrograde, you can repeat a task that you previously failed at or correct inaccurate information. I am reapplying for financial assistance for my son. My hope is that it is not too late since the deadline was March 1st and it is now May.

Outcome: Fortunately, it was not too late, and the school responded favorably with a generous financial package which included a scholarship, work-study employment at the school library, and an educational loan. This covered all of his tuition, room, and board.

An Election to Start an Investment Account

I do not advocate electional astrology for day trading or short-term risky investments. In this case, the individual was a young family member interested in long-term investments that would grow over decades, eventually into a retirement account. He asked me for an elected time to open his first individual IRA stock investment account. He had recently taken the NAIC (National Association of Investor's Corporation) course on how to pick good stocks. He planned to open an account and then save regularly for his future. He saw this as a learning experience. He had only bought one stock before, which was a total failure. This would be his first "stock portfolio." He wanted to put into practice what he had learned and understand "what" and "when" to buy, and "when" to sell given the market. Most importantly, he wanted his investment to grow over time. His plan was to pick seven stocks that he would watch closely. His original investment would be only $2200 as he did not want to lose much money while learning.

The time of the chart and opening of the account was 9:35 A.M. on April 28, 2003, a great day. This was done over the internet. Trades were made over the next several months. This date was chosen because Venus and Jupiter were trine and the Moon made good aspects to both including a parallel, contra-parallel, and conjunction to Venus.

The Venus-Jupiter trine is the focus of the chart and must be placed appropriately. There were several houses under consideration including the 2nd, 5th, and 8th. In this case, Jupiter fits nicely into the 2nd house for an increase in funds, trining Venus and the Moon in the 10th house of success. The primary goal was "increasing money." The Moon is the ruler of the 2nd house and will conjunct Venus, then trine Jupiter indicating benefit and growth. The final aspect is a sextile to Saturn showing stability over time. Both Moon and Venus trine and sextile the Jupiter opposition to Mars-Neptune, lessening the effect of the opposition. Knowing when to "sell" will be equally as important as what and when to buy. Mercury is retrograde showing a "repeat" or second attempt at investing in stocks.

Activity Election Chart

Long-term IRA Investment Account
April 28, 2003, 9:35 a.m. EDT, Catonsville, MD

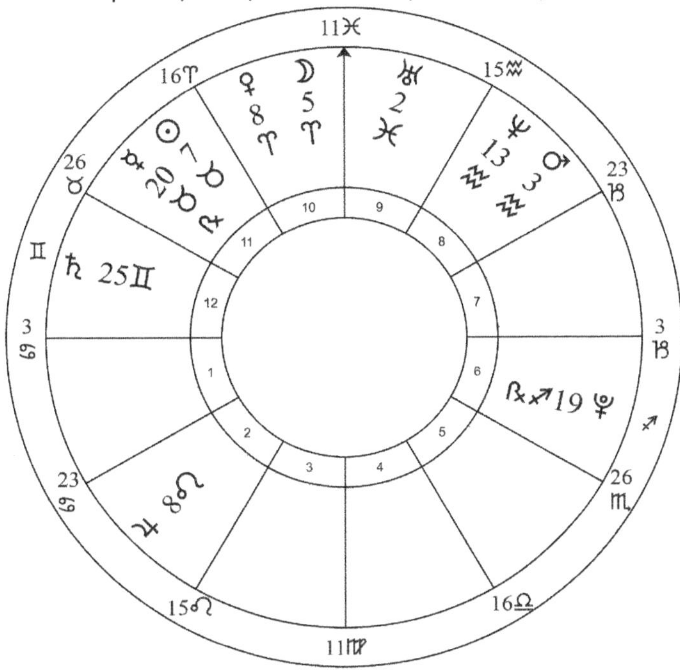

Moon's Aspects: (⚷♀) ☌♀ △♃ ✶♆ //♀ △♅ ✶♄

Outcome: The original investment was for $2200 with additions of $200 for a total investment of $2400. The original portfolio, (bought over the first months) included Abercombie & Fitch, Aflac Insurance, Dell Computers, Home Depot, Johnson & Johnson, Michael's Craft Stores, and Staples. By summer, Abercombie & Fitch, Aflac, and Johnson & Johnson were sold at a slight loss. The young man said, "They failed to thrive," and replaced them with other stocks. Total expenses for the purchases, sales and exchanges of stocks came to $103.80 which left $2296.20 invested in the portfolio. The total value of the portfolio at the end of a year was $2659.01 for a gain of $362.81. Over the past several decades, this young man has grown into a regular investor in the stock market with continued success.

Election to Secure a Bank Loan

My client, Harriet, was concerned about her ability to secure a bank loan to pay for upcoming expenses. She asked for an electional chart to help her secure the funds, and hopefully make the process as simple as possible. Harriet did not explain why she felt the need for an electional chart. I was not aware of any previous financial issues or problems with her credit score, and the process seemed fairly straight forward. She planned to drive to Carmel, New York and apply for the loan in person at her credit union. Harriet had maintained an account at this institution for many years. She would be asking for a significant amount of money and perhaps this was her concern. She wanted to use the funds to completely renovate a rental property that she owned.

Activity Election Chart

Submitting an Application for a Bank Loan
October 11, 2018, 5:20 p.m. EDT, Carmel, NY

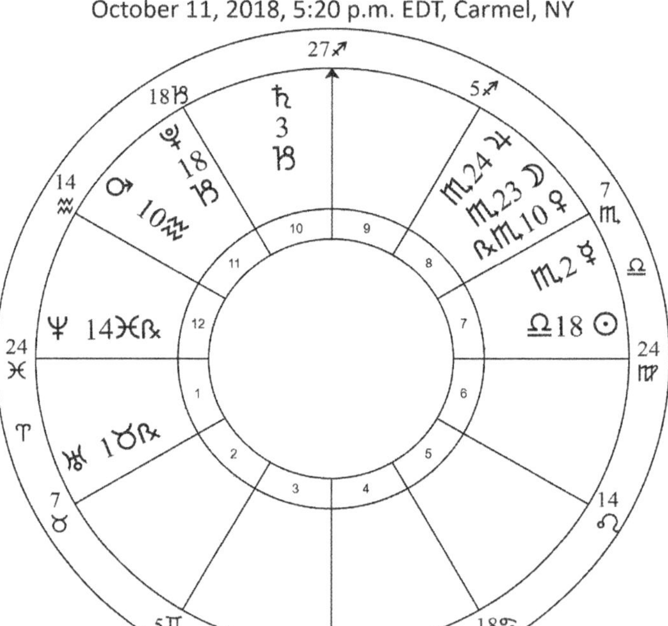

Moon's Aspects: (∥☿) ☌♃

The rulers of the Ascendant are Neptune and Jupiter. Neptune is retrograde and in the 12th house, far from the Ascendant. If there was something concerning in Harriet's financial history, Neptune's standing and placement might indicate that it was not a significant factor in the loan application process.

Her other Ascendant ruler is Jupiter in the 8th house of loans and the bank's money. Jupiter has some standing as it is in a water sign and water house. Jupiter is in its natural element as Jupiter co-rules Pisces, a water sign. Jupiter is "there" in the 8th house to secure the loan. The activity Moon is also in the 8th moving to conjunct Jupiter as the Moon's final and only aspect. This keeps the process simple and indicates that she will be approved for the loan.

Harriet's third ruler is Uranus in the 1st house. Uranus is in fall in Taurus and retrograde. This significator might be an indication that in some aspect she may not fully qualify for a loan. Uranus rules erratic behavior and it is the sign of Taurus which rules money.

Uranus is specifically kept out of the 2nd house of money so there won't be any surprise last-minute fees. Pluto was moved from the 10th house of career into the 11th house to avoid any business complications. This puts Venus in the 8th house along with Jupiter and the Moon. Venus is the natural ruler of money, but in this chart, it is also the ruler of my client's 2nd house of money. Venus connects the bank's money to Harriet's 2nd house of money. Venus is in detriment by sign and house showing that her funds were low and she needs this loan.

The Moon is in fall by sign and house showing that the bank will approve her for the loan and give her the money even though it should not. Harriet succeeds despite any strikes against her indicated by planets in detriment and fall. Venus, ruler of her money and the 2nd house, is square to Mars, ruler of the bank's money. This can indicate that there may be some restrictions or limitations associated with the loan, like promises to lower debts or requirements regarding payments drawn automatically from her checking account.

Outcome: My client secured the loan. She did use the money to renovate a rental property and was able to secure tenants.

Chapter 27
Marriage Charts

Introduction

If you are doing a marriage chart election, you want to start out asking questions. The first and most important question is, "when are you hoping to get married?" Sometimes, the couple is not very specific about when they wish to get married. They may simply say "next year." It is left up to you to choose a good time period as well as a good marriage chart. In this case, check the timing of both natal charts and look for a time period that complements both individuals.

Start by Asking Questions

People do not always get married for traditional reasons. Some marry for health insurance. It is important to ask questions about the couple's hopes and dreams regarding marriage or partnership. These questions are not just to create a good 7th house marriage chart. These questions can also help you figure out where to put the least desirable planets like Saturn. The bottom line is that you want to fit the electional chart to the couple.

- Do they want children?
- Are there children from a previous marriage?
- Do the older children get along?
- Will they share finances? (Some couples do not.)
- Is money an issue for the couple?
- Is one person supporting the other?
- Is health insurance an issue?
- How is the health of each person?
- Does the couple work together?

- Are they planning to form their own business?
- Are there religious or cultural differences?
- Why are the individuals choosing to marry?

These questions are not just to create a good marriage or partnership chart. The bottom line is that you want to fit the electional chart to the couple.

Doing a Radical Search

It is most beneficial to do a radical election search of the transits and progressions to each of the individual's natal charts when doing a marriage election. You want to choose a good time period for the marriage that complements each individual. Marriage charts are character elections. The process is more in-depth than with an activity election. Consider the upcoming transits and progressions to each natal chart. There should be significant positive aspects from Jupiter, Saturn, and/or the outer planets. Getting married is a major commitment of such magnitude that it should be reflected in planets aspecting the natal chart.

Consider compatibility when doing a marriage chart. Clashes between the individual charts and fixed outer planets can create tension and stress. You want to instill harmony. You want the marriage chart to complement the two individuals and enhance their relationship. Look at the synastry between the two individual charts or the composite chart. You might find a period when a third planet in the electional chart completes a grand trine in an individual's chart. If the man's Gemini Sun is trine the woman's Libra Sun, wouldn't a marriage Sun or Moon in Aquarius complement the natal charts? You might focus on the elements to balance out fire, earth, air, and water if the elements are very unbalanced. If you look at the marriage charts of British royalty, like Charles and Diana, you will see that they favor the male or future king. Ordinarily, you do not want a lopsided marriage chart if you can help it. Make it a good time period for both future spouses.

Natural Restraints

When researching times, keep in mind the parameters that the couple have set, such as a weekend or evening wedding, in either June or July, whether it is a religious ceremony, or Justice of the Peace. Generally, couples prefer that you find a good electional time for the wedding. They do not want to have a secret wedding at an off time that is legal, followed by a more public event. Counsel the couple on the pros and cons of any marriage chart.

General Marriage Chart Rules

You want a good Moonsign for the marriage chart. Choose a Moon with good aspects, especially a good final Moon aspect. Besides this, there are some general marriage chart rules you might wish to follow. These rules are meant to connect the 1st house with the 7th house, or the Sun with the Moon, or Venus with Mars, etc. In your marriage election chart have:

- The Sun in good aspect to the Moon

- OR, Venus in good aspect to Mars (1st house and 7th house pairing, for example Aries-Libra or Taurus-Scorpio)

- OR, Mercury in good aspect to Jupiter (1st house and 7th house pairing, for example Gemini-Sagittarius or Virgo-Pisces)

- OR, the Sun in good aspect to Saturn or Uranus (1st house and 7th house pairing, for example Leo-Aquarius)

- OR, the Moon in good aspect to Saturn (1st house and 7th house pairing, for example Cancer-Capricorn

- OR, a ruler of or in the 1st house in good aspect to a ruler of or in the 7th house

- OR, an aspect/placement showing compatibility

You want something in the chart that shows togetherness. I know some astrologers do not like certain Moonsigns for a marriage chart, and there are a lot of marriage chart dos and don'ts, but the chart has to fit the couple's intentions.

King Charles Radical Search

King Charles proposed to Princess Diana on February 6, 1981, and their engagement was announced on February 24, 1981. At that time, Charles's progressed Moon at 5 degrees Cancer was sextile to his natal Saturn at 5 degrees Virgo. They were married on July 26, 1981, when transiting Jupiter and Saturn, both at 5 degrees Libra, were sextile to Charles' natal Ascendant at 5 degrees Leo for the third time. His 7th house cusp is 5 degrees Aquarius. Charles was thirty-three years old at the time and might have felt the responsibility of producing a royal heir.

Princess Diana Radical Search

Shortly before the time of the proposal, on January 30, 1981, transiting Saturn at 9 degrees Libra was square Diana's Sun at 9 degrees Cancer. She was faced with a major decision at this time. Perhaps she knew the proposal was coming. On February 4, 1981, the progressed Moon at 3 degrees Scorpio was trine her natal Mercury at 3 degrees Cancer, and Diana was ready to accept Charles's marriage proposal. At the time of the marriage ceremony, transiting Jupiter and Saturn, both at 5 degrees Libra were trine her natal Jupiter at 5 degrees Aquarius. Note that Diana's natal Jupiter is conjunct Charles's 7th house cusp.

Natal Charts

King Charles
November 14, 1948, 9:14 p.m. GMT, London, England

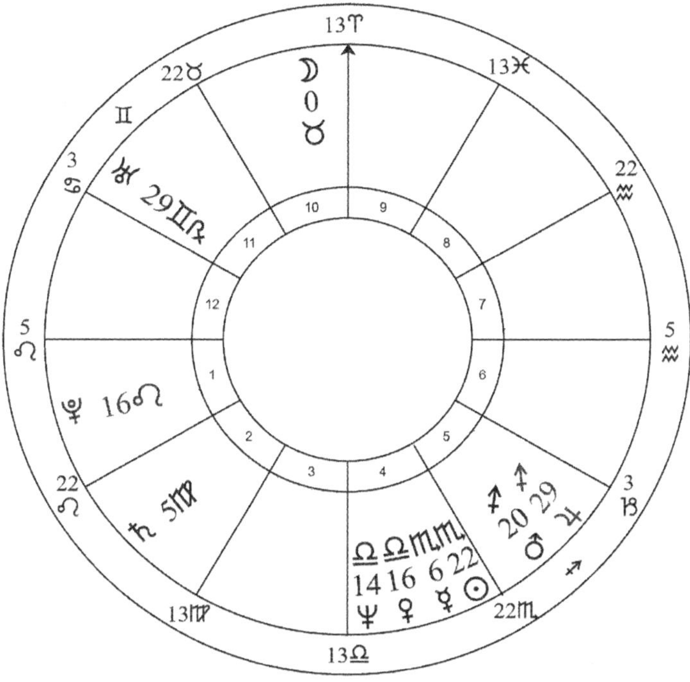

Princess Diana
July 1, 1961, 7:45 p.m. GMD, Sandringham, England

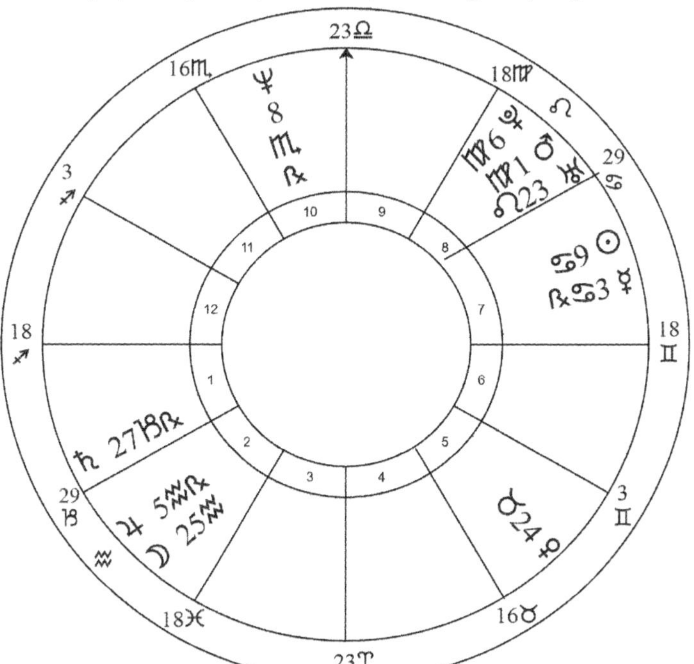

Charles and Diana Wedding Chart

This is the marriage chart for Charles and Diana. I literally watched the newsreel video to see if Diana arrived at the church on time. She did. She arrived at exactly 11 am. Then I watched the ceremony video to see when the pronouncement came, and this is as close as I could get.

Character Election Chart

Charles and Diana Wedding Pronouncement
July 29, 1981, 11:17 a.m. GMD, London, England

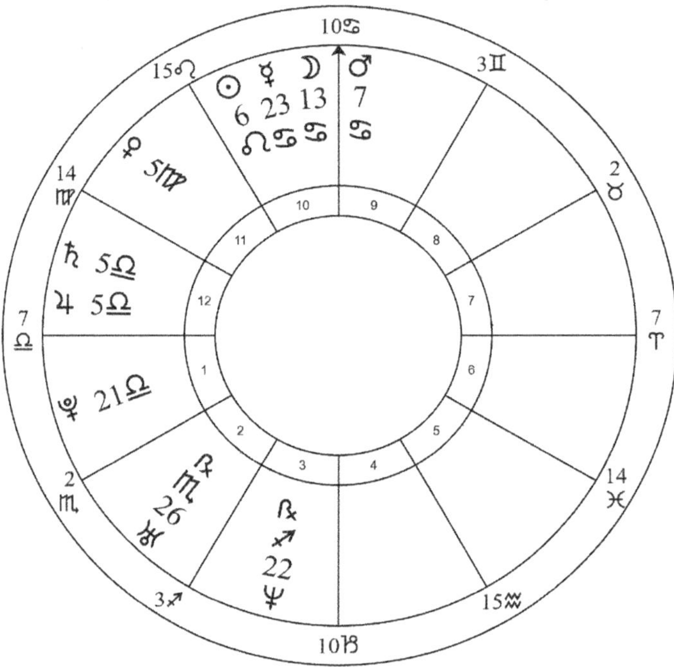

Moon's Aspects: (♂♂) ☽□♇ ⊼♆ ♂☿ △♅

The ruler of the 1st is Venus. The ruler of the 7th is Mars. They are sextile, but there is more to the story. Both are in fall. Mars in fall in Cancer can be cruel, and in this chart, Mars is square to Jupiter, the ruler for marriage legalization, and square to Saturn, the ruler of traditional roles and responsibility. Charles does not really want to get married. The Moon is last over Mars and carries the energy of Mars. Venus is also in fall in Virgo, and this is a marriage between two flawed individuals. The Moon's 1st aspect is a square to Pluto in the first house showing that there was a problem with the marriage right from the beginning. As we now know, Charles continued his affair with Camilla, the married woman he really loved. Charles is also represented in the chart by the 10th house Sun in Leo which represents the future King.

Traditional Marriage Election

You have to make the marriage chart fit the couple. This is a traditional marriage and love match. It is the second marriage for each. They each have grown children and they all get along with each other and the parents. There are no blended family issues. They have no plans to have more children. There are no health issues for either individual, but the individuals do work together in the same company. This will not be a problem.

Character Election Chart

Wedding Chart
April 26, 2022, 2:26 p.m. PDT, Las Vegas, NV

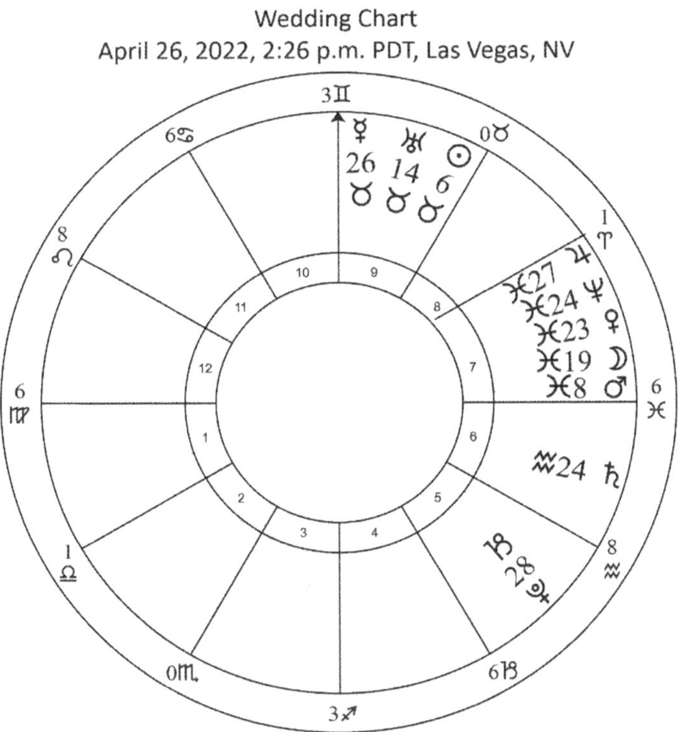

Moon Aspects: (∥♂) ☽♂♀ ♂♄ ♂♃ ✶♀ ✶♅

I presented the couple with 5 different marriage charts over several months and this is the one they liked best. I did provide short interpretations for each of the five charts.

Things of note:

1. The ruler of the Ascendant is Mercury in Taurus sextile to Jupiter, the ruler of the 7th house. Jupiter is in rulership Pisces. This brings the couple together and they love to talk and share ideas.

2. Venus exalted in Pisces is also in the 7th house with Mars. These are the traditional masculine and feminine rulers.

3. The Moon is also in the 7th house applying to a conjunction to Venus, then Neptune, then Jupiter.

4. The Moon will then sextile Mercury and the final aspect is a sextile Pluto. This was a time when Pluto, Saturn, and Neptune were all in late degree. Having the Moon in Pisces was a gentler option with the conjunction to Neptune and the sextile to Pluto.

Senior Non-Traditional Marriage

You have to make the marriage chart fit the couple. This is a senior couple in their sixties. They have been together for a long time and they are great friends. They are happy not being married and would not have gotten married except that the woman is ill and needs health insurance. They allow each other their freedom. They love to talk and share. They have a lot of fun together. Money is an issue as the woman does not have money and he is well off, or at least is in a better financial position than she is. Note that Venus is in rulership Taurus while Mars is in detriment, so there is a disparity in the couple.

The woman had tried to do the marriage chart on her own. The first chart she showed me had Saturn conjunct the Ascendant, Uranus conjunct the descendant, and Pluto on the 4th house cusp. I asked her, "If you two love freedom so much why would you put Saturn on the Ascendant? The second chart she showed me had a void of course Moon. At that point I said, "You really do not want to get married, do you?!" This is what I did with this chart:

1. I buried Saturn in the 12th house since they do not want the usual marital roles and restrictions.

2. I kept Uranus out of the 6th house of health since they are both senior citizen and the woman is already ailing. Besides, they like to be spontaneous and have fun together. Obviously, they are not planning on having children and the woman stated that all the grown children are happy with their nontraditional relationship.

3. I kept Pluto out of the 2nd house of money so there would not be a conflict. The woman mentioned that money was an issue. She wanted planets in the 7th house for togetherness. I put the best planets in the 7th house.

4. Note that the ruler of the Ascendant, Venus, is conjunct the ruler of the 7th house cusp, Mars. The Moon is between Mars and Venus. This might be considered a translation of the light from Mars to Venus except that Mars and Venus are conjunct.

5. The Moon is exalted in Taurus.

6. Jupiter is left in the 6th for good health for the woman, but it also conjunct the 7th house cusp.

7. The Moon is moving to conjunct Venus, then conjunct Mercury, and parallel the Sun. Both of these marriage charts have packed 7th houses. This is certainly not the general case. I just happened to pull these two very different situations.

Character Election Chart

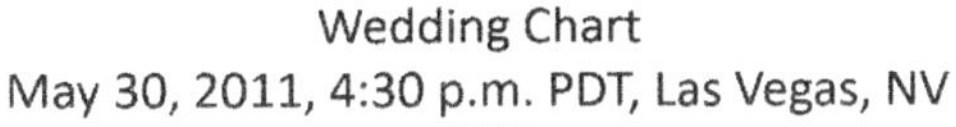

Wedding Chart
May 30, 2011, 4:30 p.m. PDT, Las Vegas, NV

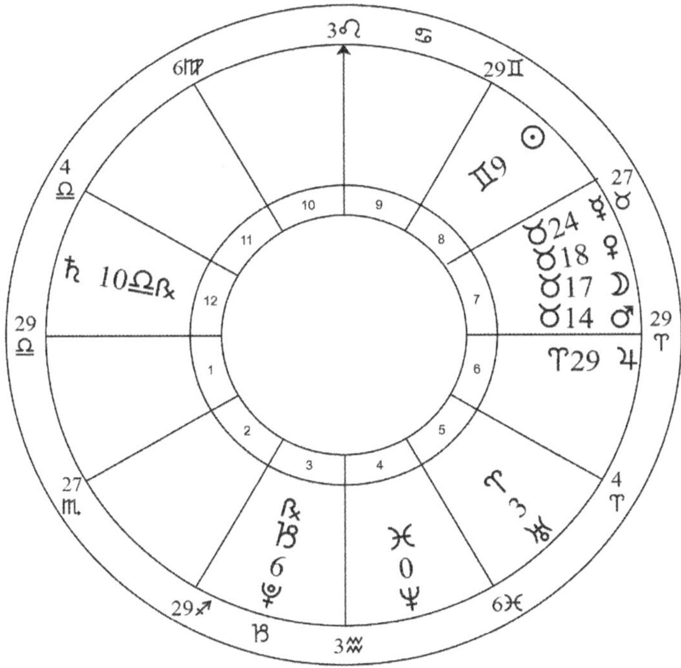

Moon Aspects: (♂♂) ☽♂♀ ♂☿ ∥ ☉

An Election to become Legal Domestic Partners

I had a request from a long-time client, Alice, for an electional chart for a "legal domestic partnership." This is something that I was not familiar with. Here is the definition:

> In Philadelphia, a Legal Domestic Partnership, known as a Life Partnership, is a city-recognized commitment for unmarried individuals, granting benefits like health coverage for partners and tax advantages. It requires that the individuals share a residence, have mutual financial responsibility, and agree to be each other's sole partner.

Alice and her partner, Ted, are senior citizens. One or both have each been married and divorced before from other respective spouses. They have been dating for a number of years, bought a house together several years ago, have been living and traveling together to visit adult children. They recently decided to legalize their relationship and become legal domestic partners. Their request had a definite time restraint. It had to be between 9 a.m. and to 5 p.m. There was also a location restraint as this is a Philadelphia-based program.

Character Election Chart

Legal Partnership
February 27, 2026, 11:25 a.m. EST, Philadelphia, PA

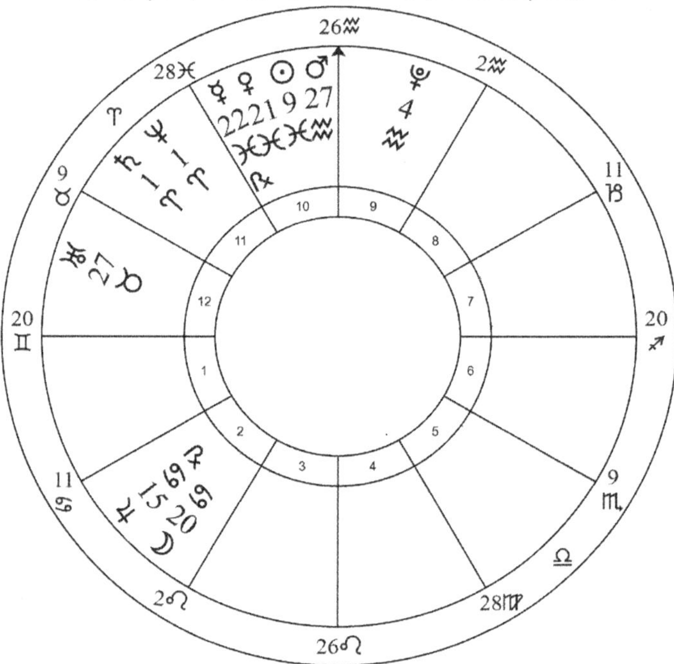

Moon's Aspects: (♂♃) ☽△♀ △☿ ⚹♅ ⚻♂

1. The ruler of the 1st house, Mercury, is trine the ruler of the 7th house, Jupiter. This shows compatible personalities and similar thinking. They do have similar ideologies, and this is a true intellectual partnership.

2. Venus, the lesser benefic, is exalted in Pisces for true affection and love. Venus is in the 10th house conjunct Mercury. The couple has a commitment to improving the lives of others on a personal, national, and global level with business goals that include education, counseling, writing, and publishing.

3. There is an emphasis on the 10th house of similar paths and the ability to either work together or in a complementary fashion. Alice's work can enhance Ted's work and vice versa even if only through creative thinking. With Mercury in the 10th house, the two can brainstorm together.

4. Jupiter, the greater benefic, is exalted in the money house with the Moon. The Moon is in rulership and shows emotional strength. In the 2nd house, it also indicates individual self-worth, shared values, and economic strength. The Moon-Jupiter conjunction is trine the Venus Mercury conjunction in the 10th house. There are a lot of trines in this chart and practically no squares.

5. Pluto is in the 9th house of teaching, publishing, and foreign travel. Pluto is sextile to Saturn and Neptune in the 11th house of goals, friendship, and humanitarian efforts.

6. Mars in the 10th house is conjunct the Midheaven indicating original thinking and the ability to act on and advocate for new creative ideas.

7. Since either or both Alice and Ted have both been married before, I am not concerned about Mercury being retrograde. They have a long history together.

Comment: This will be a newly legalized partnership, but on seeing the chart, Alice commented, "I would commit to a total stranger with a chart like this!"

Chapter 28
Spiritual Purposes

Introduction

Electional astrology isn't just for businesses, marriages, diets, or for solving problems. Electional astrology can also be used for the start of a spiritual journey, artistic endeavor, or whenever one needs insight from a higher realm.

Vision Quest

In 1991, I had the opportunity to go on a vision quest with a Cherokee Medicine Woman. The vision quest took place on the beach in the backpack area of Assateague Island National Seashore in Maryland. At the time, I wanted to remember what I had forgotten from past incarnations and begin to see my life and existence in a more meaningful way.

In the chart, it looks like the Moon's aspects will end with a trine to Jupiter (beliefs and knowledge) and then a trine to the Sun (success through an important individual), however, Mercury is set to retrograde back into Leo and become the Moon's final aspect. Mercury is exalted and in rulership in Virgo. It is a smart Mercury and indicates hidden intelligence as it is in the 12th house. Since my intent with this vision quest is to remember important teachings from past incarnations, Mercury's surprise re-entry back into Leo fits my purposes perfectly. Important, high-level information and insights might return to be accessible.

Note the Moon's aspects. First off, the Moon makes a square to Mars. Hiking into the backpack area of the island over two miles of beach sand was very difficult and hot. The temperature was near 100. There was an access road, but we were not allowed to use it. One of the requirements for our stay of several days was 5 gallons of water weighing over 40 pounds. There was a port-a-potty where we stayed, but no water other than the ocean for swimming. In addition, the Medicine Woman brought her Native American ceremonial supplies for the vision quest. We made several trips to get everything on site. It was very hot and difficult, Moon square Mars hot and difficult.

I do not handle tobacco well, but it was an essential part of the ceremony that I smoke the peace pipe at the beginning of the vision quest. This led immediately to dizziness and vomiting. While still having dry heaves several hours later, the park ranger came by and informed us that we needed to evacuate the island immediately as a hurricane was bearing down on the island. This was a fast-moving hurricane that came out of nowhere. Now we had to pack everything out that we packed in and stay at an in-land hotel.

Activity Election Chart

Vision Quest

August 18, 1991, 7:30 a.m. EDT, Ocean City, MD

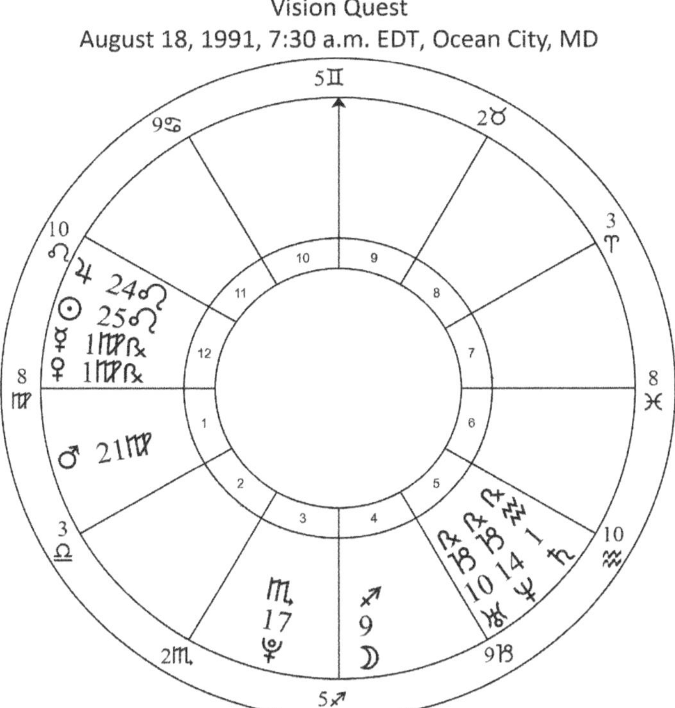

Moon's Aspects: (□♀) □♂ △♃ ☿☌♌ △☉ △☿♌

The next day we returned to the island. The hurricane had not hit the island at all, but traveled due north to New England. We returned to the beach and at that point, everything ran smoothly.

I am unable to put into words much of what I learned, but regarding my effect on the world, I knew that my very existence led to the death and nonexistence of other creatures. There was so much life in the outback. I watched a small herd of horses communicate with each other. The mare resolved a dispute between the stallion and a contender for mating rights. I watched a fox visit the campsite with no fear of humans. Crabs would have sand throwing duels to show their strength but never fought, living side-by-side in peace. But the disturbing realization was the blight of the sand crabs.

I normally visited Ocean City, Maryland. There are no sand crabs on Ocean City beaches. Assateague Island is a national seashore with a public beach. If you search for five to ten minutes, you can find a sand crab. But in the backpack area, there were millions of sand crabs. If you scooped a cup of seawater at the ocean's edge, the cup would be filled with tiny sand crabs. The backpack environment was rich with wildlife because people did not go there routinely or in large numbers. It was heartbreaking to witness the destruction we humans cause mindlessly. Simply by walking on the beach, I was crushing crab dens. My very present was destructive to the natural habitat I loved. This realization broke me because when I first arrived at the site after great difficulty, I thought the park service should install showers and toilets in the area for greater access. Now, I realized how destructive that would be. I cried for days over my shortsightedness, even after returning home.

This is only part of the realizations I had while on this vision quest. It is the one most easily spoken of. Other knowledge I recovered from past incarnations cannot be spoken off, but this was a significant experience in my life.

Chapter 29

Travel

The question of travel comes up a lot, and I feel it is important to comment on electional charts for business travel or personal vacations. Students want to know what time has the greatest finality. Is it the time of the flight? Is it when you book your ticket or make a reservation? Is it the time you leave the house or drop off your pets? I do not think any of these events matter in the end, and the timing seldom ever works out in regard to an electional chart.

In My Opinion

Creating an electional chart for business travel or personal vacation is a waste of time. It seems the timing never works out. Your flight is delayed. Your Uber doesn't arrive on time. Even if you erect an electional chart for when you will walk out the door, which is totally within your control, you suddenly remember something important that you forgot to pack. Doing an electional chart for this type of event is an inappropriate technique because it is too specific and your focus is too narrow.

I believe it is much better to do a radical search when considering upcoming travel. If you are planning a business trip, choose a time that looks successful, and then erect an electional chart for an important meeting or business event. If you are planning a personal or family vacation, choose a good time period with positive Venus, Sun, Moon, and/or Jupiter aspects. This is what I might do for myself, and then I just go with it.

Chapter 30

Book of Secrets

Introduction

Electional Astrology has allowed me to create in cooperation with Universal Forces I do not pretend to fully understand. It has taught me that co-creative manifestation through attraction is a reality. When you make a request that is in your best interest, and the best interest of all those involved, there is a response. Usually the response is supportive and moves you closer to your goal.

The electional chart is the vehicle that helped me to see this co-creative potential. Every electional search helped me define and refine my vision. In the end, every electional chart I chose helped me intuit step-by-step instructions on the best way to proceed. Sometimes the process was easy, and doors seemed to fly open unexpectedly. Sometimes the process was difficult and required much effort on my part. Sometimes my request was denied, and I was shown the reason why it should be so. I respected whatever response I got regardless of what happened, and even if there was no response at all.

This intuitive interaction has greatly enhanced my life and the lives of those I love, care for, and interact with. I am forever grateful to this Universal Force that I cannot describe, only know that it exists. It has changed me, blessed me, made me more compassionate, and gentle.

The Secret

Here is the real secret of manifestation through attraction. Co-creative collaboration with Universal Forces is available to you even if you never create an electional chart. Electional Astrology is only a tool by which you heighten and sharpen your inuition to connect and align with Universal Forces. Use it if you need to, but you can grow beyond a need for this ot any other tool. Co-creative collaboration is available to anyone who makes a request or has a vision. Call it magic, call it mysticism. I call it real, available, powerful, supportive, and protective. It is an everyday blessing that changes your world view. Only those who see the invisible can do the impossible.

I leave you with this story told to me by my Cherokee Medicine Woman friend. One day, her old car was sounding funny, so she drove into a local gas station.

When the mechanic lifted the hood, he asked, "How did you get here?"

She said, "I drove here."

He said, "That's not possible See these disconnected wires? You could not have driven here.

She replied, "What can I tell you? I pray over my car a lot!"

Your ability to invision and believe is powerful. May you be so blessed!

Index

Index

W

X

Y

Z